"Reaping insights from many paths—f [...] d clinical practice—Brian Luke Seaward's c [...] us on a transformational journey of self [...] it. Inspiring and practical, far-reaching and simple, full of compassion, love, and humor, and sprinkled with delightful stories and examples, this beautiful book demonstrates how we can simultaneously remain grounded in our everyday life while attaining fluidity and freedom. *Stand Like Mountain, Flow Like Water* can put us on the path of spirit in action and has the potential to help us transform stress into spirituality."

—Patricia Norris, Ph.D.
coauthor of *Why Me? Harnessing the Power of the Human Spirit*

"At this time in history we are experiencing another step in the evolution of our understanding of how the 'Psyche' participates in health and illness and are now able to glean the original 'soul-full' meaning of the word. Dr. Seaward is a pioneer, standing on the frontier and pointing us to a future that includes spirituality in our health and illness. I heartily recommend this marvelous book."

—L. Robert Keck, Ph.D.
author of *Sacred Eyes and Sacred Quest*

"If you've been searching for a spiritual primer with heart, you've just found it. Brian Luke Seaward's reflections and stories resonate with ancient and contemporary wisdom. They shine with love and encouragement to help us all discover more of our own truths. This is a special book for these special times."

—Susan Skog
author of *Embracing Our Essence*

"Brian Luke Seaward has a great talent for making a connection between stress and its effects on human spirituality that I never before considered. The understanding he creates in this book is so universal, it makes you wonder how one could ever question the impact of the spiritual dimension on well-being. The positive energy that emanates from this book comes from the wonderful blend of his humor, sensitivity, and articulate flow. As you read *Stand Like Mountain, Flow Like Water*, you feel as though your hands are right on the pulse of the human spirit."

—Donna Sullivan
coordinator of wellness, ConocoPhillips

STAND LIKE MOUNTAIN FLOW LIKE WATER

Reflections on Stress and Human Spirituality

BRIAN LUKE SEAWARD, PH.D.

Health Communications, Inc.
Deerfield Beach, Florida
www.hcibooks.com

Library of Congress Cataloging-in-Publication Data

Seaward, Brian Luke.
    Stand like mountain, flow like water : reflections on stress and human
spirituality / Brian Luke Seaward. — 10th anniversary ed.
        p. cm.
    Includes bibliographical references and index.
    ISBN-13: 978-0-7573-0547-4 (trade paper)
    ISBN-10: 0-7573-0547-4 (trade paper)
    1. Spiritual life. 2. Stress (Psychology)—Religious aspects. I. Title.
BL624.S423 2007
204'.4—dc22   2006037037

Publisher: Health Communications, Inc.
                 3201 S.W. 15th Street
                 Deerfield Beach, FL 33442-8190

R-07-14

Cover photo ©1996 Bonnie Montgomery
Cover and inside book design by Lawna Patterson Oldfield

For the Divine Universe,
from which all good things come

Contents

Foreword to the First Edition

I have both lived and worked at the edge of life for many years. What I have learned there is that stress does not seem to be a question of overbearing bosses, ill-behaved children, the breakdown of relationships, or even significant loss. After twenty years of working with people with cancer, I have come to realize how much stress is caused by the sad fact that many of us believe in one way and live in quite another. Our stress may be more a question of personal integrity than time pressure: a function of the distance between our authentic values and how we live our lives.

Perhaps this explains why many people in the face of what one might imagine is the most overwhelming stress, life-threatening illness, often notice their stress level has actually diminished and they feel more joy. Certainly their disease causes them concern, worry, and often fear, yet they report that their lives are less stressful now than when they were well. Such people seem to have found through their suffering a profound sense of what is most important to them, and the courage to bring their lives into alignment with it for the first time. Rather than using their strength to endure situations and relationships that betray their deepest values, they have used their strength to make needed change.

In the midst of her treatment, a woman with breast cancer told me how surprised she was to notice this change in her stress level:

> *For the first time I am sailing my boat by my own star. My God, have I sailed it by everything else! And allowed everyone else to take a turn at the tiller. All of my life I've headed against myself, against my own direction. But now I have a deep sense of my way, and I am loyal to it. This is my boat and it was made to sail in this direction, by this star. You ask why I seem so much more peaceful now? Well, I am living all in one piece.*

Each one of us has such a star. It is called the soul. Unfortunately, it is often easier to see and follow it after it has grown dark.

Perhaps the root cause of stress lies not in what so many books tell us but in the loss of a sense of our soul. If so, all of the ways in which we have attempted to ease stress cannot heal it at the deepest level. Stress heals only through the recognition that we cannot betray our spiritual nature without paying a great price. It is not that we have a soul but that we are a soul.

There are many practices that can awaken us and deepen our sense of the soul, among them prayer, meditation, chanting, fasting, and ritual. One of the most surprising of these is the experience of loss. I have learned much about the power of the soul from people who have lost almost everything they once thought was important.

Some years ago, one of my patients, a woman with cancer, told me a dream. She was a self-made woman of considerable means. One night in the midst of her rigorous chemotherapy, she dreamed that she was watching a woman build a mountain. Sweating and straining, the woman put rock on top of rock, climbing as she went, working night and day until she had constructed a majestic snow-capped peak and stood on its very top.

"A remarkable image," I commented.

"Yes," she replied, "and familiar. It was my life . . . my old life . . . working, always working . . . building my beautiful homes, my corporation, my increasing role in the international business community. Watching her standing there, I felt such a familiar thrill of pride. How competent she was! How disciplined and determined! How powerful!

"Then to my horror, I saw a great crack begin to open in the mountain close to the base. From where I was standing I could see the mountain begin to collapse in on itself. Terrified, I tried to call out a warning, but I had no voice and could only watch. Finally, the top of the mountain itself began to give way. The woman stood frozen, paralyzed. And then, at the very last second, just as the whole thing crumbled beneath her, the woman suddenly remembered how to fly."

Awed, I asked her what this dream had meant to her. Smiling she said that what we count on for support may be very different than what really supports us.

The soul is not an idea or a belief; it is an experience. It may awaken in us through dreams, or music, or art, or work, or parenthood, or sometimes for no reason at all. It overtakes us at times in the midst of daily life. Spiritual experience is not taught; it is found, uncovered, discovered, recovered. These sorts of experiences are common. They happen to all of us, sophisticated and unsophisticated, educated or uneducated, often when least expected. Many people discount them or devalue them or simply barely notice them. Yet it is just such experiences that may help us to live with less stress.

In a physician study group, Jerry told of an experience he had as a resident when he was caring for a hostile and angry young man who was in the hospital dying of AIDS. The patient had rejected all attempts to reach him. Finally, Jerry gave up trying to make a caring connection and simply delivered the best technical care he could.

Very early one morning, Jerry was awakened by a call from the hospital. His patient had just died and Jerry needed to come in to pronounce him dead and sign a death certificate. Distressed, he realized this would probably mean facing a 12-hour day with almost no sleep. Half asleep, he was driving through the dark and deserted streets, when he gradually noticed a difference in the night sky. As he put it, "I could feel the darkness as a silent and holy emptiness that went on and on, without beginning or end. In this vastness, the stars hung as countless points of radiance."

He had never seen the night in this way before and was filled with an unfamiliar sense of awe and a deep feeling of peace and gratitude. His intellect attempted to dismiss this and urged him to hurry and take care of business so he could get at least a little sleep. But he stopped his car, got out, and allowed the experience of awe to wash over him. In about fifteen minutes, it faded and he drove on to the hospital under a perfectly ordinary-looking night sky. This short experience matters to him even now, many years later. The memory of the great silence is with him still, he told us. He can call it to mind and it calms him in the midst of the most difficult times.

"I don't understand it," he said, "but I am changed by it."

The study group listened thoughtfully and then offered various interpretations of this story. My favorite is the possibility that the patient, in passing onward, may have found a way to share his greater perspective with his doctor just for a moment, as an apology and a parting gift.

Perhaps the greatest of stresses is the fear that we are alone in the dark.

—Rachel Naomi Remen, M.D.
author, *Kitchen Table Wisdom*
Riverhead, 1996

Words of Gratitude

I believe it was Maureen Stapleton who, upon receiving an Academy Award for best supporting actress in the movie *Reds*, walked up to the microphone and said, "I would like to thank everyone I ever met."

With this endeavor, I have felt much the same way. One person's name may appear on the cover of a book such as this, but no literary piece is a solitary effort. Many people, seen and unseen, are responsible for the birthing of this book, and I am grateful to them all. In the words of one of my colleagues, "It takes a whole village to write a book." Although I cannot thank each person individually, there are some people who deserve special recognition.

I am forever indebted to Laurie Kelly and Naomi Judd, who brought my work to the attention of Gary Seidler at Health Communications, Inc. in the fall of 1995. Laurie, you and Naomi are a credit to the field of health promotion.

A hearty hug goes to Linda Chapin, at the helm of the National Wellness Institute, who invited me to speak on the topic of human spirituality at the 1995 National Wellness conference, and to Elaine Sullivan, who introduced me to Naomi right before I took the stage. I think we all agree, it was a magical experience that day in Stevens Point, Wisconsin.

Profound thanks go to Gary Seidler and Peter Vegso at Health Communications, Inc., who believed in this project before reading the first sentence of the manuscript. Thanks, Gary, for your wonderful energy; and Peter, my deepest appreciation for your mission at HCI to raise human consciousness and in doing so, making this a better world to live in. A heartfelt thanks to Peter Vegso who backed the idea to come out with this tenth-anniversary edition. A big bear hug to you, Peter.

Special thanks to Christine Belleris, who as my editor skillfully guided me through the shoals of the production process. Christine, writing a book can be a stressful experience, but you made it a wonderful memory. Thanks also to Mark Colucci, Kim Weiss, Lawna Patterson Oldfield, L.A. Justice, Michele Matrisciani, Carol Rosenberg, Mary Ellen Hettinger, and everyone at HCI for your support with this endeavor.

A word of gratitude must also go to Joe Burnes and Clayton Jones at Jones and Bartlett Publishers who in 1993 released my first book *Managing Stress*, which boldly introduced the concepts of stress and human spirituality and, in doing so, has become a landmark textbook throughout college campuses and corporate wellness programs across the country.

I would like to give special thanks to Larry Dossey, who as a mentor, friend, and colleague over the years, has been one of my biggest supporters in the fields of stress management, health psychology, and alternative medicine. Larry, you are the best!

To my colleagues Deepak Chopra, Patricia Norris, Angeles Arrien, Elizabeth Roberts, Jack Canfield, Bob Keck, and Susan Skog—a big thank you for your words of endorsement. (Deepak, thanks for reminding me every now and again to enjoy the mystery.)

A very special thanks goes to my friend and colleague, Rachel Naomi Remen, who crafted such a wonderful foreword. Rachel, I am deeply touched by your unconditional generosity and support. Here's one more big bear hug and a standing ovation.

To Susan Griffin, I am so appreciative for your countless hours reading, proofing, and constructively commenting on the manuscript as each chapter unfolded; remember the Tahiti Factor! To Dan Ault, who reminded me of the wisdom of fairy tales; Tom Sarson, who constantly reminds me of the healing power of humor; and Jeff Slemons, whose creative talents made my idea for the Yogi Berra cartoon possible—thanks!

Special thanks to Judian Breitenbach, Susan Moran, Betsy Meholick, Skylar Sherman, Pat and Caleb O'Connor, Mary Jane Mees, Michelle Bowman, Andy Frank, Karen Sommers, Kate Tardiff, Jane Searles, Donna Sullivan, Claire Dineen, and Carolyn Szybist, all of whom in one way or another made a significant contribution to this book.

I must also acknowledge the longstanding support from my dear friends and family who have been my collective support group over the years, waiting for this book to be written and published.

A very special thank you goes to the great many souls I have met in my work and travels who shared their stories, giving meat to the structure of this book: Judi Billings, Nien Cheng, Brian Dalrymple, Andrew Adams, Taylor Hyman, and countless others; the divine spirit lives in your stories.

I would like to recognize the inspiring works of Carl Jung, Matthew Fox, Abraham Maslow, Lao-tzu, Black Elk, Albert Einstein, M. Scott Peck, Joseph Cambell, Yoganada, Krishnamurti, Marilyn Ferguson, Viktor Frankl, Jean Houston, Deepak Chopra, Candace Pert, Richard Gerber, Diane Dreher, Donna Eden, Mietek and Margaret Wirkus, Larry Dossey, and countless others whose profound insights and wisdom have so greatly influenced my own thoughts—becoming the synthesis found within these pages.

To the Source of Creation who goes by so many names, I offer my humble words of gratitude—every day.

Ode to Inner Peace

Have you ever seen a mountain lake at sunrise
With water so deep it resonates inner peace?
It reflects the beauty all around it
It filters the sun's light
And invites profound self-reflection.

Have you ever heard the voice of a Native American
With a tone so deep it resonates inner peace?
A voice that is grounded to the earth
A voice that lends shelter to the soul
A voice that knows the truth.

Have you ever gazed up into the stars on a cloudless night
With the constellations so close it seems you can touch them?
The sky is vast and resonates inner peace
It really gives freedom to your inner thoughts.
And should you happen to see a falling star
Or the northern lights shimmering
It steals your breath away.

I have seen a mountain lake at sunrise
There is no other time that is better.
The only thing more powerful than the sight is the quietness.

I have heard the voice of a Native American,
One of the most beautiful sounds I have ever heard,
Like a warm wool blanket on a cold damp night.
And that sky full of stars, I have seen that too, but never often enough.

—Brian Luke Seaward

Introduction to the Tenth-Anniversary Edition

I am pinching myself to make sure I am not dreaming as I write this preface to the tenth-anniversary edition of *Stand Like Mountain, Flow Like Water*, for it is every author's dream to see his or her work stand the test of time. Today, most books barely last six months on the store shelves before being replaced by another wave of titles, all competing for attention (and patrons' dollars). These days, even books that make the *New York Times* bestsellers list come and go in the blink of an eye.

Something very magical happened more than ten years ago when I first received a call from the publisher at Health Communications, Inc. to write a book on the topic of stress and human spirituality. I am forever deeply indebted. What factors contributed to its success? I asked myself this question repeatedly. It may have been the title (other authors and publishers have since told me they would kill for a title as good). Perhaps it was the cover (an inviting photograph I took of some Alaskan mountains by a cove of the Pacific Ocean at midnight one summer). People say to never judge a book by its cover, but we all know it happens. I have been told on numerous occasions that people liked the cover and simply bought the book, some not even knowing what it was about at first. Then again, perhaps the success (blush) was due to the book's content and writing style; a synthesis of insights, ageless wisdom, and stories on the topic of stress and human spirituality that I collected over the years, if not decades. The book's popularity could also be due in part to America's unyielding spiritual hunger that reached a fever pitch at the end of the millennium—and is still going strong. Most likely, it was all of these factors and a whole lot more, as well as a touch of divine grace added for good measure. For all these reasons, known and unknown, I am eternally grateful.

The world is indeed a very different place than it was when this book first arrived on bookstore shelves in April of 1997. For what appeared by all accounts to be an awakening of human consciousness, retreated in lethargic slumber (and fear) as terrorism struck New York City, the Pentagon outside Washington D.C., and the skies above a Pennsylvania farm on September 11, 2001. Over the years since this event occurred, people have become inundated with waves of fear from many sources including the media, our government, Mother Nature, corporate America, and of course an occasional terrorist cell as well. If there is one thing that has become abundantly clear, it's that fear gets our attention—immediately. But people cannot live continuously in a state of constant fear. We'd burn out! Indeed some people have. Yet for all of us, out of the proverbial ashes, comes the phoenix, and out of the ashes of fear comes a quest for inner peace. And so this quest continues, which is one reason why this book celebrates a new edition. When I first wrote *Stand Like Mountain*, I naively thought I had said all I could say on the topic of stress and spirituality. Now, with a few years behind me, I humbly stand corrected. It is with this intention that I share some new insights with you.

Reflecting back a decade ago, I began a wonderful odyssey touring with *Stand Like Mountain* in the spring of 1997. What began as an archipelago of book signings around the country developed into a series of public speaking events on the topic of stress and spirituality.

This odyssey continues to this day and the list of destinations includes the likes of ConocoPhillips, Quaker Oats, and scores of national and international conferences from Sao Paulo, Brazil and Edmonton, Canada to Ireland. To say that stress and human spirituality is a hot topic of global interest is no understatement!

Since the publication of *Stand Like Mountain*, I have been very fortunate to have been offered several other book contracts, including, *Stressed Is Desserts Spelled Backward*, *The Art of Calm*, and *Quiet Mind, Fearless Heart*. With each project, I tried very hard to craft every book with a different focus. Over time I have developed a wonderfully loyal following. Perhaps as no surprise though, when I ask people which of my books is their favorite, they all seem to give the same answer: *Stand Like Mountain, Flow Like Water*. One fan, Roger Ladd, put it best: "I didn't just read *Stand Like Mountain*. I digested it. I underlined it, I highlighted it, I took notes in the margins and then I went back and read it again."

I have since learned Roger is not alone in his approach. In fact, many people have told me that they often reread the contents of *Stand Like Mountain* over and over again because each time they get something new out of it. This comment is music to my ears because that was my intention when I first drafted the manuscript over a decade ago, and it is my intention with this edition as well.

Of the hundreds of stories that have come back to me about this book's message, I would like to share a couple with you. While autographing copies of *Desserts* at a book signing at Books-A-Million in Asheville, North Carolina, a man approached me after standing in line for twenty minutes. He politely asked if I would consider autographing his copy of *Stand Like Mountain*. He handed me his copy, which was weather-beaten and dog-eared and underlined and highlighted. As I opened the cover to inscribe my name, he shared with me that before he read the book, he was a chronic alcoholic.

"I am going on two years sobriety," he said with a shy smile. "Thanks for sharing a great message," he continued as he shook my hand and gave me a bear hug. For him, and many others, this book served not only as a critical mass of spiritual consciousness, but also as a catalyst for spiritual growth.

One day the phone rang as I was preparing dinner. It was my college roommate, Tom Sarson.

"Hey, Seaward," he said, typically using my last name as a term of endearment. "Have you seen the most recent issue of *Good Housekeeping*?"

I confided that this was not one of the periodicals that made my list of "must read" magazines.

"Well, go out and buy it and give me a call when you have it in your hands. Oh, my wife says to make sure it's the one with Joan Lunden on the cover," Tom said.

I turned off the stove, hopped in my car, and headed over to the local grocery store. I quickly ran in, bought the copy in question, and headed back home to call Tom.

"So what's the deal with *Good Housekeeping*?" I inquired.

"Turn to page 116," Tom answered. "Look at the top of the middle column. Your name appears about two inches down."

Sure enough, there was my name, alongside the title of my book, *Stand Like Mountain*. The article featured renowned "Good Morning America" host, Joan Lunden, and she credited my book as a light in the darkness regarding the collision of her career transition and failing marriage. To make a long story short, Joan and I have become friends: Not only did she offer to write the foreword to *Desserts*, she invited me to contribute a story to her bestselling book, *Joan Lunden's Wake-Up Calls*.

Equally inspiring was an e-mail from a woman in China who picked up a copy of my book while on a business trip to Seattle. She shared with me that the communist influence never acknowledges the spiritual dimension and this insight of human spirituality was a new revelation to her. Upon reading *Stand Like Mountain*, she began to "connect the dots," a process that had helped her cope with several recent significant losses.

Perhaps just as compelling are the number of stories that have filtered their way back to me from around the country (and the world) from scores of people who read the book in their church groups, support groups, and community book clubs. For this reason, I took the liberty to add a list of study guide questions at the back of this edition. I would personally like to thank all of you who have shared your thoughts of appreciation over the years regarding how this book has touched your hearts and changed your lives for the better. That was my intention then, as it is now. Moreover, it is my wish that this edition proves equally inspiring.

Over the past decade, I have lost some innocence, yet gained a bit more wisdom. In the end, I believe I have come out ahead. It is this wisdom I wish to share with you in between the covers of this book. Writing a new edition not only gives me a chance to add new material, but also to go back to tweak and update some passages that needed some revisions. This edition of *Stand Like Mountain* contains several new sections tucked into nearly every chapter, as well as a new chapter of healing stories, titled "Seeds of Change." Here is what is new in this tenth-anniversary edition:

- Twenty-first century stress in Chapter One
- A healer named Adam and the biology of belief, also in Chapter One
- The three pillars of human spirituality in Chapter Two
- The fourth pillar: the divine mystery in Chapter Two
- The hero's journey in Chapter Two
- The divine paradox in Chapter Two

- Secrets encoded in the DNA in Chapter Three
- Chapter 5: The Seeds of Change (new chapter)
- Message from water in Chapter Six
- More ways to enhance the health of the human spirit in Chapter Seven
- Uncomfortable truths (more reflections) in Chapter Eight
- Appendix 1: Healing Water Meditation
- Study guide questions
- Additional suggested reading

Having the title *Stand Like Mountain, Flow Like Water* for a popular book has also provided me with some comic relief of sorts, particularly during the introduction of countless national radio interviews, some television shows, and various public events. I became astonished, if not entertained at the number of people who, I guess out of nervousness, mispronounced (i.e., butchered) the book title. I quickly learned that many interviewers never read the books they feature on the air, but several apparently never read the title either. Place your tongue in your cheek, and enjoy a small sample of derivations I have come across over the years (with my editorial comments):

- Stand Like Water, Move Like Mountain (a dyslexic announcer?)
- Stand Like Mountain, Flow Like Fountain (cute, it rhymes)
- Stand Like Rock, Fall Like a Tree (a nice nature theme going here)
- Stank Like Mountain, Smells Like a River (??)
- Flow Like a Mountain, Stand Like a Hill (Freudian slip)
- Stand Like Everest, Flow Like Niagara (creative license?)
- Making a Mountain Out of a Mole Hill (the sequel?)
- Stand with Cane, Flow Like Metamucil (the AARP edition) and my all-time favorite . . .
- Move a Mountain, Walk on Water.

I have pinched myself many times in the course of this book's tenure, but here is one more reason. It's not every author that has a song written about his or her book, but that's exactly what happened when singer/songwriter Greg Tamblyn caught wind of my book project well before it came off the press in 1997. Greg and I have different stories about this collaboration, but since this is my book, this is the real story of how this song came to be. I met Greg at the National Wellness Conference in Stevens Point, Wisconsin, in the summer of 1996. I had just finished giving a presentation on Creative Anger Management. When the presentation was done, I found myself chatting with some people in the back of the auditorium, shaking hands and swapping business cards.

Waiting for a lull in the conversation, Greg reached out, shook my hand, introduced himself and said he would be in touch. True to his word, he sent me a package of his CDs a few weeks later. With the package was a note indicating that someday he would like to work on a song together. I played several cuts from his CDs and really liked what I heard; ballads mixed with some tongue-in-cheek parodies. In a subsequent phone call, I thanked him for the CDs and mentioned that I was an author, not a songwriter. This fact didn't deter him in the least. On a visit to Denver several months later, Greg and I sat down and brainstormed on what might make a good song. I shared with him that I was working on a new book project on the topic of stress and spirituality. When he heard the book's title, I think he actually began to levitate. I mentioned that although the title was a Chinese proverb, I could hear someone like Mary Chapin Carpenter singing this song with a touch of country flavor to it. By the end of the day, Greg said he had gathered plenty of insights and inspiration for a song. Sure enough, the song he composed (with help from his colleague Richard Helm) is a beautiful ballad and for this, I am grateful too. I mention this here because in honor of this tenth-anniversary edition, the Eversound Music label invited me to compile a new collection of relaxing, instrumental songs from their library. Upon hearing a version of Greg's song "Stand Like Mountain," they offered to include this on the CD (sold separately but cross-marketed with this new edition) for your listening pleasure. Enjoy!

It is with tremendous gratitude that I am allowed to step up to this literary podium and share my thoughts with you once again. As we begin this new millennium, may you not only stand like mountain and flow like water, but venture forth in confidence and, in the words of Gandhi, "Be the change you wish to see in the world."

Sunrise
(An Introduction)

The mountain is the metaphor.

—Ancient Proverb

I t's hard to go anywhere these days and not engage in a conversation about stress. Like the changes we encounter daily, stress is in the air. Sociologists tell us that stress is one of the few factors that knows no demographic boundaries. It is, as the expression goes, an "equal opportunity destroyer."

Likewise, spirituality also knows no bounds. If you listen closely to conversations around the globe today, the topic of spirituality is surfacing everywhere. It's no coincidence, since stress and spirituality are very much connected. In fact, as the Earth spins into the next millennium, we are realizing that everything is connected.

As another expression goes, "The darkest hour is before dawn." Yet there is no doubt that eventually a new day will begin as well. Today, the first rays of dawn are visible. I am not alone in my thinking that this is an exciting time to be alive on the planet Earth. Excitement can be realized in many ways, and, I might add, not all favorable. For some, even a good change may be perceived as troublesome. But I venture to say that this sunrise will be spectacular, as well as the promise of this new day itself.

I have been attracted to mountains since my first trip to Colorado in early childhood. There is a universal appeal of mountains that goes beyond majestic vistas and scenic beauty. For me the appeal is spiritual. Perhaps more than any other analogy, the trek toward a mountain summit, big or small, is the epitome of the spiritual journey.

In his play, *K2* (named after the second highest mountain in the Himalayas), Patrick Meyers wrote the line, "Mountains are metaphors." His voice echoes a common theme in the philosophical history of humanity. Reaching for the summit becomes the quintessential expression of the soul-searching process. Required by all but denied by many, this journey is not an easy one, for what some see as the destination, others see as an obstruction.

I was a child when the movie *The Sound of Music* first appeared. Even as a youngster, the song "Climb Every Mountain" struck a chord in my heart, for I understood both the literal and figurative interpretations behind Rogers and Hammerstein's lyrics. Soon thereafter, I was to learn that the hills really are alive with the sound of music. Whether it is the sublime beauty or the mystical melody, both the physical and spiritual attraction are undeniable. Indeed, the mountain is the metaphor for the human journey, and not a day goes by that we are not invited to become part of this metaphor and embrace it fully.

This book is not meant to serve as a guide in this time of tremendous change. Instead, it is my sole wish that the collective wisdom found among these pages serves as a reminder of what we already know, because the guidance we seek is really within us. We only need to remember our inherent wisdom and the innate potential of the human spirit.

Giving lectures and seminars in stress management, I often begin by saying that the information I am about to share is not new. It is merely common sense. However, I have quickly learned that when people are overwhelmed, common sense is anything but common. As you turn these pages, you should find comfort in knowing that the concepts, stories and insights of this ageless wisdom serve to awaken that which lies dormant in the unconscious mind. Once fully aware, we can enjoy the sunrise—not miss it by rolling over and falling back asleep.

In the preparation of this book, I read countless volumes on a host of topics, from psychology, theology, and quantum physics to philosophy, sociology, and mythology. Regarding human behavior, I have made an effort to place a positive light on each concept and example. I may be an eternal optimist, but I have found that over the course of my career as a teacher and therapist, it serves little purpose to dwell on the negative. Doing so only reinforces ideas that are contrary to those I wish to share.

This is not to say that this book was written with, or should be read with, rose-colored glasses. On the other hand, life should not be lived under a cloud of pessimism, either. We must find a balance, and that is the message of this book: *balance.*

We are well aware of examples of stress; we encounter them daily. By learning from others who have gone before us, we, too, can move along more swiftly. As with everything in life, the best approach while reading this book is to keep an open mind and open heart. When this is done, everything else will come into balance.

Writing a book about human spirituality lends itself to some significant limitations. Although limits exist, it is impossible to compose a book on this topic without making reference to the divine mystery we call God. In writing about God, it is quite easy to personify (i.e., make human) this all-encompassing and mystifying concept.

I am well aware, as many of you are, that God is not a male deity, and I have made a concerted effort not to reinforce this notion with male pronouns, such as he, him, or his. Then again, there may be those of you who question or disagree with me, and I encourage this. Some of you may even question the repeated reference to God in terms of coping with stress.

This was conveyed to me recently after giving a presentation in Dayton, Ohio, on the topic of stress and spirituality. I was approached by a woman, hand outstretched, thanking me for my lecture. After releasing her grip, she put her hand to her mouth and said, "I just want you to know that I don't believe in God, but I liked the way you weaved him in throughout your talk. It was very insightful." Then she paused, gave me a reassuring nod with a wink, and walked away.

Our relationship with God is as unique as we are ourselves. My desire in writing this book is not to explain, define, or describe God, for this simply isn't possible. But to ignore the divine concept of life, a perception often reinforced by the fruits of technology, only leads to more strife. The dawn of this new day, the maturation of human consciousness, is the realization that there is no separation from God. All things connect.

I have attempted to gently increase our comfort zones to mature and evolve our divine relationship, whatever you conceive this to be. I have done my best to leave the slate clean, so that you may continue to move toward your own understanding. Like my presentation in Dayton, I have woven the concept of God through each page. And you, like that lady in Dayton, may find yourself with a different perception than I.

So much of spiritual well-being is awareness. In an effort to promote this, I have taken the liberty of including several awareness exercises (lists). These should help increase your awareness regarding both your levels of stress and ways in which to cope with stress. So as you read this, you may want to keep a pen nearby.

Finally, knowing how important humor is as a coping technique, I included several cartoons as well. Enjoy!

We never quite know what we will find on top of a mountain. We go searching for God, but sometimes it seems that all we find are foreboding clouds and bad weather. As this new day begins, the skies are abundantly clear.

It is well known that mountain peaks are the first points of Earth to absorb and reflect the rays of sunshine at the start of each new day. There is something special about seeing the first rays of sunshine on the mountaintops. This itself is an invitation to journey and embrace the metaphor. As the ancient proverb states, "Each journey begins with the first step."

Happy trails!

CHAPTER ONE

STRESS WITH A HUMAN FACE

*I'm an old man who has known
a great many problems, most of which
never happened.*

—Mark Twain

These are stressful times. You can see it in people's eyes and hear it in their voices. Most certainly it can be observed in today's headlines and round-the-clock cable newscasts. It's a feeling that seems to be ever present, despite our best efforts to overcome it.

Living in Washington, D.C., during the Bush and Clinton administrations, I became acutely aware of the daily stress people encountered. The pulse of the nation was a constant flutter of activity, fueled by egos and paced by capitalism—thinly disguised as democracy. I was quick to learn how popular hell had become in the nation's capital: lawyers from hell, security clearance from hell, and politics from hell. And that's not counting traffic, parking, and terrorism—all from hell as well. One daunting night, I took a cab home from Reagan National Airport during an ice storm, only to hear the driver remark about the "weather from hell." It was all I could do not to think that the underworld had finally frozen over.

These truly are stressful times. The pace of life is fast and furious, and becoming more so. A quick glance through the newspaper headlines, or a few minutes of television news, is enough to confirm that humans around the world are approaching a boiling point of both anger and fear. The causes are many and varied: corporate outsourcing, workplace violence, government gridlock, AIDS, gang violence, corporate downsizing, deforestation, ozone depletion, drug addictions, international terrorism, animal extinction, and natural disasters of biblical proportions. All of these problems put our planet and its people under immense stress.

While the nation's capital seems to epitomize the frenzy of human emotions, stressful vibrations echo across the country—and beyond. This fact has not gone unnoticed by the World Health Organization (WHO). From various surveys and studies conducted in virtually every country, WHO now cites stress as "a global epidemic." The mounting tension and strife only confirm what we already know at a deeper level: Stress has become a prominent and permanent part of the human landscape. It may be hard to remember, but it wasn't always like this.

Before the 1960s, the topic of stress did not make headlines, nor was it a household word. However, the rapid rate of change, coupled with the rapid increase of technology, has infiltrated all aspects of our lifestyles. Running right alongside it are the signs and symptoms of human stress. In essence, people are trying to keep pace with a hyper-productive, 24/7 society. Sunday, once esteemed as a day of rest to honor the godliness of creation, is now merely a day to get caught up with shopping, errands, and work before the deluge starts all over again on Monday. (More heart attacks occur on Monday morning than any other day of the week!)

Technology once held the promise to make our lives simpler and more efficient, and to provide additional leisure time. Yet research studies show that instead of more leisure time, we have less. Although technology like cell phones, iPods, laptop computers, e-mail, voice mail, pagers, text messaging, TiVo, microwave ovens, fax machines, and satellite radio appear to make us organized and efficient, we have in truth become slaves to these technologies.

In his book *Modern Man in Search of a Soul* noted psychologist Carl

Jung warned that advances in technology, accompanied by increased materialism, would lead to a greater split of the conscious and unconscious mind—in other words, the ego and the soul.[1]

This prophecy, made in 1933, has come to pass as we begin the twenty-first century. The pace of life today has made us more distant from not only the elements of nature but our divine essence as well. It is no coincidence that as technology (and the cultural values associated with it) advances to dizzying heights, we find ourselves in a period of spiritual dormancy. A growing consensus suggests that this dormancy is induced by our addictions to this technology.

I believe there is an inherent relationship between stress and human spirituality. What seemed obvious to me at the intuitive level was often dismissed in graduate school seminars—until I taught an undergraduate course in stress management. Then the pieces began to fit into a larger picture.

Upon assuming the role of teacher, I became aware of a number of interesting questions. The students were not so much interested in the relaxation techniques being taught as they were concerned about the issues of relationships, values, and the purpose of life. On one hand I was surprised that none of these issues was found in any stress textbook; on the other hand these issues are so obvious, I wondered why they were not included. It became clear that these students were addressing matters of the heart and issues of the soul. Over three decades, these perennial questions have remained the same.

Detaching from my own problems and concerns, I could clearly see that stress and spirituality were not opposite ends of a continuum, but partners in the dance of life. I was delighted; one doesn't learn this in academia, especially not in graduate school. In fact, I think it's fair to say that in the mid-1980s, one didn't mention the word *spirituality* in the same breath as *science*. There was an unspoken assumption that they were mutually exclusive. In fact, *soul*, I was to discover, was a four-letter word, forbidden in the halls of academia. By and large, this perception stubbornly remains today.

What I pieced together then, and what is coming to be better understood now, is that the spiritual dimension is not only present in the human equation; it is an integral, if not essential, part of it. In order to really understand the human journey, we must acknowledge and nurture these matters of the soul on a daily basis.

Thus began my exploration into the dynamics of mind-body-spirit integration, human consciousness, and a synthesis of reflections on stress and human spirituality. This has been the focus of my own journey, both professionally and personally; I know I am not alone in this quest.

Stress with a Human Face

When we hear on the news about a crisis in a distant city or remote corner of the world, we can easily detach ourselves from it. But when stress and tension are in our own environment—at home and/or work—it is simply impossible to ignore it. For many, it is becoming increasingly difficult to cope with these overwhelming issues.

The expression "stress with a human face" reflects a sense of compassion in a tense situation. Taken literally, it means a troubled mind. Our faces clearly reflect the intensity and volume of stress in our lives. Look at photos of Jimmy Carter before and after he became president of the United States. It looks as if Carter aged twenty years during one four-year term. Bill Clinton and George W. Bush have aged similarly as well. While the job as chief executive is extremely stressful, anybody can experience the same effects of stress—even without being president.

To look at Alex now you would think he aged a decade in the past year alone. Aside from the deep lines over his forehead and the obvious weight gain, there is a loss of vitality normally seen in his powder-blue eyes. As a mid-level manager for a large corporation in the midst of restructuring and downsizing, or "right sizing," as he reminds me with a grimace, Alex is no stranger to stress.

"My life is like a Dilbert cartoon strip," he says without a smile. With two kids just starting college, Alex admits to me that he is frightened to death of seeing his research and design position outsourced overseas which, he states emphatically, is a very real possibility. The stress, he confides, goes beyond his physical appearance. It has seriously affected his health.

"I'm too young to have arthritis, ulcers, and high blood pressure," he remarked to me one day. "And it's not just my job, I'm having problems with my marriage as well. I'm working extra hours at work to cover a position that wasn't filled, leaving less time for my wife and kids. Things are just out of balance!"

Alex isn't alone with these feelings. Statistics show that he is one of millions of people feeling the squeeze of various demands placed on him, from society, culture, family, friends, colleagues, peers, and perhaps even the world at large. There are, of course, other people like Alex who make the headlines with their stressors and gain national attention, as stress knows no demographic boundaries.

Recently, I was asked to appear on a national morning news program to comment on the topic of competitive anxiety associated with Olympic athletes. Over the years I had counseled several nationally known Olympic athletes, actors, and corporate executives in stress management therapy. This particular interview was scheduled to be about five minutes in length, and as I was told, the entire topic was on competitive anxiety and the ensuing Olympic pressure on all athletes regarding the upcoming Olympic games.

Toward the end of this segment, however, the questions from the news anchor became more general in nature. With twenty seconds remaining, she asked, "Dr. Seaward, how does anyone deal with stress?"

Watching the seconds rapidly tick away, I realized I could not do justice to this question in the remaining few moments. With a smile I said, "I'm sorry, I can't answer that in a sound bite." She gave me a nasty look, thanked, me and moved on to the news.

As I left, I wondered if I could have given a better, more succinct answer, since that question is posed to me fairly often. These days I can distill the message of managing stress into one word: *balance.*

Balance is the ability to achieve a sense of symmetry in our lives. Balance is an inherent trait of the human condition. It is coded in our DNA. Balance is an innate talent that is cultivated with discipline, one that must be practiced regularly and is mindful of our spiritual essence. In other words, there are no quick fixes to chronic stress. We must look deep into the soul to answer these concerns. This can be a long, arduous process with no speedy solutions. Unfortunately, in an age of magic bullets and media sound bites, people are looking for quick answers to monumental problems.

Some of my best teachers have been my students. One day while discussing the concept of balance in my stress management class, one student raised his hand and shared an ancient proverb from his tai chi course. He explained that balance is a fundamental skill in tai chi, as well as a principle of the Taoist philosophy.

The saying is: "Stand like mountain, move like water." Now that's a sound bite.

The message is colorful, poetic, profound—yet so simple. The vision of mountains and water is one I find very soothing, but the significance of the message is even more so. The union of opposites as a means to achieve wholeness is common in the Taoist tradition. To stand like a mountain suggests a sense of stability, resistant to the winds of change. To move like water implies the ability to go with the flow, rather than trying to change things we have no control over. To move like water is to persevere, yield where necessary to gain strength, and move on once again. What this ageless wisdom advises is to have strength and security in your own being, like a mountain, yet at the same time hold the fluidity of moving water. Here was an ancient metaphor giving life to the concept of balance. I took an immediate liking to it. I don't know if Thomas Jefferson studied Taoism, but he certainly understood the concept of balance when he wrote: "In matters of style, swim with the current; in matters of principle, stand like a rock."

The concept of balance can be found in virtually every culture since the dawn of humanity. Americans may be familiar with the aspect of balance in life through the biblical passage in Ecclesiastes (3:1–8), also made popular in a 1960's hit song, "Turn, Turn, Turn," first by Pete Seeger, then again by the rock group The Byrds. Benjamin Hoff's popular book *The Tao of Pooh* also serves as a gentle reminder that the essence of Taoism is really a universal concept. Native Americans have a similar phrase, "walking in balance," which they use to describe this philosophy of a peaceful coexistence and harmony with all aspects of life. To walk in balance requires steadiness. The concept of balance is universal in appeal and ageless in wisdom. It is this wisdom that helps us address the matters of the soul when we meet resistance brought on by the winds of change.

STRESS IN THE TWENTY-FIRST CENTURY

I opened the mail the other day to receive a high school graduation announcement from the daughter of a friend of mine. I was a bit astonished to see that the Class of 2006 class motto reads as follows: "Dark and difficult times lie ahead. Soon we must all face the choice between what is right and what is easy." The quote by J. K. Rowling's character Albus Dumbledore came from the popular Harry Potter series. This expression was a far cry from my high school class motto from John Lennon: "Give peace a chance." My, how times have changed.

With each year into this new millennium I have noted that optimism has slowly given way to pessimism and despair has begun to edge out hope, perhaps at a time when we need it most. Even the optimists I know confide in me that it takes more work to be an optimist these days than it did a decade ago.

It's no exaggeration to say that a cloud of fear covers the world today in a way that was quite unforeseen, even a decade ago. Global warming, terrorism, urban sprawl, immigration issues, depletion of natural resources (e.g., oil, water, etc.), global epidemics (e.g., bird flu and SARS), natural disasters (e.g., hurricanes, floods of biblical proportions, etc.), and religious wars with no resolution top the headlines—every night. Fear itself has become a virus of sorts, and it is *highly* contagious. Fear creates division at a time when unity is needed. While there were many people who thought the world (as we knew it) would end in 2000 with Y2K, a growing number of people today fear the end times are not only near, they have arrived with a vengeance! When fear strikes the hearts and minds of people, we can either confront it head-on, or run and hide. Sadly, it appears many people have taken refuge in dogma, which, as the wisdom-keepers of all generations remind us, greatly limits rather than encourages spiritual growth.

Take a moment to look around and observe the pace of life we are living today. Does the word *frantic* come to mind? Those who aren't biting their fingernails with anxiety are grinding their teeth and pounding their fists in anger as we settle into the age of "the entitlement generation." Road rage, air rage, phone rage, sports rage, election rage, and just plain rage are all signs that people are at the breaking point of stress. But as bad as this may seem, it proposes to get worse. Current statistics suggest that Americans are overweight, depressed, financially overextended, sleep-deprived, chronically ill, burned out, and distraught about the state of world affairs, from global warming, evaporating civil liberties, and terrorism, to immigration issues, food toxins, and the next deadly flu strain to arrive on our shores. This, from the richest, best-educated nation in the world. Today people simply don't have a firm reference point to gauge the rate of change to what is known. To a growing number of people, the American Dream has become uncomfortable at best and a nightmare at worst. Moreover, information technology, which was supposed to make our lives easier, has only added to the frustration, as expressed in this famous line of graffiti: "Never before has so much technology and information been available to mankind, and never before has mankind been so confused." When one considers the likes of microwaves, synthetic plastics, and genetically engineered foods it's easy to realize that we have evolved thus far for a world that no longer exists. If you can relate to any or all of this, take comfort in the fact that you are not alone.

All of these factors and many more underlie the premise that change and stress are now thought to be synonymous. By and large people do not like change. It disrupts our comfort zones. So the question begs to be asked: Have we become too comfortable in the land of plenty? Are we drowning in the sea of consumer goods? Are we filling a spiritual void with material possessions? If so, change may not be a bad thing. It might just serve as a wake-up call. To paraphrase the sage advice of Finley Peter Dunne, we need to comfort the afflicted, and afflict the comfortable. I think it's safe to say that currently Americans, perhaps the entire planet, are being afflicted, with stress (change) coming from all directions.

While it's true that the rate of change today is markedly faster than at any time in recorded history, the truth of the matter is that change has always been part of the human landscape, and it always will be. As the expression goes, "The only way out is through." Go we must, but implicit in this wisdom is the message that we must go at a reasonable pace and not rush our way, as this will only lead to "burnout," a common expression heard from people in all demographics. Adaptation is the key!

Waiting for the feature movie to begin, I noted that over half of the seats were filled in the theater. More than a few agitated souls elected to view this documentary called *The Corporation*, a social commentary about greed and corruption. In front of me sat two couples discussing a variety of national and world events. Although they weren't speaking loudly, I had no trouble politely eavesdropping on their comments. As the lights began to dim, one of the four closed the conversation with the words, "What we have here is a consensual hallucination." I chuckled to myself, thinking, *Yes, he's right.* How (and why) did we ever agree not only to forfeit our personal power, but to adopt a frantic lifestyle that compromises our integrity, our health, and our human spirit? This is the billion-dollar question of human nature. Perhaps some insight to this answer can be found in the wisdom of comedienne Lily Tomlin, "If you are looking for fast-acting relief . . . try slowing down." To that we can add the new mantra of adaptation to stress, "Wake up, get up, and show up."

Despite the waves of uncertainty, there is always calm to be found in any storm. We have the choice of perception in all that we think and do. Take for example Carl Honoré, the Scotsman who started the "Slow Movement" as a means to seek balance in a warp-speed world. As a newspaper reporter, he lived life at eighty miles per hour in a 24/7 world. One day a light bulb went off in his head as he was reading one-minute bedtime stories to his child. You know, the ones that read like this: Little Red Riding Hood went walking in the woods on the way to her grandmother's house whereupon she encountered a wolf. She promptly killed it. The end. Now go to sleep.

Not only was Honoré aware he was cheating his child of quality bonding time, he realized that he was cheating himself of a great many things by falling prey to the guise of "quick and easy." Honoré's popular book *In Praise of Slow* approaches a host of human behaviors from eating (actually tasting the food before you swallow it) to single tasking, rather than multitasking in an effort to find true happiness in life. What started as a cultural movement in Europe has reached the shores of the United States, and none too soon. Americans, it was recently revealed, have outpaced the Japanese in the number of hours worked per week, many of whom have abandoned their vacation time to work more hours for companies that show no loyalty in return. Cultural aspects may be strong, but each and every culture eventually changes, one person at a time.

One of my favorite pearls of wisdom from Mitch Albom's bestseller, *Tuesdays with Morrie*, was Morrie's sage advice that if you don't like the culture you're in, change the culture by changing yourself. One of the ways in which we can begin to change the downside of twenty-first-century culture in our own environment is to establish healthy boundaries. This means learning to turn off cell phones, iPods, and laptops and spend some quiet time alone, in nature if possible. This also means eating healthy and learning to live within your financial means. In simple terms, it means living from a place of consciousness, fully awake. Wake up, get up, and show up.

As the world spins faster and faster into the twenty-first century we must learn to adapt by slowing down, catching our breath, and reclaiming our personal power for any and all challenges that lie ahead. This challenge may be difficult, but it's not impossible. Each day we are called upon to return to balance.

Walking in Balance

The image of balance is familiar to everyone. We learn about it early in life when we stand upright and attempt to take our first steps. From riding a bike to pulling out our checkbooks, the importance of balance cannot be understated. Indeed, it is an inherent component of every aspect of our lives. Perhaps nowhere is the aspect of balance so evident than in the examples of nature (e.g., the seasons and oceanic tides), where stability serves as the proverbial correction factor in maintaining earthly dynamics. We, too, are a part of nature, even though the walls of a home or office can seem like an impassable barrier that denies access to the great outdoors. As one close friend told me, the closest he gets to nature is the Discovery Channel and Animal Planet.

There are those who would strongly argue that the unparalleled stress we are facing today is a result of our separation from nature. Whether you agree with this premise or not, you can appreciate the connection made between stress and imbalance, for it seems obvious that when we are overwhelmed with responsibilities, challenged beyond our means or at the end of our wits, we feel imbalanced. We are first figuratively, and then perhaps quite literally, knocked off our feet.

Stress is the epitome of imbalance. Flat tires, delayed flights, bounced checks, phone tag, long checkout lines, flippant adolescents, cancerous tumors, and backed-up traffic can all disturb our psychic equilibrium.

Episodes of stress tend to hit above our center of gravity (at the point of ego) and metaphorically speaking, knock us off our feet. This metaphor becomes reality when stressors manifest as headaches, backaches, or other maladies that can literally lay us flat on our back. Perhaps in terms of effective stress management, the concept of balance is best summed up in the words of Reinhold Niebuhr, now titled "The Serenity Prayer," and used by every self-help group grounded in the tradition of Alcoholics Anonymous: "God, grant me the serenity to accept the things I cannot change, the courage to change the things I can, and wisdom to know the difference." In other words, stand like mountain, move like water!

To fully understand the dynamics of stress and how it can knock us off balance, it is best to reacquaint ourselves with the basics, starting with some definitions and progressing to the profound relationship between stress and disease. As you will see, every aspect of stress is undeniably intertwined with the essence of human spirituality.

DEFINITIONS OF STRESS

Perhaps the word stress needs no explanation. At some instinctual level we all know what it means. Feelings of being overwhelmed, impatience, panic, anger, frustration, helplessness, anxiety, as well as boredom—all are aspects of stress. Just the same, if you were to ask the first ten people you meet on the street what their definition of stress is, most likely you would hear ten completely different answers. Academicians are no closer to an agreed-upon definition either.

My definition of stress has changed and evolved over the past twenty years. I was first taught that stress was wear and tear on the body, much like repeated driving can produce wear on a car transmission.[2] To a large extent this is true. However, from a scientific point of view— grounded in Western thought in which the body is compared to a machine—this definition is incomplete. We are not machines!

Stress is often defined as the inability to cope with demands placed on a person.[3] One only need think of a frazzled mother attempting to care for newborn twins, or an office manager seated behind a mound of invoices with a phone at each ear, to understand this meaning. I have also heard stress described as "any change we encounter in our lives," and although this notion has merit, this vague definition lacks soul.

What experts do agree on is that stress is a perception—real or imagined—that is interpreted as a threat. If the threat is not resolved, then the effects will eventually produce wear and tear on the body— either in a specific organ or entire body region. What begins in the mind as a perception often ends up as a symptom of disease or illness if left unresolved. In the worst-case scenario, the body becomes the battlefield for the war games of the mind.

In the past decade a new definition has emerged from the fields of transpersonal and humanistic psychology that springs from a spiritual place. From this perspective, stress is seen as a feeling of separateness from God, a feeling of being disconnected from our divine source. This perception is really an illusion, for we are never really detached from God (whatever we conceive God to be).

Perhaps poet Maya Angelou said it best when she wrote, "I believe that Spirit is one and everywhere present. That it never leaves me. That in my ignorance I may withdraw from it, but I can realize its presence the instant I return to my senses."[4]

To say that stress is a disconnection from God holds much merit in a world where people yearn to reconnect to the divine source. While this feeling of separateness may be incorrect, the emotions generated from it are very real. Furthermore, as stress-based perceptions increase, we frequently become victims of our own attitudes and beliefs. The exposure to stress at the individual level is also occurring in society.

Matters of the soul, once left to theologians and religious leaders, are discussed today regularly among people from all walks of life, including poets, playwrights, athletes, actors, and even some politicians. And as the world quickly spins into the new millennium, the topic of human spirituality is taking a prominent, if not urgent, role in these discussions. A growing number of people feel the survival of the human race depends on it. It is here on the global stage where we see the dynamics of stress and human spirituality played out on a daily basis. Whether it involves environmental factors, economic issues, or healthcare reform, it is all related. But before we begin to understand these dynamics on a global scale, perhaps it is best to first become reacquainted with some of the basics of stress at an individual level.

THE STRESS RESPONSE (FIGHT OR FLIGHT)

Within each of us resides the means for survival, a means to confront or retreat from the dangers of physical threats. At our most primitive level, this physiological system enables us to do one of two things: to hold our ground, defend our territory, draw blood if necessary, and ward off danger . . . or to run like hell. We see examples of the fight-or-flight response (coined by physiologist Walter Cannon in the early twentieth century) all the time: the attack of a mother bear protecting her cubs, a dog that defends its master's house, or birds that fly away when a cat approaches. The flight response was never more dramatically and literally evident than when demonstrated by thousands of people fleeing the twin towers of the World Trade Center as they collapsed into a pile of rubble on September 11, 2001.

In times of physical threat, our body prepares to fight or flee. In a complex series of metabolic activities, the heart pumps quicker to get oxygenated blood to the muscles in time to move. Like a symphony preparing for the crescendo, blood pressure rises, ventilation increases, neural synapses fire, muscles begin to tighten, and digestion virtually halts, as a host of hormones and chemicals (including adrenaline) flood the bloodstream to provide various substances for energy production. It is all to one end: to survive the threat.

The fight-or-flight response is astounding when it comes to escaping from a burning building or even hustling from one airport terminal to another to catch a tight connection. As amazing as this ability to respond is, the physiological reaction is inappropriate for nonphysical threats such as sitting in traffic, playing phone tag, or standing in a long checkout line. Its purpose is inadequate to deal effectively with the many stressful situations we commonly face.

Most of our threats today are not physical. Instead they are mental (being overwhelmed or bored, emotional, worried, or guilty), or spiritual (assessing relationships, values, and one's purpose in life). Yet the body reacts to these threats, regardless of their nature, in the same fashion: with increases in heart rate, blood pressure, metabolic rate, ventilation, and muscle tension. In effect, unresolved issues and the emotions they solicit will ultimately wreak havoc on the body.

Becoming aware of our stressors is the first step in the resolution process. Ask yourself what stresses you out, makes you feel uptight, angry, anxious, or overwhelmed. Which, if any, are physical stressors?

Your Top Five Personal Stressors

1. _____
2. _____
3. _____
4. _____
5. _____

THE NATURE OF STRESS

Stress quickly begins with the perception of threat to our personal existence. Then the emotions join in—anger, fear, or both. Before long a chain reaction of neurochemical responses is triggered and released throughout the body for fight or flight. Not all stress is bad for you, however. Experts in the field of stress management agree that there is both good stress and bad stress. Good stress is anything that motivates you or inspires you to accomplish a goal or influences you to get something done. Good stress also includes those peak experiences of exhilaration. Bad stress—also called *distress*—pushes you over the edge of comfort. Distress can be acute, short-term stress or chronic, long-term stress.

Acute stress is intense but short-lived, like being pulled over for a speeding ticket or locking your keys in your car. The threat is over quickly, and life soon returns to normal (as does your body's physiology).

Chronic stress, conversely, tends to have a much longer duration— months or years, such as the stress associated with marital or financial problems, a career rut, or the boss from hell. Most stress researchers agree that chronic stressors are related to chronic disease and illness. Even at low levels, the body can only remain aroused in the stress mode for a finite time before the organs ultimately begin to show signs of dysfunction. Long-term stress also tests the strength of our inner resources such as humor, creativity, faith, patience, courage, compassion, forgiveness, and willpower.

THE STRESS EMOTIONS: ANGER AND FEAR

A multitude of feelings can and will surface at the first moment of distress: impatience, embarrassment, anxiety or frustration, to name a few. Anger shows itself through guilt, prejudice, envy, jealousy, hostility, and rage. Fear can manifest in a host of emotions, including doubt, anxiety, and paranoia. Fear can be so overpowering that it immobilizes all other thoughts and actions. While both anger and fear are linked to depression, unresolved anger issues tend to have the upper hand. In the words of comic Steven Wright, "Depression is anger without the enthusiasm."

Do anger and fear differ? Some insist that fear and anger are the same. They say that anger is merely an expression of fear. While there may be an element of truth to this notion, in terms of the stress response there are clear lines drawn between the two. Fight is not the same thing as fright. Perhaps it is best said that anger and fear are two sides of the same stress coin.[5]

Like love and joy, anger and fear are critical parts of the human equation. While they merit their respective place on the continuum of human emotions, too often there is an abundance of negativity. The result is inadequate exposure to positive emotions. Hence, there is an imbalance in one's emotional well-being. This trend toward negative thinking isn't just indicative of the younger generation; it is widespread among all age groups, professions and levels of income. In the field of psychology it is known as "victim consciousness."

When I first heard that expression, I thought it was a term used solely in upper-level psychology courses. Then I met a man at my neighborhood gas station while waiting for my car to be fixed. The man was sitting across from me when he lowered his morning newspaper and asked me point blank, "Hey, what do you do for a living?" I briefly shared my professional background with some polite but direct eye contact, then asked him the same question.

"I'm a victim!" he said boldly.

"Of the economy?" I asked.

"No," he retorted, "just a victim!"

There you have it, victim consciousness personified—a behavior that keeps us top-heavy with negative thoughts and feelings, generated by anger or fear. It can be addicting. One of my favorite expressions of victim consciousness reads: Once a victim, twice a volunteer.

This is not to say that anger and fear are bad and should be avoided. To the contrary. They are important, if not essential, to the human condition—in moderation. But not at the expense of one's emotional balance.

Both anger and fear are considered survival emotions. In times of danger, one or both of these emotions serve as a motivation to move, run, and hide. They are meant to last only long enough to get out of harm's way. However, unlike all other animals, the human species has evolved to a consciousness where we allow these feelings of anger and fear to linger for days, months, and even years. Human nature, so greatly influenced by ego, thinks, "If some is good, more has got to be better."

ANGER: THE DARK EMOTION

Phone tag. Spam. Traffic lights. Car trouble. Negative coworkers. The ex-spouse from hell. Cell phones. Everytime anger surfaces it is because of an unmet expectation. You thought the person you called would be there, but she wasn't. You thought you could make it

through the yellow traffic light, but you didn't. You thought your car would start in the cold weather. Wrong again. When things don't go as planned, it is natural to feel frustrated. To have expectations is also normal. In fact, our expectations often serve as a motivation to set and accomplish goals.

To harbor feelings of unresolved anger when desires are not met, however, becomes a control issue; we are at the mercy of our ego, controlled by unbridled emotions. Herein lies the danger. Repeated exposure to unmet expectations can turn successive bouts of frustration into perpetual resentment. The result is a sense of victimization, where we feel we have lost control of our lives. When this happens, many people feel God has ignored them, or worse, abandoned them.

Since the day Cain killed Abel in a fit of jealous rage, anger has been perceived as the darkest side of humanity. Since that time, there have been scores of examples that underlie the perception that any expression of anger is taboo. Social mores abound regarding the inexcusable displays of hostility.

It may come as no surprise to women to learn that they have been handicapped regarding expressions of anger. To show, vent, or display frustration detracts from the feminine nature that Western culture has deemed socially acceptable. In her book, *The Dance of Anger*, author Harriet Lerner highlights the social mores that have denied women the ability to feel and express anger. She writes, "The taboos against our feeling and expressing anger are so powerful that even knowing when we are angry is not a simple matter."[6]

If anger has a dark side, it is one we have placed there ourselves. Now we have learned to fear our anger. True, the countless bouts of rage and hostility that make the headlines at an alarming rate support the idea that rampant hostility is a blight on humanity. However, through research in the field of mind-body medicine, we are learning that to ignore anger is no better. Unresolved anger sows the seeds of disease and illness, including the nation's number-one killer, coronary heart disease. Research also indicates that there is a link with some forms of cancer as well. Specifically, the stress hormone cortisol, that lingers in the blood, tends to destroy white blood cells. Let there be no doubt, our emotions greatly impact our physical health.[7]

We have begun to realize that the emotional effects of unresolved anger on the body are so detrimental, they can no longer be neglected. They must be fully recognized, addressed, and resolved as quickly as possible.

There is a growing body of knowledge supporting the premise that anger is just as healthy, and perhaps as necessary, as love, compassion, and joy (remember, first and foremost, anger is a survival emotion). Energy can be generated from anger when it is channeled in a creative means, rather than toward a destructive end.

As an example, a college buddy whose father died began to lift weights as a means to erase his anger. In less than a few months, he had nearly doubled his muscle mass. The strength he needed to endure the emotional pain came in no small part from the physical strength he acquired through weight training.

Anger is not the same thing as aggression. Anger is a feeling. Aggression is a behavior. To feel angry is normal and healthy. The expression of anger, however, must be done constructively, not destructively.

Once used as a defense against physical danger, anger is now used to defend our thoughts, feelings, perceptions, beliefs, and attitudes. With these perceptions, however, come expectations. Although at times expectations can serve as a positive motivation, more often they act to undermine our best efforts when we encounter roadblocks on the human journey.

Thomas Jefferson once said, "If you get mad, count to ten. If you get really angry, count to one hundred."

While the time allotment for an anger episode will vary from person to person, anger that is left unresolved becomes a control issue. Whether we are trying to control ourselves or others, when feelings of anger exceed the circumstance that provoked these feelings, the result is that we become controlled by our anger. By clinging to our anger, we give away our power.

Throughout the history of modern psychology, anger took a back seat to the study of anxiety. Freud, who used Darwin's rage reflex theory to support his own idea that humans operate on instinct, turned his attention toward what appeared to be the lesser of two evils—anxiety. Because of Freud's penchant toward anxiety, anger was left neglected until the mid-1960s, when researchers acknowledged that personalities based on hostility (type A behavior) ran a significant risk factor for coronary heart disease.[8] When the connection between stress and disease surfaced, psychologists were led to examine more closely the dark emotion of anger. To no surprise, the findings prove that Americans do not express their feelings of anger very well. In fact, we learned that there is no shortage of ways in which we channel our anger inappropriately.

In his book *Make Anger Your Ally*, Neil Clark Warren classifies mismanaged anger styles into four categories: the somatizer, the exploder, the self-punisher, and the underhander—all commonly seen as traits of human behavior.[9] Here are descriptions of these behavior styles. As you read through these, ask yourself if you recognize any of these behaviors:

• The *somatizer* is someone who doesn't show his or her anger. In most cases this person is unaware of his or her feelings of anger. Rather than expressing anger, this person constantly suppresses these feelings and replaces them with (or hides them behind) a smile, frown, blush, or tears. These behaviors are usually learned early in life, when, fearing loss of acceptance from friends and family, these people learned to hide their anger. Since *soma* means body in Latin, the mind-body connection indicates that unresolved anger will eventually surface as disease and illness, including TMJD (jaw spasms from tooth grinding), migraine headaches, ulcers, hypertension or high blood pressure, rheumatoid arthritis, lupus, fibromyalgia, and some problems associated with the liver.

- The *exploder* is someone who has no problem showing feelings of anger. As a rule, he or she tends to erupt like a volcano, spewing hot lava in the direction of those people who can be intimidated. The exploder is typically someone who makes the headlines with this behavior when it erupts into drive-by shootings, hijackings, domestic violence, workplace violence, and mass slayings. More common explosive behavior includes swearing (the prolific use of the F word) and rude driving habits (road rage).

- The *self-punisher* is the name for the person who converts anger into guilt. In doing so, he or she substitutes rage for obsessive-compulsive (addictive) behaviors, including excessive eating, sleeping, exercise, even sex. Once while I was describing this anger style in a workshop, a woman yelled out, "Hey, you forgot shopping!" The response drew several chuckles, but after my presentation I learned this was no laughing matter. Used in vengeance toward oneself or someone else, retail therapy is no therapy at all. Left unresolved, this style of mismanaged anger will lead to depression. Sadly, this mismanaged anger style includes cutting (self-mutilation), a behavior all too common among teens. Depression also qualifies in the category. Depression, as Freud explained, is anger turned inward.

- The *underhander's* theme is "Don't get mad, get even." By displaying socially acceptable ways of revenge, the underhander tries to manipulate others passive-aggressively. Examples include sarcasm (also known as verbal sabotage), withholding information or chronic tardiness (late for meetings). This is the most common mismanaged anger style at the worksite. The motive for revenge is control, but this hunger is never fully satisfied. As the expression goes, "He who seeks revenge should dig two graves."

Although each of these inappropriate styles of anger may be present in everyone's behavior to some extent, it is now commonly believed that one anger style is prevalent in our personalities. Although you may overeat on occasion or honk your horn, your primary anger style may be that of an underhander. It should be pointed out that none of these mismanaged anger styles is advocated, since they do nothing to resolve the situation. (Once I had a workshop participant say, "Hey, I'm a somatizer. Does that mean I should change to being an exploder?" The answer was a definitive no!)

Remember, every episode of unresolved anger becomes a control issue. The irony is that while you may think you are controlling someone by staying mad (perhaps even thinking, "I'll show her"), you are actually giving your power away. Your angry feelings are controlling you and will continue to do so until you let them go. Elizabeth Kenny said it best when she wrote these words: "He who angers you, conquers you." [10]

Watching or listening to the news may not be the most accurate reflection of our world, but it does reveal the level of frustration felt by many in our society. Such expressions as voter anger, hostile takeovers, aggressive advertising, negative campaigning, in-your-face marketing, and frustrated youth are common.

In the early 1980s it was noted that Americans get angry fifteen times per day. If current polls of the entitlement generation are correct, then that number is rising. Statistics indicate that there is an upswing in wife beatings, workplace violence, and other acts of aggression. The American dream—our birthright—is no longer in reach, which means feelings of frustration continue to mount. The media now has given this phenomenon a name: floating anxiety.

To walk in balance, to move like water means to reconcile our angry feelings, and the sooner the better. Rather than cast blame, we must take responsibility for our actions. Indira Gandhi once said, "You cannot shake hands with a clenched fist," meaning that peace will not come until anger has subsided.[11] Whether we refine our expectations, change our perceptions, modify our behavior, or learn to forgive and accept without feeling violated, we must learn to resolve anger if we are to continue our progress on the human journey. Forgiveness, patience, and compassion are expressions of the human spirit.

FEAR: THE FLIGHT EMOTION

Think of a time when you were confronted with a problem and your first reaction was to turn around and walk away. Being afraid is natural, and these feelings can surface in several ways: doubt, embarrassment, guilt, worry, hope, pity, and anxiety. Like anger, fear is a survival emotion, triggered by any situation or circumstance where some aspect of danger is perceived.

Fear arises when we feel threatened. Fear motivates you to run from a burning building and compels you to hide from a growling dog. In this day and age, typical stressors that cause a fear-based reaction are grounded in the mental, emotional and spiritual aspects of our lives. Despite the nature of the problem, the initial reaction is usually the desire to run and hide. Every feeling triggered by fear is based on some issue of security or lack thereof.

There are those who suggest that the elicitation of the fear response is either functional (avoiding an accident) or dysfunctional (worrying about being late for a meeting). More often than not, it is the latter when we distort our perceptions of danger and make mountains out of molehills.

What differentiates functional fears from dysfunctional fears is ego panic. When the ego feels threatened it quickly sets up a defense. The term frequently used to describe this type of behavior is *fear-based thinking*, and examples of this thought process abound everywhere. Moreover, it is fear-based thinking that underlies the behaviors that are best known as the litany of human sins: lying, stealing, cheating, and killing.

As a healthcare professional, I encounter fear-based thinking daily. I see it surface when physicians are threatened by alternative medicine practitioners; in citizens who are afraid of losing insurance coverage; in politics over budget cuts. Anxiety, doubt, and fear are the undercurrents of many of our everyday perceptions.

Fear-based thinking is so rampant in American society, it has become the dominant thought process that runs our lives. Our fear of not having enough is fueled by a powerful corporate infrastructure that preys on our inadequacies. Advertisements tell us we need more products to satisfy this need or rectify this inadequacy. Fear does have an addictive quality to it, so quick fixes aimed to soothe the ego only create a dependency.

Think of a time you were waiting for someone who was late. Your mind begins to create a worst-case scenario: a terrible accident or disaster. This thought may prompt you to call the police station or make changes in your plans based on the sensation of fear.

COMFORT ZONES IN TWILIGHT

The roots of fear travel deep into the heart of humanity. Fear of the unknown, of rejection, of failure, of death (the grandest fear of all) lurk in the shadows of our collective soul. Yet if there is a way to describe the increase of fear-based thinking, it can be summed up in the word *change*.

As a rule we don't like change because it forces us out of our zones of comfort. To quote educator Roy Blitzer, "The only person who likes change is a wet baby."[12] Comfort is another word for security; change threatens it. It's human behavior to create a sense of comfort, not only in our living space, but also in our perceptions, ideas and beliefs. When these are challenged, the walls of the ego stiffen as a means of protection. But the elements of change can seep through these walls, like the waters that permeate the basement of a house in the midst of a flood. Nothing is sacred to the tides of change.

Being moved or pushed out of our comfort zones is not necessarily a bad thing; this is often where real growth takes place. Such was the case with Barbara, a high-powered corporate executive who found herself battling stress on two fronts: a messy divorce followed by a rumor of imminent downsizing at her company. Separating from her husband wasn't her choice; he was going through a midlife crisis. She got the house, but aside from losing the man she loved, the combined income was halved, resulting in drastic lifestyle changes. The dust hadn't even settled yet when she was fired from her job. Barbara was thrown out of her comfort zone, and the ripples of fear emanated to all other aspects of her life. But in the spirit of self-reflection, she has since changed the tack on her life's course.

As part of a weekend stress-management course, Barbara shared these thoughts with the class during an exercise in positive affirmations:

I used to place my security in both my job and my family. When those were abruptly washed away, I came to the realization that I had to search within. I began to tell myself, "I am the source of my security," or "I am the source of my power and my happiness." When I placed my security in my job or my marriage, I gave it away freely.

I don't do that anymore. I know now that whatever problems I come across, my security cannot be taken from me again.

No matter how well we fortify our comfort zones with barriers of protection, change is inevitable. It is also a fact of life. The world spins at a rate of 1,000-plus miles per hour. This alone creates fluctuation. Change keeps the world dynamic. Stagnation leads to decay or toxicity. So the question becomes: How can we be comfortable with change? The answer may sound simple, but its application is challenging. Change must be faced with an open heart.

The opposite of fear is courage. The word courage comes to us from the French, through a derivation of two words meaning "big heart." When we think of courage, we tend to think of bravery or fortitude in the face of adversity. But there is also an element of compassion, for bravery means an open heart. Through love, fear is tamed, while compassion allows us to flow gracefully as our comfort zones are expanded.

To paraphrase the words written about Jesus of Nazareth, with love, all things are possible. In every situation where change threatens our sense of security, we are offered two choices: fear and love. Like an AM/FM radio with poor reception, fear creates static that can obliterate the voice of compassion. In times of stress, it could be that we turn a deaf ear to God. When we choose the path of love, by acting through the open heart of courage, we merge divine will with that of our own. Author Gerald Jampolsky said it best when he wrote the simple words, "Love is letting go of fear."[13]

In this day and age, the rate of change is fast and furious. Just keeping up with the advances in technology is enough to make one's heart beat faster. The thought of downsizing, losing a job, changing jobs, relocating, or altering family dynamics can stir the gastric juices and tense muscles. Unresolved fear, like unresolved anger, can and will ultimately show up in the body. The body really does become the battlefield for the war games of the mind.

"Our emotions are the link between the mind and the body," says Candace Pert, a neurophysiologist who discovered that the brain and immune system have the same receptors. Emotions are in two realms. They are in the realm of the physical, but they are also in the realm of the spiritual. That's why they are so critically important.[14] Important, indeed, because left unresolved, they can lead to serious health-related problems.

STRESS AND DISEASE

Stephanie is a mother of three children. Her husband, Ted, is a sales representative for a large corporation; he travels at least four days of each week. It's a tough job raising the children alone. Despite her love for Ted, Stephanie resents his job, which has affected her health. Her story is a good example of the mind-body-spirit connection.

"Just look at me," she said to me one day. "I've lost three organs— my spleen, gall bladder, and ovaries. On top of that I'm thirty-five pounds overweight. You better believe there has been a lot of stress in my life: stress in the form of anger."

Stephanie is perhaps one of millions who has experienced the stress and disease connection. The mind understands the concept of balance; so does the body. Acute or chronic stress throws the physiological limits out of whack. Within minutes after an episode of acute stress, the body will return to a normal resting state, or homeostasis. Exposure to chronic stress, however, may prevent the body from fully regaining its physiological balance. So it is easy to see how, when various organs are denied a rest, dysfunction will follow.

Today, experts in the field of *psychoneuroimmunology* suggest that as much as 80 percent of all chronic disease is associated with stress.

Worker compensation claims to holistic practitioners' patient data document this disturbing trend. Moreover, research studies show a direct (if not causal) relationship between stress and disease, from the common cold to cancer, and nearly everything in between. Although the effects of emotional stress on our physical well-being are obvious to many, many doctors trained in a different paradigm remain unconvinced. Physicians are taught that the body is like a machine, and that only drugs and surgery can fix it. The Western approach to medicine still views the mind and body as separate entities. Moreover, this approach does not recognize the spiritual component of health.

But concepts can change. Such is the case with the emerging ideal of mind-body-spirit healing, an ancient concept that has been recently rediscovered in the West. In 1974, while researching various aspects of health behavior, Robert Ader came to the conclusion that emotional thought has a profound impact on physiological function. Recalling Pavlov's experiments with dogs, Ader was curious to know how long a conditioned response would last in laboratory rats. Teaching the rats to associate sugar water with a one-time injection of a nausea-producing drug commonly used in chemotherapy, Ader was astonished to learn that in a short period of time, the association proved lethal. He concluded that it was the rats' perception of the sugar water that led to their demise. Upon further examination, it was discovered that the rats had learned to suppress their immune system merely by associating the noxious drug with the sugar water.[15] Ader's research, later corroborated by several others, soon laid the groundwork for a new understanding of the dynamics between mind, body, spirit, and emotions. In 1981 Ader coined the word *psychoneuroimmunology*, a term now associated with the study of mind-body medicine.

While Ader was busy with his research, which looked at immune suppression, other scientists were busy looking at the mind-body connection in terms of enhancing the immune system. Since that time numerous additional studies have supported the premise that, without a doubt, our emotions can either suppress or enhance the nature of the immune system.

The emerging field of psychoneuroimmunology is composed of several different disciplines including biochemistry, behavioral medicine, complementary healing, psychology, physiology, and several others. However, what was once called mind-body medicine by those who formed this alliance in the early 1980s has slightly changed its focus to include the spirit—as in mind-body-spirit medicine. In studies investigating the remarkable recoveries of patients with terminal illnesses, it is the human spirit that takes center stage to initiate the healing process.

Times have changed since Galileo was locked in a tower by Pope Urban VIII in 1633 for going against the prevailing paradigm of the center of the universe. Today the fields of science and religion are merging onto common ground. Explorations in the fields of quantum physics, biochemistry, transpersonal psychology, and clinical medicine have shown that the reaches of human consciousness far exceed the gray matter of the brain cells. In fact, human consciousness, as a part of divine consciousness, seems to be connected to, not separated from, all aspects of life.

With regard to stress and disease, these new insights show that our thoughts and emotions can significantly affect our physical health. It should be noted that these mavericks who bushwhacked their way to the vanguard of higher consciousness didn't gain their insights solely from reading books and articles. Their exposure to this universal wisdom came equally from personal experience. So has mine.

One day while roaming the aisles of a bookstore, I found myself drawn to a picture book on healing. Flipping though the pages, I came across a photograph of a couple outside their house. Looming in the background was a rather large power plant generator with power lines reaching toward the horizon. The story that accompanied the photograph described their bouts with cancer and their concern about the effects of electrical currents (extremely low frequencies, or ELFs). It was a startling story.

Turning a few more pages, I focused on a photograph of a woman doing a technique called therapeutic touch. Not familiar with the technique, I read the story to discover a concept called the human energy field. Both stories, I was to later learn, spoke of the nature of entrainment, a term introduced through the work of Dutch mathematician Christiaan Huygens in 1665 to describe the sympathetic resonance between the oscillating vibrations of two objects. (Huygens noted this occurrence with pendulum clocks.) And while my first thought was one of skepticism, I turned back to the photo of the couple with cancer and decided this topic merited more attention.

Not long after that experience, I bought a few books on the topic of the human energy field and began to compile notes for a lecture I was giving. In the section on healing there were several books, but one caught my eye—Robert Becker's *Cross Currents*. Becker is an orthopedic surgeon with a deep interest in electromagnetic fields. Twice nominated for a Nobel prize in medicine for previous work in this area, Becker took the task in hand to elaborate on the topic of electromagnetic fields and the dangers of cancer.

Just as I was about to reach for this book, a woman beside me also reached for it. With only one copy left, I asked: "Just out of curiosity, may I ask what your interest is with the topic of the human energy field?"

"Well, my house has turned into a freak show. If I walk into the kitchen with the lights off, the lights come on. If I walk by the television, it turns off—all by itself. Appliances go on or off whenever I enter the room, and I am just trying to figure what's going on," she said.

When she paused I kindly looked her in the eyes and said, "I think you need this book more than I do."

As it turned out, the store clerk found another copy in the back room, so we both left happy. But I was reminded that the human energy field is a very real phenomenon.

Becker's book introduced me to Mietek Wirkus, a healer who can actually see the human energy field. What's more, Mietek can also detect the emergence of disease and illness in the energy field, even before symptoms appear in the body. Through a technique he calls bio-energy healing, Mietek senses distortions in the energy field as energy "clouds." Where possible he removes these emotional congestions, which then allows for the free movement of subtle energy through the chakras (energy centers located in various regions of the body that connect to the endocrine and nervous systems).

During my lecture on the human energy field, one of my students raised his hand and mentioned that he, too, had been to a healer named Mietek Wirkus who lived in the Washington area. Through the subtle mystery of synchronicity, I soon found myself at the home of Mietek and Margaret Wirkus. Under their direction I took a year-long course in bio-energy healing.

As Mietek and Margaret explained, the human entity is not composed merely of a physical body. We are mind, emotions, and spirit as well. Various layers of energy that surround and permeate the body are associated with the emotional, mental, and spiritual vibrations. Thoughts and emotions are not a result of impulses sent from one neuron to another throughout the brain; they originate in the energy field. Like water that cascades down terrace steps to collect in a pool below, thoughts and feelings cascade down through the layers of the energy field to the most dense layer of energy—the physical body.

Over time, unresolved emotions such as anger and fear tend to cause a distortion in the human aura. In essence, emotional baggage can become tumors, arthritis, and clogged arteries. From years of experience and observation, Mietek has learned to recognize illness that will result from unresolved stress. His rate of accuracy is astonishing. And he is not alone. My conversations with other renowned healers, including Donna Eden and Caroline Myss, all confirm the same premise—disease begins in the energy field.

The concepts of the human energy field and *chakras* (a Sanskrit word for spinning wheel) may be foreign to the Western scientific mind, but they are not completely unknown to those familiar with the Judeo-Christian culture, particularly in the artwork and sculptures passed down through the ages. For centuries, the crown chakra, which signifies a conscious awareness of the divine, has been painted as a halo over the head of those saintly figures who were consciously aware of a divine presence in their lives.

Recently I was reminded of the concept of the human energy field while walking through Catholic hospitals, where there are several statues of holy figures adorned in golden auras, and again when I took a trip to Santa Fe, New Mexico. It was in Santa Fe where I became most impressed with the exquisite frescoes that adorn the sides of many buildings. Paintings of the Virgin Mary, a figure highly regarded by those of the Catholic faith, typically show her enshrouded with a golden aura of light. The good news is that you don't have to be a virgin saint to have an aura. We all do!

Richard Gerber, M.D., is a radiologist who has thoroughly explored the theory of the human energy field. His interest was piqued when he experimented with Kirlian photography, using several of his cancer patients as subjects. Kirlian photography, developed in 1940 by a Russian researcher, Semyon Kirlian, is considered one of the first methods to measure one aspect of the electromagnetic field. By observing tiny electronic particles displayed in a formation of brilliant colors emanating from the body, the Kirlian photograph creates an image of what is believed to be the closest layer of energy surrounding the body. Gerber noted that the pattern and intensity of colors around the hands of cancer patients were significantly duller when compared with the vibrant colors emanating from the hands of healthy control subjects.

In his much-acclaimed book *Vibrational Medicine*, Gerber explores the theory of the human energy field, citing the results of several double-blind studies, and examining practices ranging from acupuncture and homeopathy to therapeutic touch. The human energy field is composed of several layers of consciousness, each designated by a vibrational frequency associated with it. Thoughts, perceptions, and emotions originate in various layers of the human energy field. As they cascade through the mind-body interface they are decoded at the molecular level, which then causes various biochemical changes in the body. As Gerber explains:

> *Thoughts are particles of energy. [Negative] thoughts are accompanied by emotions which also begin at the energy levels. As these particles of energy filter through the etheric levels to the physical level, the end result is immuno-incompetence.*[16]

Whereas years ago, the autonomic nervous system and endocrine system were thought to play the dominant role in the association between stress and disease, it is now the immune system that has taken on primary importance in the mind-body-spirit equation. It works both ways: Immuno-incompetence leads to disease and illness, and immuno-enhancement restores physiological homeostasis.

In an article titled "Healings, Remissions, and Miracle Cures," published in the *Whole Earth Review*, Brendan O'Regan explored the dynamics of spontaneous remission. He writes:

Remission means the act of remitting, a natural resigning or relinquishing, surrendering. Forgiveness; pardon as of sins or crimes. There are some very interesting messages locked up in those words.[17]

Various studies that report on the phenomena known as spontaneous remissions, miracles, and healings all speak to the nature of attitudinal change, or a shift in consciousness. It seems that acts of forgiveness, acceptance, optimism, and compassion not only cleanse the soul, but in several documented cases of healing, clear the distortions often detected in the human aura. In a significant handful of cases, the result is a reversal of the disease process, leading one back to health.

A more appropriate term for stress might be *energy disease.* As the explorations of human consciousness expand and merge with the investigations of quantum physics, a host of theories begin to surface that describe human consciousness as a form of energy that emanates well beyond the physical body. You've heard the expression, "Laughter is contagious." In line with that premise, fear-based thinking may be infectious as well. Healers like Mietek Wirkus and Ethel Lombardi see more than just auras around people. They also see auras around towns and cities. Sometimes the colors they see are not pretty. Negativity can cast an ugly hue similar to the worst smog hovering over Los Angeles.

The skies over Boulder, Colorado, were sunny and warm the third weekend of May in 2006. Inside the hotel, the air conditioning was attempting to compensate for the ambient temperatures. The room was somewhat dark as people lined up outside to enter the ballroom for what promised to be an extraordinary event. The afternoon session of the healing conference held at the Millennium Hotel featured a young man from Vancouver, Canada, named Adam. We would soon learn that Adam preferred a darkened room, as this allowed him to see the human energy field much better.

I first learned of Adam from an article in *Rolling Stone* magazine in 2003. One part Harry Potter (a birthmark on his forehead) and two parts X-Men (X-ray vision and the gift of energy healing), Adam could always see auras. At the tender age of fourteen, he discovered that he had an ability to heal people through a connection made via the human energy field. Adam (who only goes by a pseudonym) achieved notoriety by healing renowned musician, Ronnie Hawkins— via a photograph, no less (photographs contain an energetic imprint). First the music world paid homage, and then the entire world took notice shortly after the magazine article appeared.

Adam, now in his early twenties, took the stage and shared the story of his odyssey as a healer, a story that included mystical visions and remarkable healings, both distant and local. Adam also confirmed the stress and disease connection, explaining the emotional tie with disease and illness was not an association but a direct causal connection.[18]

As with many healers with a similar gift, Adam made it very clear that we each have this ability to work with the energy field and cultivate the powers of self-healing. The underlying message of his presentation was self-empowerment, despite the fact that many people wanted a quick fix to their health issues.

"We each have the power to heal when we can unite the powers of our conscious and unconscious minds," he explained, walking us through a powerful guided visualization that left the entire audience amazed, yet relaxed.

One of the newest voices to join the chorus of mavericks in the field of psychoneuroimmunology (or PNI for short) is that of Bruce Lipton, Ph.D. As a researcher in the field of biology, Bruce was fascinated with the structure and function of the cell membrane. His investigations transitioned from cell biology to human physiology as he noticed in his own life how his mind affected his body and various states of health. In his investigations into the stress response as explored in his landmark book, *The Biology of Belief*, Bruce writes about the concept of subpersonalities of the unconscious mind and the role of self-sabotage:

> *I call it the "belief effect" to stress that our perceptions, whether they are accurate or inaccurate, equally impact our behavior and our bodies. Ultimately our biology adapts to our beliefs.*[19]

The consequences of our thoughts, beliefs, perceptions, and attitudes (which are conscious energy) will either enhance or compromise our immune systems. Bruce reminds us that we can live a life with a focus on fear or love. Either way, our bodies will adapt to the perceptions in which we choose to see/filter the world. The choice is ours.

How does one build an immunity to negativity and fear-based thinking, either self-generated or absorbed from the company of others? Perhaps the answer lies in the development of the strength of our inner resources and the innate healing potential of the human spirit. The following stories highlight three remarkable individuals who overcame their challenges. Their stories remind us of the potential that we all have within ourselves.

PROFILES OF SPIRITUALITY: I

I have a friend, originally from Shanghai, China, who once told me there is no word for stress in her language. "We refer to it as 'opportunity,'" she said with a faint smile. If anyone has known stress, it is she. In the summer of 1966, at the age of fifty-five, Nien Cheng's life took an unimaginable turn for the worse and continued that way for over half a decade.

It was the dawn of Mao Tse-tung's cultural revolution, and tension hung heavy in the air. She was educated in London, employed by the Shell Oil corporation as a management advisor, and the widow of a former official of Chiang Kai-shek. In this political climate, the cards were stacked heavily against her. In no time, Nien was quickly targeted, then accused as a spy. First placed under house arrest, she was soon locked in solitary confinement in a cell no bigger than a walk-in closet at the Number 1 Detention House for political prisoners. All of her possessions were sold off, and her home, belongings, and way of life soon became a distant memory.

Day after day she was harassed at gunpoint to confess to a crime she did not commit. Her persistence prevailed. "In China," she told me, "personal honor is most sacred. I was committed to proving my innocence, I had no choice. If they could denounce me, they would go after my daughter and family members."

Despite repeated bouts of hunger, disease, humiliation, intimidation, and terror, Nien repeatedly defended her innocence. Today, if you were to look at her wrists, you would see the scars left by extremely tight shackles she was forced to wear for long periods of time.

Upon her release in 1972, she was declared a victim of false arrest. In her book, *Life and Death in Shanghai*, she described the harrowing ordeal of her survival and the journey to leave her country upon learning of the mysterious, if not disturbing, death of her only daughter. One cannot help but be impressed with the fortitude and strength of her human spirit to survive in an environment where others quickly perished from the torture of the Communist Red Guards.

Sitting in her living room one day, I glanced at a black-and-white photograph of her daughter Mei Ping. My mind was absorbed in the plight of Nien, an incredible story of a woman who survived a harrowing ordeal to become a living testimony of the strength of the human spirit. And this strength never wavers.

"We have a philosophy in China called Taoism," she said over a cup of tea and Chinese pastry, as she recounted various moments of those six-and-a-half years. "It describes the balance of life. The quality of patience is very important, and I knew that I must employ patience daily in my situation."

Patience, however, was not her only resource of spiritual strength. Intrigued, I gently inquired what other factors helped her get through this tribulation. She replied, "I saw my stay at the detention house as a challenge and with the grace of God, I was committed to proving my innocence." She, like others in times of stress, often cites a connection to the divine when describing the passage through a harrowing tribulation such as hers. Indeed, there is no other way. If, as Shakespeare says, the eyes are the windows of the soul, then the soul of Nien Cheng is a bright shining star in the universe of humanity.

In 2006 I made a trip to Washington D.C., for a conference on healing. I stayed an extra day to visit Nien. Although she had just turned ninety-one, she didn't look a day over seventy. She credits her tai chi, but I think a few other attributes are responsible. Patience and grace may be her strongest inner resources, but a sense of humor isn't far behind. As I knocked on her front door, I kicked off my Birkenstocks. She opened the door to greet me with a twinkle in her eye and then looked down at my feet, smiling.

Without skipping a beat she said. "Dear, please keep your shoes on. That's Japanese. I'm Chinese."

PROFILES OF SPIRITUALITY: II

There comes a time when every male teenager dreams of being the man of the house, but when it happened to Brian, even with one year of college under his belt, he wasn't prepared. It is not easy to lose a parent at any age, but to see your father die of cancer while you are still in your teens is exceptionally tough.

Before he learned of his father's diagnosis, it seemed life's road had few if any bumps. A few years earlier, he himself was diagnosed with Type I diabetes, but Brian, in his good nature, took this in stride. It never seemed to stop him from playing soccer, learning the game of rugby, going camping, participating in sweat lodges, or pursuing a degree in biology.

Unlike previous summers, June, July, and August of 1992 were grueling. Things got off to a bad start when Brian got laid off from his road construction job, and it only got worse when his dad was rushed to the hospital one afternoon for a series of tests. To Brian, the next month was the hardest to endure, as he saw his father deteriorate so rapidly before his eyes. The last trip to the hospital with his dad was almost unbearable. "When he used to take business trips, he would always mark on the calendar when he would come home. On the day of his return, my brother and I would wait with such anticipation to see him again. Only this time, we knew Joel [his father] wouldn't be coming back home," Brian explained.

The dynamics of a typical father-son relationship are often difficult, yet Brian and his dad were just beginning to bond in a way that fathers and sons can only dream about. The earrings in each ear, the buzz haircut, and Brian's nonchalant approach to life were perhaps anathema to the military style his father was accustomed to, but the bonds were there and growing, which made his father's passage all the more difficult.

Brian's reaction to the news of his dad's condition fit the classic mold of the stages of death and dying: first denial, then anger, and so on, with a prolonged layover in the anger stage. True to Brian's personality, he progressively moved toward the level of acceptance. He admits what helped in his transition from anger to acceptance was his ability to open his heart.

"At first I was really pissed, like something from my life was taken from me," he commented. "But slowly, after the first few months, my anger and frustration gave way to courage, then love. Now love is my greatest aim."

Brian will be the first to tell you that he is not a churchgoing person. "I am not religious, but that doesn't mean that I'm not spiritual. If anything, this experience has helped me become more spiritual. It may sound like a cliché, but I don't take anything for granted anymore. I find pleasure in small things, and every day I see things around me that make me happy. My father's death has opened up a lot of doors, and although it was a big price to pay, I wouldn't change a thing."

PROFILES OF SPIRITUALITY: III

If there is one word that best describes Judith Billings, it would be resilient. She embodies the essence of that word. She also describes herself as a survivor, yet these two words don't do justice to the strength of her human spirit, which has proved to be her greatest ally since she learned in March of 1995 that she has AIDS.

Judi is not exactly sure when she became infected with the HIV virus, although she thinks it may have been a couple of decades ago, when she tried unsuccessfully to get pregnant by means of artificial insemination. In the early days of the AIDS epidemic, sperm bank samples were rarely screened for the virus. It's a moot point now. The fact is that for Judi, the HIV virus had progressed to AIDS.

Having been ill with respiratory problems for six months, she underwent a series of diagnostic tests, yet the mystery remained unsolved. Not knowing the cause of her illness became a stressor in itself. When her physician suggested they run an AIDS test, Judi thought to herself, "Well, at least it's one more thing to rule out."

Reflecting on that fateful day, she explained, "I remember how I felt when I found out. I had learned earlier that same day, from the results of a lung biopsy, that I had pneumocystic pneumonia, which meant either cancer or AIDS." Then, hours later came the diagnosis. Her doctor informed her that the results were positive. At that point she said she felt both shock at the reality of testing positive for the AIDS virus, yet at the same time, relieved that the mystery was now solved.

For Judi, the diagnosis was a temporary setback, but true to her nature, then came resiliency.

"Like other people, I thought I was well educated about the AIDS virus, until I was diagnosed with it. Then I realized I knew very little," she explained. "So I wrote down pages and pages of questions. I wanted to know everything, and not just the frilly stuff; I wanted all the facts and details. I brought these pages to my doctor, not satisfied till I came home with each question answered."

One part curiosity, one part defiance, and two parts compassion constitute her definition of resiliency. "I wasn't going to play the role of a victim. Inasmuch as is humanly possible, I control my destiny," Judi said. "I made up my mind I was going to learn to live with AIDS, not die from it." And that she has. A superintendent of public instruction in Washington State, Judi has not let the diagnosis stop her from functioning in her position, nor has it impeded her efforts to consider running for Congress. The combination of medications AZT, DDC, and a protease inhibitor has been a big help but comprises only one aspect of her healing journey. Resiliency requires more than medications.

In February of 1996, a year after her initial diagnosis, I asked Judi what inner resources she accesses to help her on a daily basis. She began by talking about her family—her parents, husband, and children—whom she said have been totally supportive, not just in the past year, but throughout her entire life. She also spoke of her faith in God.

"I have a very personal connection with the supreme force. We all have to realize that there is someone or something a whole lot bigger than we are. There is something there, and I rely upon this as well. I find each day I must strike a balance between taking an active role in my life, yet at the same time surrendering to God."

After a pause, Judi said with a chuckle in her voice, "Oh, I can't forget humor. Humor has helped me immensely. You cannot take yourself too seriously. Laughter is the next best thing to love."

In the summer of 2006, I placed a phone call to Judy to say hi and visit a bit. We chatted about our lives over the past ten years including the loss of her parents, her passion as an educator, and AIDS, a decade she called a hybrid of "blessings and bombshells."

"I am as busy now as I was working full time. This rite of passage has been a mixed blessing for sure. I have participated in events I could never have dreamed of prior to this passage in my life. In the past ten years, I have served on numerous national committees, including President Clinton's National AIDS Council. I have met some of the most wonderful people from around the world. I have traveled to several international AIDS conferences and heard some remarkable stories. Having AIDS puts one in touch with one's mortality quite quickly. You find out really fast what's important in life, and live your life with this focus."

I asked Judi if she would be willing to share a new message with my readers and she didn't hesitate one moment.

"The message I would like to share is one that I have shared with many people over the past decade: Faith, family, and friends is an unbeatable combination of support for any crisis. For me, whether it's my husband, my friends, or God, I always have someone to talk to. For me it's a great stress reliever."

CHAPTER TWO

SPIRITS ON
A HUMAN PATH

We are not humans on
a spiritual path.
Rather we are spirits on
a human path.

—Jean Shinoda Bolen

As the last person sat down, a flight attendant made the standard announcement reminding all passengers to stow their belongings under the seat in front of them, and then the plane rolled away from the gate. The runways at Denver International Airport are quite long, and we waited patiently to become airborne. The silence was broken when the captain announced that we were number two for takeoff, at which point the plane began to roll forward, and we were airborne at last.

Forty-five minutes later, a flight attendant rushed toward the cockpit, her face anything but serene. The flurry of activity continued for several minutes while we all sat patiently, waiting to learn of our fate. The captain's voice broke the silence. It appeared there was smoke coming from one engine, he explained. A woman across the aisle gasped.

"It doesn't look too serious," he continued with a commanding, steady voice. "But we'll be making an emergency landing in Iowa."

It didn't take a psychic to read the minds of the passengers as we quickly descended toward fields of corn and soybean in the nation's heartland. Our faces had fright written all over them. Looking through the window, I saw fire equipment lined up for what seemed like miles. The plane landed safely, but we were stranded in Iowa for most of the day. Despite the safe landing, people's flight schedules were disrupted and they were none too happy about it. What could have been a disaster soon became a memory. By 7:00 that evening, everyone had continued on their way, and life went on. As I boarded my next flight, I overheard a passenger in front of me compare this day to her entire life.

No metaphor more aptly describes the human experience than that of a journey or path. When we attempt to articulate our spiritual nature, this analogy strongly resonates between the mind and heart, for within each of us resides a drive to reach a destination—no matter how grand or humble. Planes and cars may be the obvious vehicles for the transportation of the physical body, but what encourages the evolution of the human soul is the pure essence of spirituality: to achieve our highest potential, with an open heart.

The human voyage reveals the full spectrum of experiences: bumpy takeoffs, clear blue skies, colorful horizons, moments of unbearable turbulence, unscheduled stops, and more often than not, smooth landings. However, the destination of our life's journey cannot be measured in miles, nor can our success be measured in material wealth. The evolution of the soul is gauged entirely by our capacity to love. There are some who say that the spiritual journey is measured not in miles but inches. Twelve to fourteen inches to be exact . . . the distance from your head to your heart. Those who have shared the moments of a near-death experience remind us that the most important lesson in life is to expand our capacity to love by giving and receiving unconditionally. This may be a tall order to fill, but it is not impossible.

Our lives are a series of events strung together through the spirit of each breath and heartbeat. Some circumstances may appear more important than others because they mark vital changes in the growth and development of our existence; marriage, childbirth, divorce, and death are rites of passage—milestones for each human journey. In truth, every aspect of life has meaning, even if we cannot see it as it unfolds.

Human spirituality does not merely reflect the dynamic peak experiences, although they make up life's more memorable moments. Spirituality is as subtle as it is dynamic, perhaps even more so. Moments of strife, conflict, boredom, and tension offer their spiritual perspectives as well. When viewed in hindsight, the focal point is remarkably clear. That's when we say to ourselves, "Oh, that's why that happened!"

Stressors, which appear like thick clouds overhead, usually turn out to have silver linings. As the Hawaiian expression goes, "No rain, no rainbows." The eighteenth-century writer William Cowper expressed the thought of clouds this way in his hymn, "O God in a Mysterious Way":

> Oh fearful saints, fresh courage take;
> The clouds you so much dread
> Are big with mercy and shall break
> In blessings on your head.

And while you could say that the road to happiness is always under construction, I prefer this clever adage: "*Stressed* spelled backward is *desserts!*"

Embarking on any journey requires vision and direction. The human expedition is no exception, even though our perspective may be limited. Like binoculars used the wrong way, words and phrases can distort a perspective. This often happens when describing the spiritual nature of humanity. Some of the best attempts to articulate human spirituality have been lost in the translation; we mistake the map for the territory it represents.

In his effort to clarify the mystery of life and turn the perspective of the human journey right-side up, theologian Pierre Teilhard de Chardin once explained, "We are not humans having a spiritual experience. Instead, we are spirits having a human experience." Jungian analyst Jean Shinoda Bolen put a different slant on the same concept: "We are spirits on a human path."

DEFINITIONS OF SPIRITUALITY

How does one describe the indescribable? It would be fair to say that the topic of human spirituality has been the focus of countless conversations dating back to antiquity. Yet despite the millions of words used to elaborate on this concept, human spirituality is a phenomenon in which no one definition seems adequate. In truth, there are no sufficient words in the human language that come close to explaining this ineffable concept. The moment we entrap the essence of spirit in the confines of words, all we are left with is an empty cage.

A definition separates that which it attempts to define from everything else long enough to gain a sense of clarity on the concept. Yet spirituality is inclusive in nature, not exclusive. In fact, human spirituality encompasses so many factors that to separate anything out denies a full understanding of its true meaning. To eliminate or delete any aspect would be a gross injustice.

Spirituality is ageless. It knows no bounds. It holds no allegiance to one group, continent, or religion. Author Aldous Huxley once described spirituality as the perennial philosophy, a timeless wisdom that transcends religion, politics, and egos.[1] True to the nature of inclusiveness, spirituality is all-encompassing, despite our best efforts to describe it otherwise.

In many cultures the word spirit means breath—that which enters our physical being with the first inhalation at birth. To inspire, to breathe, is to be inspired by the breath of God. The Hebrews refer to breath as *ruah* and even as this word is spoken, you can hear the rush of wind pass through your lips. In the Eastern culture, *pranayama*, or diaphragmatic breathing, is thought to have a spiritual essence that enhances a physical calmness by uniting the body and mind as one. This occurs by breathing with the flow of universal energy. Likewise, the ancient Greeks used the words *pneuma* to connote spirit and *psyche* to describe the human soul. The word *psychology* is now commonly associated with the study of human behavior. Psychology, however, gives less than tacit acknowledgment to the spiritual dimension. Theologian Thomas Moore said it best when he stated, "The field of psychology has done little to promote the soul growth process." [2]

Undoubtedly, the human spirit includes the facets of higher consciousness, transcendence, self-reliance, self-efficacy, self-actualization, love, faith, compassion, enlightenment, creativity, self-assertiveness, community, and bonding, as well as a multitude of other components. Yet each aspect alone is not sufficient to describe the essence of human spirituality. Even when strung together, these words barely begin to scratch the surface. Because the concept of spirituality is so ineffable, we are left with the option to describe it through analogy, simile, or metaphor. Think of a time when you found yourself in conscious recognition of your divine connection. Perhaps it was coming face-to-face with a deer in the woods. Perhaps it was holding your child for the first time. Or maybe it was sharing a brief instant of jubilation with several friends. This type of experience can and does leave one speechless. In our best attempts to express in words our thoughts and feelings, we search our memory banks to explain how we feel, only to come up short. So we reach for a comparison: "It was like . . . it was as if . . . it was similar to . . ." Such is the nature of human spirituality.

This doesn't mean we should abandon efforts to acknowledge this essential aspect of the human condition. The consequences would be horrendous. In recognition of this fact, the World Health Organization (WHO) made an attempt to place the spiritual dimension prominently on the healthcare map. Although this definition may itself appear inadequate, the significance of the statement cannot be denied. WHO defines human spirituality as "that which is in total harmony with the perceptual and non-perceptual environment."[3] First and foremost, spirituality is experiential and there is no substitute for personal experience.

SPIRITUALITY AND RELIGION

Several years ago I heard a symphony conductor interviewed on National Public Radio. In his attempt to express the essence of classical compositions, he said music was a universal language that could be understood at some level by everyone.

"Music," he said, "has a very spiritual essence. When we listen to music, we eavesdrop on the thoughts of God." What he said next really grabbed my attention. "We must distinguish the difference between spirituality and religion. Spirituality unites, where religions divide and separate."

When you hear the truth you feel it in your gut; it vibrates in every cell of your body. Upon hearing his words, I got goose bumps at the recognition of this wisdom. Since first hearing these words, I have shared this story in various presentations around the country and I never fail to see reassuring nods and smiles of recognition.

Sometimes defining what a concept *is not* becomes an explanation in itself. For instance, human spirituality is neither a religion nor the practice of a religion.[4] Each religion is based upon a specific dogma: a living application of a specific set of organized rules based on the ideology of the human spirit. It is generally agreed that being actively involved in a particular religion is a way to enhance one's spirituality—

to bring one closer to God. This is the primary objective of all religions. On the whole they are effective. But recently several experts in the field of humanistic psychology have noted that religion can often stifle the growth of the human spirit. Religion may serve as a path, but it can also form a roadblock.

This fact has led some behavioral psychologists to observe that people can form an addiction to a religion as a means of validating one's existence. By the same token, the practice of extreme rituals, such as prolonged sessions of meditation, are considered unhealthy if they eclipse other essential aspects of one's life. Religion can certainly promote spiritual evolution; the two are very compatible. Yet individuals can be very spiritual and not religious, just as people can be religious but have a poor awareness of their own spirituality.

I have a clergy friend who states it this way: "God has many the Church has not, and the Church has many God has not."

Recently a workshop participant shared with me a similar perspective, one that I'm sure came from her personal experience. She explained, "Religion is for those who are trying to avoid hell; spirituality is for those who have already been there."

Borrowing from the language of metaphor, I describe spirituality as water that flows freely everywhere. Water, like spirit, may take on different shapes but it is found everywhere. Religions are like containers that hold water; they come in all shapes and sizes. But water doesn't need a container to exist. To understand the concept of spirituality you have to experience it; rarely will two interpretations be the same. Although spirituality and religion are separate but related concepts, it is impossible to separate the concept of spirituality from the divine aspect of the universe. The poet Maya Angelou said:

> *Spirit is an invisible force made visible in all life. I believe that Spirit is one and is everywhere present. That it never leaves me. I*

may withdraw from it, but I can realize its presence the instant I return to my senses. I cannot separate what I conceive as Spirit from my concept of God.[5]

This is the most exciting time to be alive. At no other point in our history has so much information become accessible to so many people at one time. We have an unprecedented freedom to assimilate the great wisdom from around the world. By comparison, centuries ago the vast majority of the world's population could not read. Information was spoon-fed and the control over what information was released was immense. Now, as pieces of the cosmic puzzle become assembled from all cultures, religions and societies—specifically those pieces that highlight various aspects of ageless wisdom— we begin to see that there are common denominators that bind the human spirit. Spirituality unites, whereas religions divide and separate. In this critical time of humanity, it is clearly time to put aside our differences and unite as one people.

In the words of Christian theologian Matthew Fox, "We are living in a post-denominational age."[6] Bearing this in mind, it becomes imperative that we learn to set aside our cultural, religious, and political differences and work together as one people. Today, the world is experiencing many wake-up calls in an effort to raise consciousness. The answers to global problems will not come from separateness, but from unity.

Of Spirit and Soul

A divine life force permeates every inch of the universe. Spirit animates matter and inspires the dreams of humanity. Gifted healers and sages claim to see spirit as energy, yet it would be naive to think of spirit merely as tiny particles of mystic light randomly floating in the cosmos. There is a divine order to all life, even if we see it as chaos at times. Spirit exists despite the disbelief of some and the skepticism of others. It delights in appreciation, yet never wavers in those who doubt.

There is a part of ourselves, our divinity, that is universal in nature. There is also a part of our essence that is unique—the aspect we call soul. Ancient myths and legends suggest that the Source, or Prime Creator, scattered itself to the four directions in an adventure called human existence. The promise was to return at some point and share the meaning of those life experiences. Like a diary that records memories of a journey, so, too, our experiences are stitched into the fabric of our souls. The spirit of life binds us to the Source of God at all times; this connection can never be broken, despite illusions to the contrary. The wisdom of spirit and soul is as old as time itself, best described as a symbiotic relationship. Spirit nourishes soul. Soul invigorates spirit.

God's last instructions to little Yogi Berra.

God, The Source, Prime Creator, All-That-Is, The Great Mystery, is said to be omnipotent—all-knowing. Glancing at the bigger picture, however, I question this. An all-knowing God would never be surprised, would not be spontaneous, would not be curious. A God who is all-knowing would be bored. Anyone who has attempted to understand the thoughts of God is reluctant to admit that there is a lack of surprise, spontaneity, curiosity, and excitement in the divine order of the universe. Ageless wisdom suggests that we are the eyes and ears of God.

In our effort to explore the human landscape, we channel our experience back to a collective source far greater than the individual human mind, so that God can have self-knowledge in every conceivable way. An ancient proverb reminds us that only brave souls walk the human path, for the earthly existence is enshrouded in a veil of illusion. It is a brave soul on a noble adventure who attempts to lift these veils. In doing so, courageous souls are no strangers to stress.

From this perspective, exactly what is stress?

- Stress is the tension between divine will and free will.
- Stress is the tension between ego and soul.
- Stress is coming to terms with the responsibility to venture in uncharted territories.
- Stress is resistance to living in the present moment.
- Stress is forgetting (or ignoring the need) to employ the power of spirit through love at times when it is needed the most.
- Stress provides the greatest opportunity for the growth of the soul.

Whenever we encounter stress, it serves as an invitation to explore and develop one or more of the following parts of the human landscape: the relationship we hold with ourselves; our relationship with God, however we conceive God to be; our relationship with others;

and our personal value system, thus fulfilling a meaningful purpose in life.

From various corners of the globe, Earth has often been described as a grand classroom where assignments are given and pop quizzes appear frequently.[7] It is said that at a higher level of consciousness, we choose these lessons to test the courage of our soul. Regardless of how events are selected or encountered, the task is still the same: to shed light where there is darkness, to overcome fear with love.

Shakespeare once said that all the world is a stage, and all its people actors. If it is true that we are all equal in our divinity despite the roles we play, yet unique in our humanity, then our bodies are nothing more than costumes in which we act out our roles in the drama of life. Some of the most difficult people we meet are some of the greatest actors to grace the earthly stage. They are also our greatest teachers.

The philosopher and poet Kahlil Gibran once said, "I have learned silence from the talkative, tolerance from the intolerant, and kindness from the unkind. I should not be ungrateful to those teachers."[8]

We must remind ourselves not to confuse the costume for the actor inside, nor must we forget that every experience is a lesson, a reminder and an opportunity to practice the art of unconditional love.

THE THREE PILLARS OF HUMAN SPIRITUALITY

Listen closely to the wisdom of the shamans, sages, healers, and mystics and you will hear a common theme regarding the essence of human spirituality: relationships, values, and a meaningful purpose in life. These are known as the three pillars of human spirituality, and they permeate every aspect of the human condition. They are also at the root of every stressor, problem, and dilemma we encounter on the human journey. Take a moment to itemize your list of current stressors and you may notice that they tend to fall into one of these categories, perhaps all three at the same time: relationships, values, and a meaningful purpose in life. Let's take a closer look.

Relationships

The aspect of relationships is twofold: internal (that which we have with ourselves and our higher self) and external relationships (those we have with everybody and everything else). How well do you know yourself? How well do you trust yourself? How often do you take time to soul search? What is your relationship with your higher self? The answers to these questions form the basis of understanding of our internal relationship. Friends, family, colleagues, neighbors, and peers (even strangers) might seem to be the hallmark of external relationships, but the wisdom of the Native Americans would remind us that we also hold a sacred relationship with the air we breathe, the water we drink, the land we walk on, as well as all of the Earth's creatures. All life is relationship. Stress often occurs between and among relationships when egos collide and control for power is exercised.

Values

What are your values? This is a heavy question to ask, I know. By and large, people tend not to talk directly about their values until some crisis surfaces (e.g., the Columbine massacre, 9/11, Hurricane Katrina). Values may be abstract in nature, but they underscore what we believe to be most important in our lives. Love, privacy, health, wealth, creativity, and leisure are all values. These represent the core of what we hold to be the most important aspects of our lives. Stress often arises when these values, like the tectonic plates of the Earth, collide. In spiritual terms this is known as a values conflict. The most common example of a values conflict is freedom versus responsibility, and this affects nearly everyone alive.

A Meaningful Purpose in Life

Career. Family. Education. Pets. If there is a cornerstone to human spirituality, then look no further. A meaningful purpose in life is it. "Why am I here?" and "What is my purpose in life?" are perhaps the most profound questions you can ever ask yourself. A purpose-driven life is a life fulfilled; however, the sages remind us that in the course of our lives, we will have many purposes and many voids in the search to fulfill each purpose. Stress often arises when the meaning of life evaporates, thus creating a vacuum. At times the pain can be almost unbearable. This can happen with the death of a child, the end of a marriage, the loss of a job, or any event that shakes the foundations of your soul. But we must never lose faith. In the words of Nazi concentration camp survivor Gerta Weissman Klein "Giving up is the final solution to a temporary problem."

Once you were able to digest and demonstrate this ageless wisdom shared by the sages, they would take you in their confidence and share with you one more pillar of human spirituality: the divine mystery.

THE FOURTH PILLAR: THE DIVINE MYSTERY

Can you keep a secret? I have had several mystical experiences in my life. This may come as little or no surprise to many of you reading this book, as you may have had several yourself. The problem is that rarely does anyone seem to talk about them publicly, for fear of being castigated as a lunatic and hauled away by the men in white coats. For this reason, I am a little guarded about sharing these experiences. I imagine that if, indeed, we did share these on a regular basis, we might be living in a much different world. Perhaps a better world, indeed.

Organized religions are not particularly fond of mystical experiences. In fact, they often go out of their way to disprove them. Why? This is clearly something they have no control over. Angels, miracle cures, colossal synchronistic events, weeping statues of the Virgin Mary, healing waters (such as those at Lourdes), and holy apparitions top the list of mystical experiences but there are many, many more. Science doesn't like mystical experiences either, as they tend to make a mockery of the scientific method (spontaneous healings are a prime example). Science has come a long way to explain a great many things (the aurora borealis comes to mind), but there will always be things that can never fully be explained by science. They can and must be merely appreciated.

You don't have to levitate, bi-locate, or walk on water to be a good mystic. All you need do is simply appreciate the mystery. This is the only prerequisite to becoming a good mystic. This appreciation takes practice and discipline, but the rewards of a mystical life are immeasurable.

Of the several mystical experiences I have had (including premonitions, visions, psychic dreams, and healings) what I am about to share ranks at the top of the list.

One morning several years ago, I awoke to find a symbol imprinted on my right hand. I didn't actually notice it until I was in the shower, getting ready to shampoo my hair. (This was at a time when I had a full head of hair.) I looked into my hand to find a circle with lines emanating from the center, out beyond the circle's perimeter. The imprint of this symbol lasted for at least an hour before fading away, but not before I could make a sketch of it.

When one encounters the unexplainable, one first looks for a rational explanation. My first thought was that I must have been sleep-walking. I combed the house looking for any and all objects that might match the indentation found imprinted on my hand, but to no avail.

Silly as this sounds, my next thought was that perhaps I was abducted by aliens (when the mind runs out of rational explanations, it starts to explore irrational ones). I can recall talking to several friends and colleagues about aliens only to learn that I could find no one who would admit to believing in other life forms in the universe (apparently they didn't wish to be hauled away by the men in white coats either). Several friends hinted that I might actually be an alien and inquired why they would want to steal one of their own!

One colleague was a Catholic priest who used hypnosis as a means to help promote smoking cessation. One day I asked him if he might consider placing me under hypnosis to solve the mystery of the symbol, which by this time had reappeared on the same hand several times in the course of the year. Upon learning of my newfound symbol, he said, "I don't want anything to do with this," and walked away. This experience did nothing to solidify my relationship with the Catholic Church. I was to learn that religions of all types (Buddhism excluded) are very leery of mystical experiences, primarily because they have no sanction over them. After all, if you have a direct line to the Supreme Being, why would you need the church?

One day, I awoke to find the symbol appear for the seventh time, but this time, uniquely on my left hand. Moreover, printed on my index finger were the letters VID. Shaken, but not stirred, I once again stepped out of the shower and sketched the symbol and the word. Coincidently, that same day, a colleague gave me a collection of audiotapes by renowned mythologist Joseph Campbell. It was while listening to these tapes that I discovered the translation of the word *vid*. Campbell states that the word is a Sanskrit word meaning wisdom. Although I wasn't sure how all the pieces fit together, I knew enough to pay attention to the signs and synchronicity of it all.

My search to seek the meaning of this mysterious message led me to many people who claimed to be in the know (and more who did not), but I never resonated with any of their interpretations. Finally, it was a reputable psychic (often used by the FBI and police detectives) who gave the best insight that turned out to be most accurate. What did it all mean? Perhaps what any and all mystical experiences mean:

They unveil the simplistic reality to reveal a deeper, more complex essence of the grand universe, and an opportunity to appreciate it. In the sage words of one of the greatest minds of all times, Albert Einstein, "The most beautiful and profound emotion we can experience is the sensation of the mystical. It is the power of all true science."

It is often said that the fourth pillar of human spirituality remains invisible (subtle) to those who cannot master the dynamics of the first three. Yet being a mystic doesn't ensure an easier path to life. To the contrary, it can become quite difficult to walk in two worlds at the same time.

The Hero's Journey Revisited

Everyone loves an underdog, perhaps because deep down inside we each see ourselves as underdogs many, many times in the course of our lives. Everyone also loves a good story. The fact that more than 80 million copies of *Chicken Soup for the Soul* have been sold supports this fact, as does America's fascination with the Hollywood film industry, from movies such as *Spiderman* to *The Lord of the Rings*. When lovable underdogs are intertwined in the plot of a great story, we have the makings of more than just good entertainment. We have the fabric of a coded road map for the long and arduous human journey of our own lives.

Why do we love a good story? From a spiritual perspective, good stories act not only like a map, but also like a compass, which in unison help steer us in the direction of home. Stress, in all its countless manifestations, can not only throw us off "the path," it can distract us from getting back on the path. By hearing or learning of someone's plight in overcoming adversity and shifting roles from the victim to victor, we re-energize our own human spirit to pick up and start moving on our own journey once again. In simple terms, we gravitate to these stories to give us inner strength and help lead us safely home. Stories are the language of the soul. Whether it be Frodo, Harry Potter, Dorothy, Jason and the Argonauts, or Stanley Yelnats, we quickly resonate with each character as a reflection of our human spirit. These heroes are not merely two-dimensional characters. Lance Armstrong, Rosa Parks, Christopher Reeve, and Naomi Judd are real-life examples of the underdog who overcame staggering odds to become victorious. In their celebration, we celebrate too.

The fact that the human spirit craves a good story was no surprise to renowned mythologist Joseph Campbell, author of the acclaimed book *The Hero with a Thousand Faces*. In his quest to understand the appeal of powerful stories, Campbell studied the myths and legends of virtually all cultures throughout the history of mankind. To no one's surprise (and everyone's delight), the central character of each mythical legend began his (or her) humble journey with the odds stacked against him; the quintessential underdog. Why? Because to have the odds stacked high thickens the plot. In the course of each story, the underdog matures into the role of hero, a conscious evolution of the soul.

In his understanding of the mythical hero, Campbell outlined what has since become regarded as the classic stages of "the hero's journey." In simplest terms, there are three stages of this journey: the departure, the initiation, and the return home. Let's take a closer look at each one. As you read through this template, try to identify the coordinates of your own hero's journey.

THE DEPARTURE

The departure is an exit from home. Sometimes carefully planned, more often abrupt, this first stage of the hero's journey is the transition from the known to the unknown. Campbell refers to this stage as "the call to adventure," where curiosity, sometimes combined with either boredom or necessity, lures the hero out of the comforts of the known and into uncharted territory. While some heroes listen to the call to adventure, others ignore the call, preferring to simply stay at home. Sitting out the hero's journey is not an option, however. Frodo accepted the challenge to return the ring to Mount Doom, Jason (and the Argonauts) departed in search of several items needed to secure the release of his mother. Hansel and Gretel, Pinocchio and Ariel, the Little Mermaid, all made their departures too. Once out the door, the hero must cross the threshold of adventure and confront the guardian of the gate, the first test to measure one's spiritual fortitude.

How does the departure translate to the average everyday hero? It might be the end of a relationship. It could be the termination from a job. In fact, it could be any event that pushes you out of your comfort zone. Leaving the known and going into the unknown can and will happen many times in the course of our lifetimes. As one workshop participant explained to me quite aptly, "I begin the departure stage of the hero's journey every morning I get on the L.A. freeway."

THE INITIATION

For some, the departure from home is stressful enough, but a note of caution is necessary: More difficult challenges lie ahead. This stage, as Campbell called it, is "baptism by fire." The hero is put to the test to see what he or she is really made of. In this stage the hero is given an arduous task, perhaps several. Dorothy had to retrieve the Wicked Witch's broom. Frodo had to destroy the ring. Jason had to get the golden fleece (among other things). Along the way the hero will most assuredly meet a nasty villain: The Wicked Witch of the West, Rumplestiltskin, or Darth Vader are classic examples. Any good author will tell you that these characters are really personifications of our own fear, that which we must overcome to complete the journey success-fully. The hero's mantra throughout this stage is "Never give up."

No hero stands alone in this stage of the journey. Each has help, both seen and unseen. Campbell referred to this aspect as "the assistance of spiritual aids." In mythology this might include magical potions, unbreakable swords, horses with wings, angels, talking lions, good witches, or sorcerers, all of whom lend a helping hand. The implied message from each of these characters is that through thick and thin, we are never disconnected from our divine source. We are never alone. Additionally, the hero also is called upon to use his or her own inner resources—what I call muscles of the soul. These include, but are not limited to, patience, humor, forgiveness, compassion, tolerance, creativity, bravery, faith, honesty, and courage. As horrendous as the challenge is, we have the means to meet the challenge, resolve or conquer it, and move on. Now, it should be known that some heroes, after making their initial conquest, get a little arrogant. Given the chance to return home, they opt to face more challenges and rack up more trophies, but ultimately they become mired down by their own egos. Remember, no one likes a cocky hero.

THE RETURN HOME

The return home marks a pivotal turning point in the hero's journey. Achieving success with his or her mission, the hero returns home to share the spoils. In doing so, he or she becomes what Campbell calls "the master of two worlds": the world they conquered, and the world they returned home to. Because greed is not a spiritual value, it is incumbent upon the hero to pass along any and all wisdom gained in this odyssey to family and friends who stayed home so that they too can learn and evolve their own spiritual growth. Frodo came home to Bag End. Dorothy made it home to Kansas. Luke Skywalker landed back home in his spaceship, and Lucy, Peter, Edmund, and Susan made it home through the wardrobe to England. The good news is

that you will make it home too. This is the promise of the hero's journey. This is the promise of the divine universe.

Campbell saw mythology not as exaggerated historical fact but
rather a spiritual covenant endowed to all those still struggling to get
home. In essence, we are all on the hero's journey. Remember that no
matter how stressful your life is at the present moment, you are never
alone, and those waiting for you at home beckon you to return.

The Path as a Metaphor

Ask any mountain climber what his or her destination is, and the
answer will be the summit. Why? Because the view is unparalleled. If
life is an expedition, then the realization of our divine connection is
like reaching the summit. To stand on a mountain peak epitomizes the
expression, "I have touched the face of God." Initially, a mountain
peak may offer itself as a metaphor of the completion of the journey,
but the life's odyssey never ends on a mountaintop. One stays there
only long enough to enjoy the view and become inspired before beginning the descent.

There is no best route up a mountain. There are several paths, each
offering a different experience. Ask any sage, shaman, healer, or wisdom keeper who speaks from the heart which is the best path to the
divine source. Without doubt you will be told there is no one path,
only a path that is best for you. As Carlos Castaneda writes in *The
Teachings of Don Juan*:

> *Look at every path closely and deliberately. Try it as many times
> as you feel is necessary. Then ask yourself and yourself alone, one
> question: Does this path have a heart? If it does, it is good; if it
> doesn't, then it is of no use.*[9]

In matters of the heart and issues of the soul, our paths will frequently intersect or align parallel with other trails. It matters not which path you take: Christianity, Judaism, Islam, Mother Earth spirituality, or another. What matters is that you keep moving forward—growing—on the path you have chosen. Resting on the sidelines indefinitely is perhaps the greatest sin known to humanity. In fact, the word *sin* is derived from the word *inertia*. Doing nothing serves no one.

For a path to enhance the evolution of your spiritual well-being, there are some recommended caveats. The spiritual path must be creative, not destructive; progressive, not regressive. It must stimulate and enhance—not stifle—spiritual well-being. True to the nature of any expedition, it is important to pack light. As author Glen Clark reminds us, "If you wish to travel far and fast, travel light. Take off all your envies, jealousies, unforgiveness, selfishness, and fears." [10] There are no Sherpas or porters on the spiritual path. We each have to carry our own baggage.

The path of human experience would be mighty crowded if everyone were to embark at the same point in time during the soul growth process. Therefore, it would stand to reason that not only are there numerous paths, but we each move at a pace conducive to our soul's growth process. Take a moment to look around the spiritual landscape, and you will notice that it appears anything but congested. In fact, the stressors we face often make us feel isolated and forgotten, but it is impossible to get lost on the spiritual path. We can only be immobilized by our own fears.

Is there a certain formula to follow that enables the soul to stay on schedule with its growth process? Probably not! As the expression goes, water finds its own level. Yet there does seem to be a pattern of spiritual maturity that closely resembles the development from infancy to adulthood, from dependence to independence to interdependence.

Sometimes before the final leg of the journey to interdependence we encounter a layover in codependence. This too, can become a distraction.

The common theme in this pattern of spiritual growth is summed up in the question: How can one best nurture a relationship with God?

One such reflection comes from the insight and wisdom of psychiatrist M. Scott Peck, author of the books *The Road Less Traveled* and *The Different Drum*. In the latter book, Peck describes a pattern of soul growth process he noticed after years of observing his patients and their encounters with stress. Similar in concept to theologian James Fowler's stages of faith (even Campbell's hero's journey), Peck's framework consists of four systematic or hierarchical stages of spiritual growth and development.[11] These include: the chaotic anti-social individual, the formal institutional individual, the skeptic individual, and the mystic-communal individual. Each of these stages addresses recognition, awareness, and fulfillment of our relationship to the divine. To best explain this evolution of higher consciousness through the soul growth process, I have depicted the stories of four people who embody the traits found in each developmental stage.

Stage 1: The First Leg of the Spiritual Path

Joanne, a financial analyst from the West Coast, is not the kind of person you would wish to spend a free afternoon with unless, of course, you are a glutton for punishment. She berates, belittles, and bemoans everything and everyone; she is known as the Dragon Lady at work. It's a title she cherishes. Some even called her the Antichrist! Unabashedly, Joanne admits her favorite role model is Prince Machiavelli, but she has others. One Halloween she wore ruby slippers to work in honor of the Wicked Witch of the West. Her employees were not amused. The words *shrewd, intimidating, manipulating, backstabbing,* and *cunning* come to mind when one attempts to describe her—those are her better qualities.

Joanne is a lonely person. She is what Peck would refer to as a "chaotic-antisocial individual." And her behaviors are not uncommon. There are many people like her—people who wish to control everything and everybody. Accordingly, chaotic anti-social individuals can be very manipulative and unprincipled. They often find that controlling others is easier than taking responsibility for their own lives.

This type of individual conveys the message, "I don't need God. I can do it myself!" They may act like they are God, but more likely they give the impression of being spiritually bankrupt. Persons at this stage will push the limits of tolerance, while deep down inside they are frightened of being alone. Perhaps because of a weak relationship with God, these people attract an inordinate amount of difficulty and chaos in their lives. In some cases it is magnified by drug and alcohol abuse, to the point of serious active addiction.

There are those people who remain at this stage their whole lives. It may take a life-threatening situation to move a person from this stage to the next phase of spiritual growth. In a desperate attempt to leave a place of turmoil, a person at this stage of spiritual growth will search for some type of group or organization to help make order out of his or her personal chaos.

STAGE 2: THE SECOND LEG OF THE SPIRITUAL PATH

Trisha strives constantly to maintain her ideal weight. Recently, while planning a trip to Cancun, Mexico, she set a goal to lose ten pounds. Not having the willpower to adhere to a diet, Trisha turned to Weight Watchers, which has a structured program to help people lose weight and a fine reputation for success. When Trisha tried to join she was told that based on the height/weight charts, she didn't meet the weight criteria. Determined, she returned the next week wearing extra clothing and carrying several stones in all of her pockets. It worked!

As strange as it may sound, there are people who commit crimes to go to prison, where there is food, clothing, and shelter. There are people who enlist in a branch of the military service to straighten out their lives. And there are people who become members of a church, temple, or religious group for guidance. Institutions like these offer their followers rules and guidelines to minimize personal strife, leave chaos behind, and rebuild a life based on a more stable foundation.

Stories abound of lives that were dramatically turned around. By and large, people who make a quick transition to this stage from the first desperately need doctrines, discipline, and guidance to progress with their spiritual well-being. But there are times when personal empowerment seems less than zero. Those who give their power away begin to foster codependent behavior. The result can be a vicious unbroken cycle of approval seeking.

In this stage one's relationship with God parallels the child-parent relationship, where God is a loving but punitive deity. In the words of Peck, "God becomes an Irish cop in the sky." A Supreme Being is personified in human terms. Visions of God resemble Michelangelo's Sistine Chapel painting: a white God on a white cloud wearing a white toga. At this stage, God is typically an external figure, much like Santa Claus.

People who advance to this stage are looking for their personal needs to be met. They also come with lifelong questions, but they see life's answers in terms of black and white; there is no room for gray. To a point, their needs are fulfilled. Comfortable with this stage, many people stay at this level for the remainder of their lives. Some, however, may slip back into the first stage and continue an oscillation process to quench a thirst for control and power. Others who come to a point of stability may eventually leave this stage because of unmet needs that surface after they have become comfortable. So they shop around for another organization to meet those needs. At some point they may become skeptical of all religious institutions, yet they remain spiritually stable enough to avoid slipping back to stage one. At this point such people begin a free-floating process, unanchored to anything, moving toward a sense of independence.

STAGE 3: THE THIRD LEG OF THE SPIRITUAL PATH

Don't talk to Ian about God. He doesn't want to hear it. If you persist, Ian might tell you there is no God, not the one he was raised to believe in. He has his reasons. Raised a Roman Catholic, he began to question some of the Church rules and regulations when he started dating a woman from Canada who was also raised Catholic. After a trip to Montreal, he learned that different countries do not honor the same days of holy obligation. In other words, you could commit a sin in the States if you missed church on the feast of the Immaculate Conception, but if you crossed the border, you were exempt. Ian discovered that the Catholic God apparently has different sins for different countries. That was the first red flag. There were enough others to make him question why he belonged to an organization with rules he didn't agree with. So at age twenty-three he walked out of church and never turned back. Ian is the epitome of what Peck calls the skeptic individual.

When a person questions the dogma or finds a lack of appropriate answers, he or she will likely depart from the organization. Frustration may turn into mistrust. Cynicism may be the first sign that the seeds of independence are taking root. With tongue in cheek, Peck calls people in this stage "born-again atheists." Healthy doubt provokes an individual to seek truth. Matthew Fox calls this necessary process "demasking the face of God." In an evolutionary step of consciousness, the perceptions of God introduced at a young age are removed.

Through repeated questioning, an exploration of universal conscious-ness begins anew. This is considered a crucial stage of spiritual devel-opment—when one begins to question the basis of understanding that an institution represents. Skeptics question every aspect of truth. Why is this stage critical? Because this is where one shifts from being spoon-fed to being self-fed. Independence.

The goal of raising a child is his or her self-reliance—leaving the nest and discovering the world on one's own. However, as one pro-gresses on the spiritual path, there are no guaranteed answers. In this stage there is no black or white, only perpetual gray. According to Peck, a person at this stage of the human journey is more spiritually developed than many habitual churchgoers. But it offers no sense of security. This third passage of spiritual development is like skydiving: Once airborne there is an incredible sense of freedom, but at some point a person must land.

Soon after declaring independence, two outcomes are likely. First, like Ian, a person may sample other church institutions, still searching for a morsel of truth to understanding the universe and our role in it. Second, he or she may progress to the next and final stage of spiritual development. Images of the prodigal son surface when encountering this stage, but remember, upon the return home, this individual will not be the same.

STAGE 4: THE FOURTH LEG OF THE SPIRITUAL PATH

Sarah called the first episode a "cosmic bread crumb." Others might have called it a mystical coincidence. On a flight from New York to Washington, a flight attendant asked her if she would change seats to allow a mother and young child to sit together. The person Sarah ended up sitting next to was a publisher who just happened to be reading her manuscript on board that very flight. Since that first significant bread crumb, there have been dozens more. The bread crumbs offer glimpses into the mind of God, Sarah explains with a smile, adding that every time she finds a piece of the cosmic puzzle to help make sense of the universe, the perimeter of the puzzle increases. On a grander scale, Sarah's whole life has taken on mystical proportions. She reminds herself daily to simply enjoy the mystery.

In the continual search for answers to life's questions, people like Sarah eventually realize that there are several questions that have no definitive answers. Unlike the skeptic who initially fights this premise, a person at this stage takes delight in life's paradoxes. These people find comfort in the unanswerable, yet like a sleuth who loves a good challenge, they are hungry for possible clues to the mystery of life. Peck refers to people at this stage as mystic-communals.

In this stage, God has been depersonified and demasked, yet fully embraced. Moreover, one comes to the realization that God is equally an internal source (the power of love, faith, and will) as well as an external source (an unexplained energy or consciousness).

Mystic-communals begin to see an outline of the whole picture, even with several significant pieces missing. They see spirituality—the good, bad, and ugly—as a living process, not merely an outcome, reward, or heaven-oriented goal.

Equally important is the role these individuals play in their community. They see the connection of all life and the importance of service. Individuals who reach this level feel a need to build and maintain a strong community by nurturing quality relationships through acceptance, tolerance, love, and respect. They know the importance of being connected. Standing on a mountaintop is akin to kissing the face of God. But no journey ends on a mountaintop. Those who gain perspective from this vantage point know that to raise consciousness for all, they must share what they have seen. People who achieve a footing upon this stage of spiritual development realize it is only the beginning of a long, fruitful pilgrimage.

In any board game, a toss of the dice or a specific card drawn can send you back to square one. The spiritual path is no different; stressors can cause us to lose our footing, tumble, and backslide a stage or two. A person embracing life's mystery who suddenly experiences the death of a loved one may have feelings of anger or guilt when the death is perceived as a form of divine punishment. "Why me?" they ask. "What did I do to deserve this?"

No matter what stage you find yourself in, a union of stressful situations may cause you to focus on the external side of God, or lack thereof, causing you to backslide a stage or two. But having once journeyed ahead, it is easier to regain lost ground. Ultimately, the journey of the human path is an individual effort; no one can do it for us. However, we are not entirely alone on this journey. Love and grace serve as guides to lead the way—when we choose to listen.

ROADBLOCKS ON THE HUMAN PATH

The spiritual path is not a straight line on a flat plane. That would be too easy, too boring, and quite unproductive. The spiritual landscape is equally filled with rugged beauty and elegant charm, all of which promote the evolution of the human soul. How does the soul evolve? Metaphorically speaking, we begin our life with many rough edges. As we travel on the human path, we encounter a host of opportunities to polish them. Like a rock that is tumbled and smoothed till it becomes a polished gem, the human soul also evolves from the lessons in each experience. Where there is friction, there is often pain. Yet as the soul evolves, painful moments make way for strength and beauty. In the words of German philosopher Friedrich Nietzsche, "That which does not kill me, makes me stronger." Such is the case with Jennifer.

On the surface Jennifer seemed to be the epitome of success—an artist with an international reputation. Whereas her exterior seemed calm, inside there was turmoil. It began before the divorce and worsened when she fell in love with a man who lived five hundred miles away. This new dynamic threw the issue of child custody between Jennifer and her former husband back into the courts.

"It was not a pretty picture," she says. Standing six-foot-four, her ex-husband was an emotional and physical roadblock. At times his presence became intimidating, which he used to full advantage. Throughout her entire marriage, Jennifer was afraid of him; it kept her immobilized for years. She would avoid confrontation at all costs. But as her new relationship began to develop, choices had to be made. Avoidance was no longer an option.

"Standing up to my former husband was the toughest act I ever had to face," she says. "But having done this, now I can face anything." In her studio is a quote from Richard Bach's book *Illusions*: "Every problem holds a gift for you in its hands. We seek problems because we need their gifts."

Roadblocks may appear to take many forms, such as a belligerent spouse, an alcoholic parent, an unfulfilled job, a terminal illness, or a difficult child, but these are not in themselves the obstruction. They are the tip of the iceberg—a reflection of our perceptions, beliefs, attitudes, and opinions that stagnate the flow of spirit and keep us immobilized.

The forces behind the roadblocks are fear, anger, greed, laziness, guilt, and worry. These perceptions can result not only in immobilization but also paralysis of the human spirit. As perceptions, the real roadblocks on the human path are less tangible but more potent because they act to immobilize our life energy. In nonmetaphorical terms, they are best described as those daily problems that drain our energy and eventually seem to stop us dead in our tracks. Perhaps as no surprise, the two biggest roadblocks on the path of human experience are the primary stress emotions: fear and anger. Left unresolved, they can be as disabling as four flat tires.

Taking the path of least resistance is an admired skill—one that has been advocated for ages. This is how water flows. But the path of least resistance does not mean complete avoidance or passivity to the point of emotional abuse. Resistance can be persistence when there is no other choice. Roadblocks may not appear so, but they are an essential element for the soul's growth. Simply stated, roadblocks and obstructions are part of the spiritual journey. To avoid working through the problem is like skipping school. What was avoided on one stretch of the human highway will eventually surface somewhere else down the road until it is acknowledged, processed, and resolved. Singer/songwriter Harry Chapin once wrote about the road of life in a song titled "All My Life's a Circle" where he sings, "No straight lines make up my life, and all my roads have bends, there's no clear-cut beginnings, and so far there's no dead ends."[12]

DISTRACTIONS ON THE HUMAN PATH

It is easy to become distracted; the human attention span has shrunk dramatically since the advent of television, even more so with the addictive use of the remote control.[13] Especially since the human mind craves stimulation, in this age of high technology, there is no shortage of distractions.

When the thought process is intense, the mind craves diversions to offer mental relief. This is why we daydream. Whereas an occasional shift in attention is healthy, a prolonged digression can be hazardous. The greater the distraction, the more difficult it is to redirect our attention inward. The wise adage comes to mind, "Look, but don't touch."

Anything that lures our attention long enough to pull us off track can be a distraction. Distractions begin as attractions. Fairy tales and fables are filled with messages that warn of potential dangers. Inevitably the character becomes distracted and gets lost. Art surely imitates life. Distractions are every bit as real on the human journey as they are in fiction. Cell phones, iPods, television, the Internet, drugs, alcohol, food, and even other people can serve as diversions. In the Judeo-Christian culture they are called temptations. While not all temptations are bad, we have a tendency to overindulge (if some is good, more is better), which sets the stage for conflict and turmoil, as expressed through addictions.

Wisdom reminds us to stop and *smell* the roses, not eat them. Prolonged distractions can be downright hazardous. Distractions dull the senses and dampen the spirit. Moreover, detours can zap our spiritual strength and rob us of our destiny. In fairy tales, the characters always find their way home and learn a lesson, too. In real life, people are not always as lucky. More often they are perpetually sidetracked by their own ego, never reaching their full potential.

Think for a moment of the distractions in your life and list them below:

1. _____
2. _____
3. _____
4. _____
5. _____

THE GIFT OF INNER RESOURCES
(MUSCLES OF THE SOUL)

Years ago, I had a vision where I was seated at the foot of a richly engraved, wooden chair. Although it seemed empty, I knew it was occupied by a brilliant light. Comfortably seated, I waited patiently for a message. Then it came. I was to be sent on a mission. Not only was I selected, I volunteered. I was told to take nothing except that which resided in my heart—my inner resources. I would have some spiritual guidance, but I would be unaware of this assistance. I returned from this vision with a sense of peace and contentment.

In sharing this experience with a few friends, I found it was more common than I had originally believed. Is it possible that we all volunteered to come into human existence? If so, then we do not appear on Earth spiritually naked. The operating instructions are clearly written in a language that the heart understands and strives to articulate through our inner resources.

What are our inner resources? A short list might include humor, creativity, optimism, courage, willpower, patience, acceptance, forgiveness, intuition, compassion, curiosity, humility, faith, and love. Inner resources are those intangible assets that help us cope with everyday problems. In times of stress, no matter the intensity, it is these remarkable qualities that help us dismantle, remove, circumscribe, or transcend the barriers that fall in our path. These resources are not gifts for a chosen few; they are birthrights for each and every individual. Our inner resources are the sinew of our spiritual muscle. However, like muscles that atrophy with disuse, our inner resources will also fail to help us meet the challenge that we encounter if we neglect them.

Recently I had the chance to talk with anthropologist Angeles Arrien. She refers to inner resources as "medicine of the soul," a term she found common among many cultures. "What's your medicine?" she asked me point blank. We agreed that for both of us, it is love.

Medicine is one way to describe these gifts. There are other expressions. In the Western world we talk about the five senses, but as we all know, there are more. A sense of humor, a sense of imagination, and a sense of intuition are a few more in this collection. Why should we limit ourselves to just five? I have often thought if corporations and educational institutions were to explore and acknowledge these human resources—the department of intuition, the vice president of imagination, the division of patience and courage—we would be living in a more altruistic and compassionate world.

As a stress-management therapist, I often meet remarkable people who have gone over, around, and under difficult roadblocks. They arrive on the other side the victor, not the victim. When I ask what helped them get through their ordeal, they always describe some aspect of inner resources.

One such case was Andrew, who at the age of thirteen dove into the deep end of a backyard pool and snapped his neck. He is now confined to a wheelchair and will be for the rest of his life. Andrew doesn't live on sympathy or pity. Instead, he thrives on humor. With a smile that spans ear-to-ear, he says one part of his anatomy that is exercised regularly is his funny bone. Humor therapy has been so critical to his recovery that Andrew is studying to become a physician, hoping to use his talents as a goodwill ambassador for comic relief.

Another case is Pete. When he was ten, Pete was diagnosed with bone cancer. Within months the cancer permeated his left femur. To know Pete is to know the meaning of optimism. Many people perceive cancer not as a roadblock, but as a dead end. For Pete, however, it was a mere pothole. Hearing about kids with a similar fate who had sought the assistance of the Make-A-Wish Foundation, Pete soon found himself on board a plane to Florida to swim with dolphins. This was an extraordinary healing experience. His wish came true. In his heart he knew it would. Optimists know these things.

A third role model for spiritual health is Stephanie. The daughter of an alcoholic father, Stephanie was sexually molested and emotionally abused the first ten years of her childhood. It took a long time for her to sort out the strife in her early life, and she would be the first to tell you that she not only resented her father, but also her mother for not stopping the abuse. Stephanie's adult life began to mirror her father's addictive tendencies. After a car accident while driving under the influence, she went for counseling and therapy treatment. She began to see behavior patterns with deep family roots. On the first anniversary of her sobriety, Stephanie found herself at her father's bedside awaiting his final moments in his bout with liver cancer. During his remaining days, Stephanie comforted him with her words of forgiveness, reconciling his past behaviors and her feelings of anger toward him for these actions.

We don't need to meet catastrophe head-on to utilize our inner resources. They can and should be employed every day. Standing in line at the grocery store may require unyielding patience. Dealing with an alcoholic parent demands a strong degree of acceptance. Resolving a conflict with a fellow coworker or roommate may require swallowing some pride and using humility. Each inner resource is represented by a color in the heart's rainbow. There are no stressors that will not give way to the strength of our inner resources. We are never asked to carry a burden that we cannot bear.

Considering the magnitude of our inner resources, our spiritual potential is awesome. Yet the degree to which we utilize our inner resources determines the true health of the human spirit. This is what author Marianne Williamson says about it:

> *Our deepest fear is not that we are inadequate. Our deepest fear is that we are powerful beyond measure. It is our light, not our darkness, that most frightens us. We ask ourselves, who am I to be brilliant, gorgeous, talented, and fabulous? Actually who are you not to be? You are a child of God. Your playing small doesn't serve the world. There is nothing enlightened about shrinking so that other people won't feel insecure around you.*

We were born to make manifest the glory of God that is within us. It is not just in some of us. It's in everyone. And as we let our own light shine, we unconsciously give others permission to do the same. As we are liberated from our own fear, our presence automatically liberates others. [14]

What is the medicine of your soul? List five inner resources that help you face the tough times. If one or more of these spiritual muscles has withered, think about how you can get them back into action.

1. _____
2. _____
3. _____
4. _____
5. _____

Spiritual Potential and Spiritual Health

To stand like mountain is the ability *to recognize* the potential of our inner resources. To flow like water is *to act on* this potential. Our inner resources are not gifts for a chosen few as much as they are birthrights for everyone. Every day we are called upon to use and expand our potential by employing these inner resources. Our spiritual potential, as expressed through humor, compassion, faith, forgiveness, courage, creativity, and intuition, is like a group of instruments. Our spiritual health is demonstrated when we play those instruments. With practice we are all capable of making beautiful music. Life may be a journey, but with God as the maestro, it is also a marvelous symphony.

The Divine Paradox

A budding sense of interest is known to be the initial catalyst for spiritual hunger pangs; few people start this craving solely with a simple curiosity. Undeniably, stress is the real catalyst for spiritual growth; a deep longing for answers that give perspective and understanding to some of life's biggest problems. We look for answers, first as a call for help. Only with the first few insights does curiosity ignite to lead us further down this enigmatic path. Through it all, we continue to seek clues to the dynamics of how the universe works and our purpose in it. Spiritual growth often leads to spiritual exploration, abandoning common (sometimes dogmatic) knowledge for the distant shores of divine insights and mystic revelations. What you may find if you keep looking is that some answers generate new questions. Moreover, some inquiries have very complicated answers, while other questions appear to have no earthly answers whatsoever! When you reach this point on the spiritual path, you have entered into the landscape of the "divine paradox" where a comfortable sense of dualism, if not illusions, gives way to a seemingly ambiguous, yet astounding oneness. The following are but four of the more common paradoxes found on this journey.

1. You are God, but you are not God.

   If you were to explore the tenets of all religions, you might discover a common similarity: Humans are seen as a divine creation. "Children of God" is a common expression to describe this concept. Mythology from all corners of the Earth speaks of man's divine nature, from the story of Adam and Eve to the parable of the Hopi Corn People. Other terms used to illustrate this impression include a "human tabernacle," "a spark of divine creation" and the "breath of God." While some may cry blasphemy at this notion (and many have), every spiritual luminary from Jesus and Buddha to Gandhi has tried to elucidate this concept of our divinity. But don't let this notion go to your head, because you are not God. Unless you are keeping a mighty secret, you cannot create new galaxies with a bang, walk on water, or raise folks from the dead.

One of the first steps to understanding this paradox is to see the divine in all people, all things and to realize and then appreciate that you too are a part of this cosmic puzzle. Realizing that we each contain the spark of divine essence also means that we are all equal. No one person is better (or worse) than anyone else, despite wealth, education, property, good looks, or athletic prowess. We are all special. To know and act with the realization of one's divinity is not a task to be taken lightly. Conversely, it calls to mind another divine irony: the unbearable lightness of being. As you begin to grow comfortable with this paradox, you may begin to realize that everything we do, from our thoughts and actions, is a cocreative process. Please use this wisely!

2. You are your body, but you are not your body.

We live in an illusion of sorts (perhaps many). We inhabit a body, a marvelous vehicle that transports us everywhere. Legs to walk, arms to carry, and the five senses to receive a wealth of information that the brain spends untold hours, night and day, processing. We identify with our bodies. We are our bodies, right? To the unassuming eye, we most definitely are our bodies. Under the influence of the material world in which we live, untold attention and time is placed on the body, often to extremes. Tatoos, Botox injections, face lifts, liposuction, and hair transplants top the list. From aerobics and enamel bleaching to food and fashion, the human body becomes an object of intense, if not hypnotic, fascination. Yet we are no more our bodies than a driver is part of the car he or she drives. Remember this: Despite how much pain we feel when the body aches, we are not just our bodies. While research now reveals that consciousness inhabits every cell of our bodies, consciousness is a little more complicated than neurons and cell memory. Consciousness appears to exist not only within, but also outside the body, as revealed through the research of remote viewing, near-death experiences, and the death/afterlife reality itself. Perhaps this paradox is best put this way: Your body is what you are; your soul is who you are. So take good care of your body, the vehicle that transports your soul, but as the saying goes, "Don't mistake the car for the driver."

3. You are separate from everything, but you are connected.

One of the first things we learn as humans is to see ourselves as separate beings from our parents. Once the ego makes this distinction, we enter the illusion of separation. In the developmental life cycle process, we make a beeline for independence. Sometimes the consequences are deadly. Under this veil of illusion, we take note of all things different (perhaps even threatening) from us, particularly with other people. The ego can be very discriminating. Through the filter of the ego, we quickly perceive, if not judge, how great these differences are: skin color, accents, percent body fat, hair, height, and weight, to name a few. Furthermore, we as independent bodies are not attached at the hip to everyone else. We are separate entities. We come and go as we please. And this, ultimately, is a good thing.

Indeed, there are differences and divisions, but as science explores the differences at the atomic level, a curious observation is detected. Everything is energy. As such, everything appears to be connected energetically. There is no separation. The lines of division are merely an illusion. The field of quantum physics reveals that indeed, everything is connected energetically. The word used to describe this concept is *entanglement*. Quantum entanglement is now used to describe everything from dark matter to synchronistic events. There is a great responsibility in understanding the concept of entanglement. Our thoughts and feelings, like stones thrown in to a big pond of life, affect everything in the pond.

Carl Jung also talked about the concept of entanglement, though he called it the "collective unconscious," a point where all minds connect. As it turns out, Carl Jung conceived this idea after having lunch with Albert Einstein. Not only are the fields of psychology and physics connected, but *everything* is connected. Perceptions of separateness are only an illusion. So enjoy your uniqueness. Enjoy the illusion of your separation, but remember, it is an illusion. You are separate, but you are connected . . . to everything.

4. You are insignificant, but you are essential to the universe.

In a crowded world of 6 billion people and counting, it may seem a little daunting to think of oneself as an essential part of humanity, or even the planet, let alone the entire universe. Rather, the word *insignificant* comes to mind. The words *humble* and *modest* are not far behind either. When one begins to ponder the broad ramifications of such a perspective of our significance, it is humbling indeed. A peek at the time-space continuum only exaggerates the seemingly insignificant aspect of our lives. For instance, when people look back on their lives to determine what legacy, if any, is left for posterity, most people tend to think of themselves as a mere blip on the radar screen of life. Under stress, this insignificance seems to be magnified. Yet, we are anything but insignificant. What appears to be such is an illusion, a mis-realization. Suicides are the epitome of this mis-realization. As such, suicides are a gross injustice to the universe. Perhaps the real question to ask is, what makes a life significant? It's not fame. Surely it's not wealth. A brief romp through history does not adequately portray the real measure of significance either, for history by all accounts is often distorted by the lust of material gain rather than the spiritual essence of life (to the victor go the spoils). Can you image how a history of the world would appear through the lens of compassion rather than a chronicle of wars and empires?

Just as every cell is important to the functioning of the body, every person is essential to the balance of the universe. If we look further we might see that our capacity to love, as expressed through compassion in action, is the realization of our essential nature. Perhaps this was most clearly demonstrated in the classic movie *It's a Wonderful Life*. Truly we have no idea how many lives we touch in the course of our earthly existence, but rest assured the impact is astounding and the number of people is countless. Nor can we even fathom what significance the planet Earth plays in our solar system, galaxy, and beyond, but know too, it is equally astounding. Can one person really make a difference in the world? The answer is yes, and this difference manifests every day, millions of times each day. Let your essence consciously be essential every day. This paradox and perhaps all the rest can best be summed up in the wisdom of this timeless proverb: "Be humble, for you are made of Earth. Be noble, for you are made of stars."

THE YELLOW BRICK ROAD REVISITED

Somewhere over the rainbow, we seek a glimpse of truth to help guide us on our journey. Dorothy from Kansas was no different. Since the release of the movie in 1939, the story of the Wizard of Oz has captured our attention because it deals with the essence of a human spirit. While many people cited political overtones to L. Frank Baum's work, I see it from a different perspective. This story is the epitome of the hero's journey. My understanding became even clearer when I learned of Baum's interest in human spirituality and his association with Helena Blavatsky, cofounder of the theosophy movement. Here are some of my reflections on the ageless wisdom of this story as a spiritual metaphor of life.

After a traumatic landing, Dorothy finds herself in a strange but colorful land. In an effort to find her way home, she is repeatedly advised to follow the yellow brick road (the spiritual path). She is joined by the Scarecrow, the Tinman, and the Lion who personify her inner resources of intuition, compassion, and courage. Indeed, these are weak muscles of the soul, but they stand by her side to assist her on her journey. Along the path, she encounters both good and evil. The Wicked Witch of the West poses a formidable roadblock (fear), which Dorothy overcomes by throwing water (an act of compassion for the Scarecrow) on the witch, causing her to melt.

The field of red poppy flowers—which began as an attraction— soon becomes a distraction and pulls them off the path. Eventually the group falls asleep (falling asleep on the spiritual path). The miracle of snow is their spiritual wake-up call, and they resume the journey to meet the Wizard.

When they finally meet the powerful one, they find that behind the curtain is a man no different from themselves. In the end, Dorothy is told that she had the means to get home all along—the ruby slippers.

We have been told this, too, in the expression, "The kingdom of God is within us."

While making the book into a movie, many spiritual events unfolded. Among them was the story of the Wizard's coat. Frank Morgan was said to be displeased with the selection of clothes presented to him for his costume as the Wizard. In talking with the head of the wardrobe department, he struck a deal. He would head over to the Salvation Army for a more suitable coat. It didn't take him long to find one. Even his wife agreed it was the perfect coat for his character to wear. The head of costumes also agreed, and Morgan's wife took the jacket home to be dry-cleaned. When Morgan came home from shooting that day, his wife smiled from ear to ear. She told him that the coat he had selected was no ordinary coat. Searching the coat's pockets, she found the name of the previous owner sewn inside: L. Frank Baum.

CHAPTER THREE

THE DANCE OF EGO AND SOUL

*Tension is who you
think you should be, relaxation
is who you are.*

—Ancient Chinese Proverb

A rimbaugh is an ancient, Celtic puzzle with two odd-shaped halves that appear as if they don't belong together. But when interlocked in just the right fashion, they reveal their inherent connection. The same can be said for the dynamics between ego and soul, for at times these two seem as distant as the moon and the Earth. The ego and soul are two wheels of the same bike, each necessary, both important. Without soul, the ego would be completely misdirected. The soul without ego would be endangered.

We live in a world where it is common to notice the polarities of life: good and bad, masculine and feminine, hard and soft. To comprehend the true nature of opposites, we must understand that what appears to be polarities are really two parts of the same whole. While it may seem as if each is an independent entity, on the human journey the two unite to become one, like the rimbaugh. Describing the dynamics between ego and soul reminds me of the expression, "It takes two to tango."

THE ANATOMY OF EGO

The concept of human spirituality is difficult to put into words. Equally challenging are attempts to explain the ego—that part of our being expressed through personality, identity and self. Freud tried his best with the latter, but over the past century his concepts have been misunderstood. Perhaps other people's egos got in the way. It is hard to discuss a topic objectively when everyone thinks he or she has a personal expertise in the area. Be that as it may, let's take a closer look at the dynamics of ego and its relationship to the soul.

The word ego comes from the Latin word "I," as in "I am happy" or "I own a new house." Over time, the word ego has come to be used interchangeably with the word "self" or "persona." These words paint an incomplete picture of this intangible aspect of our human identity. The egg helps illustrate that part of ourselves that is sensitive and is protected by a hard shell. Yet the shell itself is fragile. Both the outside and inside are delicate and vulnerable.

Sigmund Freud, who popularized the concept of the "id," was convinced that stress was inevitable, due to the insecure nature of the ego. The ego is quite easily threatened by a host of various perceptions; therefore, some level of tension is always present. In Freud's opinion, stress isn't an overwhelming sensation but a constant level of tension one must learn to tolerate. Not only is the ego easily threatened by outside forces, it is extremely vulnerable to internal messages, produced by what Freud called the id (our impetuously selfish and demanding self).[1]

Insisting that human behavior was instinctual, Freud reasoned that the id was responsible for what appears to be animalistic urges (primitive sexual impulses), which the ego is then called upon to satisfy or subvert. Incessant tension exists between id and I, as each tries to manipulate the other. To have the ego and id work together was Freud's greatest aim in therapy, but he understood that anxiety was an inseparable part of the human condition. He never left much hope for attaining inner peace—or for that matter world peace, since all things are connected. (It should be noted that although Freud was the first to coin the word *ego*, he wasn't the first to acknowledge it. For over a thousand years, Tibetan Buddhists have referred to this aspect of each individual as the "lower self" or "self.")

Freud's protégé Carl Jung took a different road. Inspired by the belief that humans are spiritual rather than instinctual, Jung saw the human experience as a vehicle for the evolution of the soul. He explored the process of self-realization and termed it "individuation," where self-awareness through self-discovery and soul-searching leads one to a greater understanding of one's own life purpose.[2]

Jung, an ardent advocate of dream analysis, said that the conscious and unconscious minds speak entirely different languages. The former is well-versed in analytical, critical, rational, and linear thought, while the latter is fluent in metaphor, simile, symbols, imagination, and intuition. According to Jung, the ego acts as a censor, keeping information from the conscious mind if there is potential to cause emotional or spiritual pain. From Jung's perspective, based on decades of research, the unconscious mind contains a wealth of information freely accessible to the conscious mind, except for the censoring role of the ego.

He explained tension as the absence of "psychic equilibrium," produced by the miscommunication between the conscious and unconscious minds. In some cases the ego goes beyond filtering thoughts from the unconscious mind; it erects monumental barriers, making communication nearly impossible.[3]

THE ILLUSION OF SEPARATION

The ego is a bodyguard for the soul. Not satisfied with this supporting role, the ego, encouraged by the id, demands more attention. This tendency to dominate is so strong, it can eclipse not only the ego's true purpose, but shadow the intentions of the soul.

Like a military coup, this small rebel faction of the ego claims autonomy every chance it gets, thus denying a connection to our higher self. The result is a perceived loss of our divine connection; a separation from God. From a holistic perspective, stress is defined as "a perceived separation from God." This definition has gained greater acceptance by those in the field of mind-body-spirit healing who see the disconnection played out. Others simply use the acronym E.G.O. (Edging God Out). The illusion of separation (commonly known in the East as the "veils of illusion") is a breeding ground for more fear, thus repeating the cycle again and again. In times of stress, ask yourself if it is anger and/or fear that blinds you to your divine connection.

When you look in the mirror you see a reflection—an image of the external you. To confuse the likeness with who you really are may seem puzzling, but this is exactly what happens when this faction of ego (the alter ego) dominates the partnership of ego and soul. Identifying with the body and ignoring the soul only perpetuates the illusion of separation.

Mystics talk about transcending the ego through meditation to gain insight, intuitive wisdom, and enlightenment from our higher self— which then guides us farther along the human journey. The practice of meditation quiets the incessant chatter of the ego/alter ego so that the mind becomes open and the connection to the higher self is realized. Some Western religions scorn meditation as the work of the devil, but Christian theologian C. S. Lewis hit the nail on the head in his book *The Screwtape Letters*. The devil, he wrote, says, "It's funny how mortals always picture us putting things into their minds: in reality our best work is done by keeping things out."[4]

Stimulated by fear, the ego confuses caution for control. Called to action by one or more of the five senses, it weaves a thick illusory veil around the soul. Held in darkness and caught in the layers of veil, the soul tends to lose sight of its mission. With a hypnotic effect, the illusion evokes a state similar to amnesia. Some say the soul, in a period of darkness, falls asleep. The image of a slumbering soul brings to mind this quote from Dr. Albert Schweitzer:

> *You know of the disease in Central Africa called sleeping sickness. . . . There also exists a sleeping sickness of the soul. Its most dangerous aspect is that one is unaware of its coming. That is why you have to be careful. As soon as you notice the slightest sign of indifference, the moment you become aware of the loss of a certain seriousness, of longing, of enthusiasm and zest, take it as a warning. You should realize your soul suffers if you live superficially.*[5]

Freud thought the id was motivated by instinct, but others say that it is fear that directs the ego. Fear reinforces the veils of illusion, reflecting separation rather than union with the true self. As such, the ego, fueled by fear, declares mutiny and thus becomes the soul's biggest obstacle or impediment on the human journey. In an unguarded moment, we might acknowledge this fact. Have you ever said, "Things could be much better if I didn't get in the way of myself"?

Whether it is called id, alter ego, the shadow, subpersonality, or the mask, there is an intangible part of the persona that delights in taking control. It builds walls rather than bridges and favors separation rather than unity. This is what most people refer to as the problem associated with ego. But you don't solve a problem by chopping it off and getting rid of it—certainly not when it is an essential part of the human condition. Like a house pet, the ego must be domesticated or you are going to have poop all over the place. Any parent who has experienced the terrible two's or encountered a rebellious teenager will tell you it is discipline and love, not avoidance and indifference, that help one get through this challenging period. Similarly, anyone who has ever taken dance lessons knows that you have to continually practice the steps to get the moves right. And so it is with ego as the human journey unfolds.

Consider the Taoist yin/yang symbol. It is made up of two equal but opposite halves, one black, the other white. The bridge between opposites is contained in each half—there is a small aspect of the feminine in the masculine, and vice versa. Even the darkest area holds the potential to accept light. As such, that part of the ego that is manipulative holds promise for change. And change we must if we are to walk in balance.

The Chinese philosopher Lao-tzu said, "A journey of a thousand miles must begin with a single step." The message of ego and soul is also present in the ancient Chinese proverb, "Tension (ego) is who you think you should be, relaxation (soul) is who you are." Our first step is the recognition of the role our ego plays as we strive to move forward.

EN GARDE, EGO!

Stress is a perceived threat. Once threatened, the ego must protect itself. Freud referred to this as "defense mechanisms." Accordingly, we access various defenses from the arsenal to constantly guard the ego from pain. These behaviors, ingrained from a very young age, become second nature and operate unconsciously throughout life. Although they may be hard to detect in our own behavior, we have no problem observing them in others. In the short term, these defenses may seem helpful, but in the long term, they only promote more stress. In the words of psychiatrist and renowned author Brian L. Weiss, "Anxiety is being lost in the ego."[6]

Imagine the ego like a young child—sensitive and insecure—to understand how the ego twists perceptions to soften the impact of perceived threats. Defense mechanisms are a distortion of the truth, bending reality to soothe the ego and save face. The Ten Commandments are related to Freud's theory of ego protection. Stealing, lying, cheating, and killing are symptoms of an insecure ego. You will recognize the names of these defense mechanisms since they are played out every day as we interact with others. Labeling these behaviors allows us to free their grip on the soul. Freud recognized and coined terms for a dozen of these. These are five of the most common ego defenses: [7]

Denial

It's hard to embrace our imperfections. Who wants to look stupid or feel embarrassed? It's much easier to deny our foibles. This happens regularly when the ego is threatened by one's behavior. People tend to deny they have a drinking problem, a drug addiction, or deviant sexual habits. Children are masters of denial. "I didn't do it," they say, when they are about to get in trouble. Honing that skill over the years allows adults to become quite adept at denial as well.

Repression

When we do things we wish we hadn't, or when things are done to us that we'd like to forget, we push them from our minds. If they are extremely embarrassing or painful, we may subconsciously choose to bury them in the unconscious mind, far from conscious thought. Thus the memories are effectively repressed.

Projection

By the time we become adults, we know what is and what isn't acceptable behavior. Should anger, fear, or lust arise and be deemed inappropriate, we shift the focus of this feeling by attributing it to someone else. Think about negative campaigning, where party leaders regularly project their feelings onto their opponents. Examples are also abundant on most career paths.

Displacement

This is behavior where inappropriate feelings toward one person are put onto someone or something else. Remember the aspirin commercial whose slogan was, "Sure you have a headache, but don't take it out on the kids"?

Rationalization

When we blame others for our problems, we rationalize. To get laid off from a job or to have your spouse walk out on you is unflattering to the ego. So attention is shifted away from self and directed toward the cause of discomfort. Typically rationalization is used when individuals lose their job because of insubordination, yet tell people they hated the job and are glad to be leaving. A good friend often reminds me just how common rationalization is every time he engages in it, by repeating this clever phrase, "Rationalization is okay, because everyone does it."

Here is a quick summary of Freud's defense mechanisms:

Denial: I didn't do it
Repression: I don't remember doing it.
Projection: He did it.
Displacement: He made me do it.
Rationalization: Everyone does it!

Defense mechanisms ease the emotional pain, even if they don't eliminate it. Stress does penetrate the barriers and when it is deemed threatening, anger, fear, or both quickly surface. Sometimes the fright is so great, the ego becomes extreme in its effort to maintain a sense of control. What may start as an emotional ripple of unresolved anger becomes a tidal wave of cancer by the time it manifests itself in the mind-body-spirit connection. In rare times of real danger, it is the job of the ego to exert a sense of control. Nonetheless, control is a double-edged sword; it cuts on both sides.

The ego, like an office manager on a good day, keeps matters of the mind orderly and self-esteem intact. To paraphrase the thoughts of Integral psychologist Ken Wilber, "The ego in its purest form is best suited to organize and give unity to the mind."[8]

Where some control is good, more is not necessarily better. There is an addictive quality to authority. When the scales of control (ego) and empowerment (soul) are tipped out of balance, the dance between ego and soul comes to a halt as the ego attempts to go solo. The story of control is as old as humanity itself. To put it bluntly, the ego being quite full of itself at this stage needs an enema.

Albert Einstein was once asked what he would recommend to improve imagination and creativity in children. His reply was, "Read to them fairy tales." His answer might have been the same if the question was, "How can one best learn the dynamics of ego and soul?" "Read to them fairy tales." Thumb through the pages of Grimms' fairy tales, *Aesop's Fables*, or *The Arabian Nights* and it's not hard to find several stories that focus on the nature of ego—from the greedy dog with the bone to the story of the fisherman and his avaricious wife. And let us not forget the story of Pinocchio! The Bible is also filled with stories and parables that address the relationship of ego and soul—as are the sacred texts and the legends of all cultures.

Remember the story of the three little pigs? As with all fables that aim to teach a message, this one is about the nature of boundaries and defenses. The wolf is the stressor. Each encounter forces the pigs to defend themselves to avoid becoming bacon and ham sandwiches. From straw to stick to brick, the defenses become more effective, but so does the creative process to avert disaster.

Like the three little pigs, it is natural to protect ourselves. Without the defense mechanism, we would fall prey to the whims and fancies of others, only to lose our identity and direction in life. Conversely, defenses can become so dense that the light of day cannot penetrate and obstructs that which nurtures the soul. In darkness the soul falls asleep.

Each time a stressor penetrates the ego's defense system, emotional pain results. At this point, there are two options: either build stronger walls or examine the options. The first is a reaction. The second, a response, involves reasoning—learning from the problem and growing from the experience.

The ego reacts, the soul responds. When ego boundaries are expanded, like when you repot a house plant, the soul doesn't become root-bound and stifled; it flourishes. Without getting caught up in semantics, a strong ego is one that allows room for spiritual growth, whereas a weak ego is pretty thick (giving the impression of strength) and stunts the maturation of the soul.

BIG EGO, LARGE HEART

We are all familiar with the concept and inherent problems of the ego, if not ours (denial), then certainly the ego of those who irritate us (projection). When we say, "My, he has a big ego," we mean a person whose personality is overbearing, or whose identity needs constant stroking. We might think big-ego people are insecure; however, chances are that repeated stress has caused that person's self to adapt in this way. Although our first inclination is to react, reactions are seldom appropriate. Each encounter, no matter how difficult, necessitates empathy and compassion, not arrogance or indifference. Arrogance only throws gasoline on the ego's fire, causing more anxiety and stress.

While the ego isn't an organ, a comparison to the heart offers some insight. The expressions "a big ego" and "an enlarged heart" have much in common. When endurance athletes are given a graded exercise stress test to examine the capacity of their cardiovascular systems, it is evident that the adaptation of stress (miles of endurance training) results in an enlarged heart.

Conversely, athletes who pursue the path of anaerobic exercise, specifically weight training, also see an enlargement, but of the heart wall. Externally, they may both look developed; however, the difference is an increased capacity to pump blood versus an increased wall thickness, the latter being a significant health risk later in life.[9] A thick-walled ego is also a deterrent to our health.

The expression "big ego" is seldom a term of endearment, although it could be. Like the long-distance runner who trains to run a marathon, life allows us to increase our capacity to grow emotionally and spiritually. When the limits of ego expand, so does the realization of self toward a greater consciousness that all is one. On the other hand, an increase in heart wall thickness is analogous to the thick protective wall of the ego—more commonly referred to as a defensive ego. Ego expansion is a good thing; ego constriction is not because it leads to atrophy of the soul.

One more comparison to the heart is also worth mentioning. An open heart is full of compassion and joy—motivated by love. A closed heart is a hardened heart—steeped in fear and barricaded by anger—which cuts off the flow of blood to itself and all other body organs. The clinical name for this phenomenon is atherosclerosis, where plaque buildup occludes the flow of blood in the coronary arteries. Currently, coronary heart disease is the leading cause of death in the United States.

Once thought irreversible, landmark research by Dean Ornish, M.D., reveals it is now possible to reverse the trend of blocked arteries through diet, exercise, support groups, and meditation, without invasive surgical procedures or pharmaceutical drugs. What Ornish teaches for meditation is no ordinary method. Having spent time in

India learning about the subtle anatomy of chakras and the human aura, Ornish made an intuitive connection between a closed (hardened) heart chakra (unresolved anger and fear) and closed (hardened) coronary arteries.[10]

Consequently, the meditation technique he incorporated into his heart disease reversal program involved dismantling the barriers of ego and opening the heart—first spiritually, then anatomically. His holistic approach has proved quite successful and has now become a recognized program practiced nationwide.

SECRETS ENCODED IN OUR DNA

I don't own a television by choice, but I do read a tremendous volume of books, mostly nonfiction. One of the books that has had the greatest influence on me in the past ten years is *The Cosmic Serpent* by Jeremy Narby. For me, this book began to connect a great many dots (questions) that were hanging suspended in space and time in my own spiritual quest. Not only was it a book I couldn't put down, I highlighted it, underlined countless passages, and took notes in the margins. Then I went back and read several passages again.

Narby's book begins as a personal journey to the Amazon rain forest with a scientific study of the hallucinogenic *ayahuasca* plant, but develops into a stunning exposé on human DNA. This magical double-helix strand, it turns out, holds a vast body of knowledge far more extensive than an encyclopedia. Narby not only highlights the current research ranging from DNA's chemical structure to photon emissions, he explores the ancient/ageless wisdom passed down through the eons of time in artwork. Aside from all the snake images, which symbolically represent wisdom, my favorite was the Taoist yin/yang symbol, which from a different perspective could certainly represent an aerial view of the DNA molecule.

Simply stated, a coiled serpentine DNA strand is a coded library of knowledge, yet one might suggest that for some unknown reason much of this knowledge is off-limits. One of the topics Narby addresses is what scientists call "junk DNA." Medical scientists coined this term to describe the overwhelming portion (95 percent) of the DNA molecule that currently serves no *known* purpose. That's right! We only use approximately 5 percent of our DNA. The rest gets a free ride. Intuition suggests that there must be another explanation.

In my understanding of human nature I am puzzled if not baffled at the downside of human behavior. After so many hundreds of years of conscious evolution (all jokes aside), why is the default mode of human emotions still locked into the gear of fight or flight? This doesn't make sense to me. Why is it that, when given the opportunity, the ego trumps the soul? With access to only 5 percent of each DNA strand, do we really know "just enough to be dangerous"?

As I read Narby's book, a slew of profound questions popped into my head. Does the ego have its own gene? And if so, did this gene somehow deactivate the other 95 percent of our DNA? What we would be like as a species if we had full access to the entire strand of DNA? What would humanity be like if each person rose to his or her highest potential? What would life be like on planet Earth under this condition? Would we have heaven on Earth? Does the soul have a gene? If so, why does it appear to be recessive in a great number of people?

Jeremy Narby's quest led to an experience with the drug *ayahuasca* (another name for this plant is Amazonian spirit vine) to reveal some amazing insights to the nature of human consciousness. As it turns out, one needn't fly to the Amazon to follow in Narby's footsteps to achieve the same means. Wisdom keepers from the dawn of time have illuminated a path that leads to the same destination. The path is called meditation and unlike any natural hallucinogenic substance, this practice holds the promise to keep the balance of power between

the ego and soul. The training effect of meditation acts to domesticate the ego thereby providing access to untold divine wisdom.

MATTERS OF THE SOUL

The conscious, analytical, rational mind begs to know what the soul looks like, what it is made of. But these questions are irrelevant. Unlike the ego, which is well-versed in the language of the five senses, the soul comes from a realm familiar with, but invisible to, sensory perception—an ethereal realm rich in energy beyond the comprehension of conscious thought. The soul—curious, eager, and enthusiastic—incarnates in physical form with a body. With this vehicle and personality, it can explore the human landscape and gain wisdom through experience. This experience includes the good, the bad, and the ugly. The eternal soul comes from a place of divine origin. At some point it will return to that place with its wealth of experience. Strange as it may seem, each soul is identical in its divinity but unique in its personality and mission. Furthermore, all souls gifted in various talents are diverse in their dreams but united in the noble effort to raise consciousness through love. Sadly, the earthly plane is dense with fear, which often causes many souls to forget their mission, thus denying the fulfillment of compassion in action.

In Latin, the word for soul is *psyche*, a unique aspect that distinguishes humans from all other members of the animal kingdom. To date, no metaphor has been fully accepted to describe the soul's nature or its constituents. In the words of maverick theologian Matthew Fox, "We need to move beyond theology toward a cosmology where the work of soul is seen as limitless, not limited in its human scope." [11]

The soul is always aware of its divine connection—its higher self. Although it knows it is never alone, this recognition and memory are often eclipsed by the shadow of ego. Through the myopic vision of ego, division and separation are all that is perceived—hence the inclination to fear and its reaction to it. We may use the expression "lost souls," but in the eyes of God, no souls are ever truly lost. What may appear to be confusion or stepping off the beaten path are merely those souls lured by curiosity but soon distracted by doubt and fear. As difficult as it may be, we are not to judge or interfere, only assist when called upon. What may look like a lost soul could be that individual's life mission. It is not our purpose to criticize an individual's path, just as we should not pass judgment on someone's choice of a career major in college.

On occasion the soul has been compared to a diamond caked with earthen soil; the collection of human experiences makes certain facets not only visible, but noteworthy as well. Various references to soul include a ledger where our earthly experiences are continually recorded. Stories have been told about selling the soul, but the soul is not a piece of real estate that can be bought, sold, or negotiated. Shamanism notwithstanding, souls are not property to be retrieved from the lost and found. The soul is a gift from God, and, as the saying goes, how we nurture it, how we live our life, is our gift in return.

The soul cannot be measured, although some have tried. I am reminded of a story about such efforts told by Elmer Green, a preeminent researcher of human consciousness and healing at the Menninger Clinic in Topeka, Kansas. Curious to probe the specific indices of the human soul, early scientists were known to have weighed bodies promptly before and quickly after patients died. With the scales unaffected, their only conclusion was that if a soul did exist, it didn't weigh anything. To my knowledge, this is the extent of the scientific research, though I am sure that more attempts are being made elsewhere.

Scientifically speaking, we are quite naive about the complex relationship between body and soul. This we do know: The body is the vehicle of the soul, but the soul does not die with the body. It returns to the place from where it came, more polished, more refined, more educated, and more divine.

Compassion, intuition, imagination, faith, courage, free will, humor, and humbleness are just several of the aspects that constitute the muscles of the soul. These inner resources make up the human journey as the soul gravitates toward people and circumstances that allow for its growth. If you are in doubt as to the direction of your soul's journey, or if you are curious about what lessons are being offered to you, take a careful look at the people in your life. The planet Earth is a school where lessons are offered nonstop. We are surrounded by teachers.

Gary Zukav, author of *The Seat of the Soul*, describes the soul this way:

> *Your soul is not a passive or theoretical entity that occupies a space in the vicinity of your chest cavity. It is a positive, purposeful force at the core of your being. It is a part of you that understands the impersonal nature of the energy dynamics in which you are involved, that loves without restriction, and accepts without judgment.* [12]

SOUL WORK

Optimally, the soul and ego work in partnership toward the soul's mission and evolution. The ego gains information from the five senses, the soul attains knowledge from intuition and wisdom from experience. Like Lewis and Clark, they explore the frontiers of human consciousness. It is the job of the ego to help guide the soul on its path of evolution. It is the task of the soul to remind the ego that separation from our divine source is only an illusion. With this understood, the work of soul begins.

What is soul work? Perhaps it can best be described in terms of our capacity to love, a capacity exercised through each of our inner resources. The soul is called to work when it encounters intolerance, blame, greed, anger, cynicism, fear, and negativity. Jungian scholar James Hillman refers to this as a "downward movement in the psyche" where we are called upon to bring light into a place of darkness. The human body maintains its physical strength by exercising; the soul also needs exercise to grow and evolve. This is done through relationships with family and friends or interactions with acquaintances and strangers and the challenges we encounter on the human journey. The path of least resistance may look safe and appealing, but in the words of author Steven Levine, "Safety is the most unsafe spiritual path you can take."[13]

Zukav describes the work of the soul as a promise to God, through which we express our talents, the gifts we bring into the world. The realization of these gifts is what psychologist Jean Houston refers to as the *entelechy*. Entelechy, she explains, is a word she coined to describe "the dynamic purposeful unfolding of what propels us to actualize our essence."[14]

Like the acorn that becomes the mighty oak, the work of the soul is to unfold its gifts so that it may reach its highest potential. Both Houston and Zukav suggest that the expression of our talents, the dynamic unfolding of our entelechy, is stifled when it is hampered by inertia and fear. On a grander scale, the work of the soul is to move from fear to love, and by doing so to elevate human consciousness toward the next step of our evolutionary journey.

The work of the soul also involves play, as we are called upon to remember and engage in the wonder, creativity, and sacredness of life. Hillman refers to this as "movement of spirit." When the sacredness of life is absorbed, it truly invigorates the soul. There is a cartoon with a figure somewhat resembling Calvin of Calvin and Hobbes fame. Alongside Calvin is a phrase that says, "God put me on this Earth to do a certain number of tasks. Right now I am so far behind that I'm never going to die."

Is it really possible to accomplish our tasks, to master the lesson of unconditional love, and evolve the soul in one lifetime? Western philosophy has shunned the notion of reincarnation, but recently it has taken on greater interest as psychiatrist Brian L. Weiss and psychologist Ian Stevenson share their extraordinary past-life case studies.

In his book *Many Lives, Many Masters,* Weiss describes a remarkable story of a woman named Catherine who, under hypnosis for treatment of anxiety, described her soul work through a collection of several past lives. Weiss, a clinically trained M.D., did not believe what he was hearing at first. His surprise was genuine, but he is not alone. Other people under hypnosis have described their journey on the earthly plane as an evolutionary process beyond the comprehension of space and time. Weiss writes:

> *Our task here is to become more Godlike, to recognize the divine and spiritual nature of our soul. To do that, we need to unlearn fear, violence, greed, ego, and power; then kindness, joy, love, and spiritual wisdom are all there.* [15]

Those who believe in reincarnation are not obsessed by it. They follow the recommendation of Siddhartha Gautama, the Buddha, who taught his followers this sage advice, "If you wish to know the past, look at your present life. If you wish to know the future, look at your present life." [16]

FROM FIGHTING TO DANCING

Peek inside the cockpit of a 747 and you will notice dual controls for both pilot and copilot. Even with computer wizardry, flying a plane of that size is no easy task. It requires the collaboration of many people to get from one destination to another successfully. The human journey also requires that the ego and soul work as a team rather than adversaries. We tend to think of ego as a spoiled brat, but the role of the ego is crucial to the human journey. Its supporting role is critical when situations arise where caution must be exercised.

A young boy once explained it to me this way: "You see," he said matter of factly, "the soul is like a kite. It likes to soar, but it needs something to hold it down so it won't wander endlessly. We are like the anchor that keeps the soul grounded." Tugging his baseball cap down over his right eye, he paused for a moment, then added with a voice of excitement, "Imagine the view from up there."

For the partnership of ego and soul to dance, there must be balance. For balance, the ego must relinquish all but the necessary control so the soul may become empowered. As the expression goes, "One cannot discover new oceans until one has the courage to lose sight of the shore."

LETTING GO OF STRESS

It is the soul's desire to travel lightly, while the ego is a pack rat. For better or worse, the soul is responsible for all the actions of the ego, and consequently it gets weighed down with the ego's possessions—both perceptions and material goods.

Because the ego collects things for security, the two are equally encumbered. Letting go of stress is a way of releasing those possessions, attitudes, and beliefs of the ego. Lighten the load. Here are three ways to start and continue this process of letting go of stress:

1. Respond Rather Than React

If there is an instinctual side of the ego, it shows during times of stress. As a reflex, the ego reacts to threats within milliseconds. A snide remark, a sarcastic comment, a hand gesture, silence, or an act of hostility are examples of reactions to a perceived threat. When you do these yourself or see others do them, realize that each reaction is a reflex. But the ego, like a housebroken dog or cat, can be trained to respond.

Research in the fields of health psychology and behavioral medicine reveal that these reactive behaviors can be modified: first, by becoming aware of how you act under duress; second, by choosing a more appropriate response. Like the un-housebroken pet, when the ego reacts there is usually a mess to clean up. When the soul responds, it surveys the situation, looks at options, and acts accordingly—either waiting patiently or not acting at all.

The soul is patient. A response utilizes one or several inner resources when a threat surfaces to the mental, physical, emotional, or spiritual aspects. Letting go of stress invites us to respond, rather than react, each time we encounter a stressor.

2. Surrender the Ego

Originally the ego was designed as a partner to the soul, not its saboteur. The fall from grace, a universal story shared through myth, legend, and parable, is really an insight to the struggle between ego and soul. But it is only through balance that harmony can occur. Eastern philosophy teaches that pure ego is one that is absolute with pure spirit. In the highly acclaimed book *Sex, Ecology, Spirituality,* Ken Wilber writes, "Pure Ego or pure Self is virtually identical with what the Hindus call Atman (or the pure Witness that itself is never witnessed—is never an object—but contains all objects in itself)." Wilber continues to explain that pure ego is synonymous with the Sanskrit term *Atman*, also known as Brahman or the divine source.[15]

Surrendering the ego is an expression to remind the self to work with the soul, not against it. Stated another way, you must become as objective as possible by detaching from your emotions long enough to observe your behavior and how it impedes progress toward self-awareness.

Think of the time you locked your keys in your car (or some equivalent event) and said to yourself, "A year from now, this will be funny, but right now, this is not funny!" This is an example of initiating that first stage as the observer, to step completely outside yourself and see how best to handle the situation. Remember, surrendering the ego should not be confused with abandoning responsibility. In fact, when threatened, the ego is quick to avoid responsibility. Surrendering the ego is the first step necessary to assume responsibility and resolve the stressful situation at hand. Examples abound of people whose egos became a roadblock rather than a guide. We are all familiar with those people who have refined the art of manipulation and control.

Here's a humorous story on the concept of surrender. A professional colleague of mine teaches an adult education course called "Coping with Difficult People." One day we shared stories from our respective teaching experiences. Explaining the history of this particular course, she chuckled, saying, "Unfortunately and ironically, the title attracts the difficult people—those who have spent their whole life trying to figure out why everyone else is so difficult to work with. It makes for a challenging course!"

The ego can be a friend or a foe to the soul. As a friend, it keeps a cautious eye out for roadblocks and distractions. As a foe, the ego undermines the journey by trying to control everything, which is an impossible task. Taming the ego is learning the difference between knowing when to control things and knowing when to go with the flow, or as the ancient Chinese proverb suggests, "Stand like mountain, move like water."

This balancing act requires continuous practice. Unlike house-training a pet, the ego is prone to make repeated messes. Of course, almost everything can be cleaned up with an open heart and an honest apology. Like a well-trained puppy, the occurrences will be fewer when the ego is kept in balance. Remember, the ego has a susceptibility to fear, which brings on the desire to control. Become aware of the circumstances that trigger fear so you can address the problem more readily with your inner resources.

Take a moment to reflect on some issues you are dealing with right now. During this period of reflection, become the observer and ask yourself which of these issues you are able to detach from, surrender to, and work to resolve.

1. _____
2. _____
3. _____
4. _____
5. _____

3. Follow Your Dreams

It would be incorrect to say that the ego, astute in judgment, rationale, and analysis, resides in the brain's left hemisphere, patrolling the border of the subconscious mind. It would be equally inaccurate to infer that the soul resides in the brain's right hemisphere, even though intuition and imagination are cognitive functions that engage the soul's inner resources. However, we can presume that the soul uses the unconscious mind to communicate to our conscious mind through thoughts, memories, insights, and dreams.

It was Jung's opinion that dreams were a unique way to reveal insights and solutions to help us deal with the everyday problems encountered during our wakeful state. Jung was so convinced that dreams played an important role in guiding the soul that he dedicated the majority of his career to the study of dreams. Stories surface regularly of people whose dreams provided insights to overcome and resolve problems and move ahead.

By and large the language of dreams is anything but obvious, and for this reason we are most likely to ignore the messages they contain. Viewing a herd of elk roaming the attic, holding intelligent conversations with famous people long dead, or flying a hot air balloon underwater borders on the bizarre to the conscious, rational, linear mind. Not so to the unconscious, which is rich in symbols and fluent in a language that it begs to share with the conscious mind. Jung felt that the skill of dream interpretation could be learned by anyone; he insisted it is the dreamer, not an encyclopedia of dream interpretations, that ultimately decodes the message of each dream symbol.

How do your dreams speak to you? If you are like most people you may not remember them. Recalling dreams is a skill that proves quite effective with practice. If there is a specific dream, perhaps a recurring dream, write it down, play with the dream fragments, and see if they can be encoded. Next, reflect on the dreams of your soul. How well are these manifesting themselves? What steps can be taken to start this process?

Dream Fragments and Symbols	Dreams and Life Mission
1.	
2.	
3.	
4.	

The expression, "Follow your dreams," speaks to both ego and soul. This expression brings to mind ambitions, wishes, or a life goal. Indeed, each person incarnates on Earth with a soul dream—a life mission to fulfill. But following our dreams also means processing the clues of dream fragments presented by the unconscious mind in an effort to help resolve issues and reconcile our problems. By increasing our fluency in the language of dream symbols and processing their messages, we release the stress that holds us captive. In turn, we fulfill the promise of our life purpose. Jung gave some friendly advice to those who are eager to let go of stress: Follow the insight of your dreams, for to ignore these messages, just because they may seem irrelevant or incoherent, is unwise and unproductive to the soul's growth.

A TALE OF TWO BROTHERS

Since the ego has a short attention span, it needs constant reminders on how it can best serve the soul. There are many fables and parables that describe the relationship between ego and soul; each offers a similar perspective on the nature of this dance. This Celtic tale is a variation on this theme.

Once upon a time, two brothers—fraternal twins—lived in a remote village. As boys they were friends, but as they matured into young men, their relationship became less amicable and more adversarial. The taller one, dominant in his views, was quite outspoken and aggressive. The handsome one was reserved and passive but equally strong in physical stature. The two were soon-to-be heirs of a prominent, wealthy farmer.

The father's wish was to leave the farm to both sons, for he knew that neither could run the business alone. The taller one had an innate business acumen and a quick wit. The handsome one was grounded to the soil and spoke the language of the seasons.

The taller brother, jealous of his twin, schemed to have his sibling kidnapped so he would become the sole heir to his father's fortune. The plot to abduct his brother was successful. One night while returning from town alone, the handsome one was clubbed over the head and later thrown into a hay wagon bound for the coast. Months passed and not a trace of the handsome lad was found; he was presumed dead. And so it came to pass that the heartbroken father died and willed his property to the remaining son.

One night after the first harvest, the tall lad went into town and drank himself into a stupor. His arrogance brought him face-to-face with trouble, and a raucous fight lasted into the wee hours. Early the next morning he was found by a traveler along the side of the

*road, not far from the inn. He had been badly beaten and left for
dead. The kind traveler carried him home. For days he dressed his
wounds, cared for him, and attended to his needs.*

*Days turned to weeks, until one afternoon the beaten man
regained consciousness. He found himself in his own bed, in his own
house, not knowing how he had returned. He was delighted to be
alive. Just then his brother came to dress his wounds. The beaten
man, recognizing his twin, began to cry.*

*After confessions and apologies, the two resumed their father's
wish to maintain the farm together. The next year the taller man,
with his strong business skills, negotiated honest deals to acquire
neighboring land. At the same time, the handsome brother engineered a new irrigation system to increase the size of the harvest,
and business did extremely well. The following year the spring rains
came and never seemed to end. The rivers flooded and several lives
were lost. All crops throughout the valley were damaged, save one
farm whose owners harvested an early crop. When the rains ended
and the sun broke through to dry the land, the two brothers held a
celebration and donated all their harvest to the townsfolk.*

Like the relationship between the two brothers, the dance of ego
and soul is a dance of balance, where both halves contribute equally
to the progression of the soul's maturity; the energy of both is
focused in the same forward direction. The dance then becomes the
journey of life.

SEASONS OF THE SOUL

To everything turn, turn, turn

There is a season, turn, turn, turn

And a time for every purpose under heaven.

—Pete Seeger[1]
"Turn, Turn, Turn"

If you were to talk to the wisdom keepers, the shamans, the healers, the sages, and the prophets of all cultures through human existence, you would learn there is no one curriculum for spiritual growth. Nor is there a specific series of sacred rituals for spiritual evolution. In fact, the paths of human spirituality are as varied as the people on them. Instead you will find four processes that continually nurture the health of the human spirit. These seasons of the soul include:

- **Centering:** a time of solitude to quiet the mind, lower the ego walls, and tune into the voice of the higher self.
- **Emptying:** cleansing the mind and soul by releasing old thoughts, perceptions, attitudes, and stressful toxins that obstruct one's attention.
- **Grounding:** cultivating one's powers of intuition, imagination, and intellect.
- **Connecting:** sharing the insights, creative expressions, and compassion gained in the grounding process to enrich lives and raise consciousness for all of humanity.

While the seasons of the Earth, phases of the moon, and the oceanic tides repeat with regularity, the timetable associated with the seasons of the soul are less predictable, yet no less dynamic. What makes life so interesting, at times even chaotic, is that every person operates on his or her own schedule. And unlike the seasons and cycles of nature, the soul is also influenced by free will.

The cycle of the seasons—centering, emptying, grounding, connecting—follows a rhythmical pattern, a natural flow in the process of the soul's growth. As dark gives way to dawn, it is impossible to become grounded in intuitive wisdom before the soul is emptied of doubt.

The human agenda varies from day to day and person to person. Moreover, it is not uncommon to see the soul's growth rate finishing one experience while starting another. The intensity and duration of each soul season is clearly dependent on the experiences we encounter and our level of soul maturation.

The journey of the soul is an evolutionary process grounded through each and every experience we encounter—whether pleasant or unpleasant, sublime or undesirable. There are no exceptions. Every situation is important. By taking the time to explore these seasons, we can attempt to understand the meaning of those experiences that so greatly affect us. On occasion you may ask yourself, "Is there really meaning and purpose to the less than desirable experiences that make me feel victimized and violated?" Caught in the midst of these encounters, it often seems impossible to make sense out of them. As a result, one often feels like the victim; this is a natural response. But when we choose to first listen then learn from the lessons by emotionally detaching from the experience, we mature spiritually—like the rough rock that becomes a smooth gemstone.

This process of soul growth is as inevitable as the phases of the moon, and as natural as the dawn of each day. So the seasons of the soul offer us the unique opportunity to examine the landscape of the human journey—the spiritual path. In turn, these seasons offer insight into two of the most important questions: Who am I? Why am I here?

Four aspects of the human condition compose the whole: mind, body, spirit, and emotions. Of these four components, the spiritual dimension—more specifically, the evolution of the soul—is the most difficult to comprehend. Perhaps for this reason, it is the most trying. From a physical perspective, the challenges put forth are very tangible. We can see obvious changes in our body as we age. Likewise, our mental processes sharpen over our life span. Our emotional maturity—the ability to feel and express the entire range of human emotions—may be stifled now and then, but it is seldom compromised.

Nevertheless, it is the soul's growth process, our evolution of higher consciousness—the realization of the divine nature of our inner selves—that is the least understood, the most challenging, yet ultimately the most rewarding.

Is it possible to embrace each season of the soul, each cycle of soul growth with equal enthusiasm? Perhaps not. Indeed, some seasons are more difficult than others.

A colleague of mine, a Vermont pediatrician, gives out more smiles than medicine. Jack is no stranger to the marked differences between bone-chilling winters and the humidity of summer. No matter which season, if you're in Jack's company, you will often hear him say, "This is my favorite time of year." We, too, should embrace the seasons of the soul in much the same way, for the insights they offer are invaluable.

These four processes, like the planetary seasons they represent—centering (autumn), emptying (winter), grounding (spring) and connecting (summer)—are equally subtle and dynamic, challenging and uplifting. All provide a sense of balance to the soul's growth process.

Seasons of the Soul

| Autumn | Winter | Spring | Summer |
| Centering | Emptying | Grounding | Connecting |

THE CENTERING PROCESS

To center means to enter the heart. The centering process is an approach to go within, to quiet the mind, and to explore the landscape of the soul. In its truest sense, centering is the first step of the soul-searching process, for a quiet space must exist before the wisdom of the heart can be heard. Like the shorter days of autumn, which gently usher us inside at an earlier hour, the centering process invites us to tune into our inner self by unplugging from the external world. For just as there is a world to discover through our five senses, there is a whole universe to explore within the human mind.

Through the centering process, the conscious mind is encouraged to pause in silence and then listen to the deep-seated wisdom that guides us. To center ourselves is a way to achieve balance, to bring equity back to the soul; we do this by making a concerted effort to reconnect with that part of our consciousness we know as the Higher Self, the divine essence or God. Chinese philosopher Lao-tzu wrote these words in his philosophical teachings of Taoism:

> *Be still and discover your center of peace. Through nature, the ten thousand things move along, but each returns to its source. Returning to center is peace. Find Tao by returning to source.*[2]

The spiritual teacher Paramahansa Yogananda gave the same message in these words: "Calm the mind, that without distortion, it may mirror Omnipresence."[3]

Jung felt that much of the stress and turmoil we experience was a result of what he called psychic imbalance—the inability of the conscious and unconscious mind to speak to each other directly. As mentioned in Chapter Three, this imbalance is due in large part to the language barrier between the conscious and unconscious minds. Jung was convinced that if we made a habit of turning our thoughts inward, by delving beneath the waters of the conscious mind, we would become fluent in the language of the unconscious. Once proficient, we would be able to tap the reservoir of divine wisdom, or that aspect of universal consciousness that connects us all.

Centering is a process where rather than doing, we take time to simply be. In the words of Jesus of Nazareth, "Be still and know that I am God." Sometimes the simplest truths can be found in the strangest places, like bumper stickers, greeting cards, bathroom graffiti, and tea bags. Recently I came across one of these simple truths, which reminded me of the importance of centering. It was on a T-shirt I found in Virginia Beach: "The irony is, if you don't go in you can't find out." Find out what? The answer: the simple truths that lie hidden under the layers of the ego. When we take the time to tune into our thoughts, feelings, perceptions, and attitudes, we begin to discover the inner wisdom that lies dormant under the layers of consciousness, waiting to be revealed to us. The renowned spiritual teacher Jiddu Krishnamurti wrote, "When the whole consciousness is silent and tranquil, free from all becoming, which is spontaneity, then only does the immeasurable come into being."[4]

A CONFLUENCE OF DAILY DISTRACTIONS

Centering is as natural and necessary as eating and sleeping. Yet due to a constant barrage of mental distractions, going within is usually postponed. More often it is abandoned altogether. As such, the soul receives less than adequate attention, like a house plant that hasn't been watered. Ultimately this neglect manifests itself in the physical body, and we get sick. If there is a deterrent to our soul's growth, it lies in an overabundance of distractions, both external and self-generated.

There is no denying that we live in a world of constant sensory stimulation also known as TMI—too much information! The human mind, far more sophisticated than any machine, is constantly deciding what is important and what is not. In addition, the alter ego, with the self-appointed task to censor most of this information, prowls the edge of the five senses, looking for anything that can be perceived as a threat. When the ego is alarmed, all attention is directed externally, rather than toward the focus of the soul. In this warp-speed, consumerist world, spiritual bankruptcy is at an all-time high. With all senses turned outward, the spiritual coffers are empty.

There was a time when it was easier to quiet the mind. Today the challenge is monumental, but not impossible. Stop for a moment and listen to the sounds around you. What do you hear? The TV, the satellite radio, your iPod, the refrigerator, street traffic, or the ring of your cellphone? This cacophony of noise creates a barrier to the deeper levels of consciousness. Furthermore, we are so accustomed to noise that we have become desensitized to the wedge it places between our mind and our soul. Sad to say, even if there were an absence of external distractions, the conscious mind—under the direction of the alter ego— has no problem coming up with its own distractions. The voice of the alter ego babbles incessantly.

A cluttered mind is a stressful mind. The preoccupation of fear-based thoughts distracts the mind of the soul's importance. In the 1960s the technique of Transcendental Meditation hit mainstream America. Through various research studies by Herbert Benson and others, we learned how effective meditation is in its ability to quiet the mind.[5] In essence, meditation became a way to subdue the thoughts of the alter ego. As a prime example of the mind-body connection, the practice of meditation showed some beneficial physical effects such as reducing the heart rate, lowering blood pressure, reducing muscle tension, increasing resistance to colds and flu, increasing the quality of sleep, and minimizing other factors associated with chronic stress.

The basic premise of meditation is to clear the mind of distracting thoughts. Like a broom that cleans a dusty floor or a strong breeze that clears the sky of clouds, meditation through mantras, breathwork, and so on cleanses the mind of mental chatter and ego distractions. This makes room for new insights, intuition, and aspects of higher consciousness to guide us further on our journey. While the practice of meditation provides a sense of mental balance, centering narrows the gap between alter ego and soul. Again, in the words of Krishnamurti:

> *When the mind is still, reality, the indescribable, comes into being. So the mind must be simple, unburdened by belief, by ideation. And when there is stillness, when there is no desire, no longing, when the mind is absolutely quiet with a stillness that is not induced, then reality comes. . . . And when that happens, it is a blessing.*[6]

Entering the Center of the Heart

It is clear that we need a balance between external stimuli and turning our attention inward. While it may seem difficult to find that quiet space, there are things you can do to create healthy boundaries to minimize the distractions and interruptions thereby dedicating some quality time to be alone.

1. Designate a time each day to center yourself. Many find early morning hours best for meditation, but only you know your schedule, so find a time to call your own.

2. Designate a quiet space specifically for the centering process. It can be a corner of a room furnished with pillows, or a special chair by a window full of sunlight. Find time in your daily schedule to occupy that space, making it a high priority if only for a few minutes a day, by sitting still for as long as you feel comfortable. If you are not used to doing this, it will feel strange and your initial thought will be to fight it. Five minutes may seem like an hour, but like anything you may first try, it will take some practice to find your comfort level. If you live with others, let it be known that this is time when you are not to be interrupted, and ask them to honor your request.

3. Close the windows, unplug the phone, and turn off the radio and TV.

Initially, my meditation practice came through exercise, primarily running and swimming. What first started as a routine for outdoor physical activity quickly became a ritual for cleansing my mind, particularly in the pool, as I felt the water caress my body with each stroke. For the most part, physical exercise really did the job of clearing my thoughts and providing a sense of psychic equilibrium. But with a change of jobs and some additional life challenges, my routine soon became inadequate. I found that I needed something more. So in addition to my physical workout, I actively took up a more passive form of meditation. I sat quietly on the floor of my bedroom and simply concentrated on my breathing. Like most people beginning this practice, minutes seemed like hours to me.

For the first few days I only sat still for three to five minutes before convincing myself that I had done all I could possibly do that day. My patience was thin, but my dedication was immense. Eventually, each morning the period grew comfortable so that after a month I could sit for thirty minutes straight. It didn't take long to notice the effects.

Aside from the calming presence I felt throughout the day, I had also rid myself of allergies.

As for the best way to meditate, there is no one best way that's right for all people. Try various techniques and see which feels most comfortable for you. Some people begin by sipping a cup of tea. Others fill the air with soft instrumental music or white noise and read a passage from a meditation book. Still others find a comfortable place to sit, close their eyes, hold an object in their hands (such as a sea shell, a polished gemstone, rosary beads, or a crystal) and monitor their breathing. There really is no best way to meditate, only a way that is best for *you*.

Enlightenment doesn't come easily—and there are no guarantees that when you first initiate the centering process you will open the doors to divine wisdom. Like beginning a weight-loss program, the changes won't be immediate. But through practice and self-discipline, the chasm between alter ego and soul is narrowed, enabling you to walk in balance with greater confidence.

There is an ancient proverb, "When the student is ready, the teacher will come." The centering process is an exercise in readiness, of calming the mind. For when the mind is calm, then the voice of wisdom and insight is able to speak. We are both the student *and* teacher!

Centering Exercise #1

Breathing Clouds

A friend of mine met with a Chinese healer to discuss the importance of breath work. "There are forty different ways to breathe," he said.

"Really?" asked Michelle. "I thought there were only two: inhale and exhale." She was soon to learn that there are many ways to breathe consciously, as a means to center one's thought to the heart and to clear the mind as well. Concentration of the breath by following the breath inward is considered one of the most fundamental ways to begin the centering process. The following technique, breathing clouds, is an exercise to help you focus on your breathing. By using the metaphor of clouds, you will clear your mind of extraneous thoughts.

Gently close your eyes and focus all your attention on the flow of air as you breathe in and exhale. After three to five breaths, visualize the air that you breathe into your lungs as a cloud of clean, pure, energized air. Tell yourself that the clean, fresh air that you breathe in through your nose has the power to clear your mind of distracting thoughts, as well as to cleanse and heal your body. As you slowly inhale this clean, pure air, feel the air enter your nose and travel up through the sinus cavity toward the top of your head. Visualize the air traveling down your spinal column and circulating throughout your abdominal area.

Now, as you exhale slowly and deeply, visualize that the air leaving your body is a dark dirty cloud. This dark cloud of exhaled air symbolizes all your stressors, frustrations, and toxins. With each breath you take, allow the clean fresh air to enter and circulate and rejuvenate your body, while the exhalation of dark cloudy air helps to rid your body of its stress and tension. Repeat this breathing cycle for five to ten minutes. As you continue this cycle of breathing clouds, you may notice that as the body becomes more relaxed through the release of stress and tension, the visual color of the breath exhaled begins to change from dark to gray, perhaps even an off-white, a message from your mind that it is cleansed and refreshed.

The Body Flame

Imagine that the energy we burn all day is not just physical energy (calories), but mental and emotional as well. Imagine that this source of energy resides in the center of your body (the Japanese call this reservoir of energy the *hara*). When this energy is excessive, we feel frantic and overwhelmed. The body flame meditation, like the breathing clouds exercise, is a way to help clear your mind of excess thoughts and excess energy.

Begin by lying comfortably on your back, keeping your spine aligned from your head to your hips. Concentrate on your breathing by making each breath comfortably slow, deep, and relaxed. Close your eyes and try to locate the center of your body, your center of gravity, which is about an inch or two below your belly button. Next, imagine a flame hovering over that point of your body. Metaphorically speaking, this flame is a symbol of your state of relaxation. It feeds off your body's energy. When the body has an abundance of energy—nervous or negative energy—this flame will be quite tall, perhaps like a blow torch. When you are completely relaxed, your flame will be quite small. I call this a "maintenance flame," like a pilot light in a gas stove. Imagine the size of your flame. See its size relative to your body's level of energy. Look at its color. It may be an intense brilliant yellow/white color. Now look at its shape. At the bottom it is round or oval-shaped. As you look toward the top, you will see it comes to a jagged point. Your flame may even dance around a bit. As you look at this flame, feel it feed off the excess energy in your body. Let your flame burn off any excess energy you feel detracts from your ability to relax. If you find your mind distracted by wandering thoughts that pull your attention away from the image of the flame, try to send these from your head up through the flame, and redirect your thoughts back to this image. As you continue to watch this image of the flame, feel your body slowly become calm and relaxed. As your body becomes tranquil, notice the flame decrease in height. Soon you will notice your flame decreasing in size—to one-half-inch tall.

Continue to notice the color, shape, and size. And feel your body relax as your attention is affixed to this image. Continue to keep your mind's eye focused on your body flame. When you feel completely relaxed, with your flame very small, very still, allow this image to fade from your mind, but retain this feeling of relaxation, knowing that your mind is now clear, with fewer and fewer distractions.

DILBERT reprinted by permission of United Feature Syndicate, Inc.

THE EMPTYING PROCESS

Nature provides many wonderful examples to remind us of our growth and balance on the human path. A still pond on a cool, quiet morning offers a host of images of self-reflection through the centering process. The darkness of night and the ebb of the ocean waters also help to illustrate the fullness of the soul's growth process.

As the chilly winds of autumn usher in the harsh winter, the human soul is constantly invited to empty itself.

This soul season is a time of cleansing, letting go, and releasing the nonessentials we have outgrown or no longer need. These nonessentials—sometimes referred to as emotional baggage—may be thoughts, perceptions, beliefs, attitudes, memories, and feelings that were once useful but that no longer serve us. They may also be represented by material possessions or relationships.

As so eloquently expressed through the voice of Ecclesiastes, "There is a time for keeping, and a time for throwing away." The emptying process is the time for throwing away to allow more room for personal growth.

The emptying process allows space for new insights, ideas, intuitive thoughts—or even enlightenment. But this can only happen when there is room. Sadly, we are usually reluctant to clean our mental/spiritual house. Stated differently, the emptying process is a time to weed the garden of the soul. The natural world craves a time of emptying, and the human soul is no different. For our spiritual essence to thrive, we must regularly cleanse that part of our consciousness that stagnates our spiritual growth. A parable from the Eastern culture brings this point home quite clearly:

An American professor on sabbatical took a trip to the Himalayas to research a new book. Inquiries he made regarding mystical consciousness in the town of Katmandu led him to venture up a mountain path in search of a wise old yogi. After days of travel, he happened upon a hut where there resided a man, matching the description given to him.

Once invited in for tea, the professor graciously sat down, patiently held a tea cup, and awaited the chance to converse with the yogi. As the tea was poured, the professor noted the cup was soon full, only to see the yogi keep pouring, next filling the saucer, and then spilling tea onto the floor. Politely, the professor insisted the yogi stop.

The yogi replied, "Your mind is like this tea cup. You came to me searching for insights, yet your mind, like this tea cup, is quite full. It is so full of concepts and beliefs that there is no room for new wisdom."[7]

Of the four seasons of the soul, the emptying process is the most painful and difficult to work through. Just as clouds contain moisture, the emptying process contains grief, and there will surely be grieving in this season. My most recent encounter with this season was the loss of my beloved dog Shasta. Shasta entered my life in January of 1999. He was a rescued dog about three years old. If ever a Siberian husky had a face to charm people and steal hearts, Shasta indeed had that face—and a personality to match. People adored him, including all my workshop participants (Shasta was my perennial pet therapy guest speaker). I adored him too. In the summer of 2006, Shasta was diagnosed with bone spurs on his vertebra, a condition so bad that his spine had fused together. Within weeks his condition worsened as his spinal column became crushed. My vet said it was the worst case he had ever seen. Non-pet owners will never understand this, but my dog was my family, friend, roommate, soulmate. The day I took him in to be put to sleep was one of the worst days of my life. I cried uncontrollably. (I have since discovered that men who "never cry" will be reduced to tears when their dogs die, thus giving credence to the expression, "man's best friend".) Death of anyone close can create a void in our lives, and Shasta has left a very big hole in my heart. But life goes on, and I take comfort in the words, "This too shall pass."

Although we may seek guidance, no one can complete this painful part of the journey for us. More often than not, whenever possible we tend to avoid the emptying process altogether either by turning about-face and retreating, or stopping dead in our tracks. Did you know that avoidance is the number-one ineffective stress coping technique? If there is such a concept as a spiritual couch potato, the spud stops here. Do you silently moan, "I'm not budging" when this season approaches?

The resistance to emptiness comes from many sources. In the tradition of our ancient ancestors, it is common to want to hold on to possessions—whether they consist of material goods or our beliefs and opinions. Although we may be living in the high-tech age, we are still hunters and gatherers. Now we not only collect a wealth of material possessions, we also gather information to which we attach our opinions, attitudes, and beliefs. All of this supports the identity of our egos. If you doubt this fact, initiate an objective conversation on the topic of politics or religion with anyone who holds a view other than your own.

It is very hard to "let go" of our perceptions and beliefs because these are the very possessions in which we place our security. To move outside our comfort zones triggers the fear alarm, which in turn allows the alter ego to enact a host of defense mechanisms—from denial to rationalization—all of which inhibit or immobilize the soul's growth process. Fear keeps us frozen in place. It is faith that melts the fear and gently guides us through the darkness of the void.

Releasing the accumulation of our perceptions, beliefs, and opinions is what the emptying process encourages us to do. In the Eastern culture this process is called detachment. We must let go of those material or abstract things that immobilize our level of consciousness—detachment without ego involvement. Similarly, in the words of Jesus, the emptying process invites us to "be in this world but not of it."

Lessons in detachment don't come easily. When John lost his job in a corporate restructuring move, he threw up his hands and said, "I quit!" After realizing the irony of this comment, he found himself laughing out loud. Later he told me how he watched himself move through the death and dying process for the job he once felt was secure. First denial, then anger, next some bargaining around corporate benefits, and finally acceptance of the situation at hand.

"There was plenty of rationalization at first," he confided. But forced to look at the situation realistically, he opted for optimism rather than pessimism. "To be honest, at first I felt used. I worked for this company fifteen years! But it didn't take long to realize I was free to make some choices that I would not have done otherwise, being in a comfortable rut."

Within a month, John started his own consulting firm and now finds more time to spend with his family than his previous job ever afforded him. "Losing my job was the best thing that ever happened to me," he said.

Consider the process of emptying and the avoidance that accompanies it. Nowhere is this better understood than with the thought of a young child who will do anything to get out of taking a bath. Like that child, we often enter this season kicking and screaming, trying to avoid the inevitable. Yet as we all know, stepping out of a bath or shower and feeling clean and fresh is a wonderful sensation. The same holds true when we emerge from the void and see the first rays of dawn after endless hours of darkness.

The emptying process holds the promise that whatever is released will always, without exception, be replaced by something of equal or greater importance. Yet no matter how many times we rotate through the emptying process, we always seem to forget this part. Perched at the precipice, we are reluctant to take the next step. At these times we must remember that nature provides us with many wonderful examples of our growth and balance: Winter is always followed by spring, the new moon is always followed by a full moon, and darkness is always followed by light. The same promise awaits the human soul as we emerge from the void, cleansed, refreshed, and invigorated. Sadly, this transition becomes impossible for those who fear letting go.

FEAR OF THE VOID

The sensation of emptiness is neither appealing nor desired in the American culture. In fact, we are constantly barraged with media messages to buy, consume, and fill up, not empty, cleanse, and eliminate. So the emptying process is mixed with feelings of fear and avoidance. (Notice the word *avoidance* contains the word *void*.) Fear eclipses faith, resulting in spiritual stagnation.

The void represents change and transition. Change, as we learned in the first chapter, is often synonymous with stress. So when we approach the edge of the void—a space of uncertain possibilities—we are often filled with anxiety. We want to run and hide. If there is pain on the human journey, it occurs in the emptying process: what Jung described as "the dark night of the soul," what theologian Matthew Fox calls "Via Negativa," what philosopher Lao-tzu referred to as "the dangers of excess," and what the average person calls "growing pains." Perhaps as no surprise, the emptying process is also known as "the winter of our discontent."

A colleague of mine lost an earring of great sentimental value. I gently reminded her to let go spiritually that which she had already separated from physically. "Yes," she replied, "but the spiritual letting go is so much harder." Her words speak for us all as we ourselves encounter similar circumstances.

Of all the seasons of the soul, the emptying process is, by far, hardest to endure, and thus the easiest phase to avoid. Those who try to skip this process usually end up in what I call a state of "spiritual constipation." Several experts in the field of humanistic and transpersonal psychology admit that the spiritual dimension is the last aspect of our lives to which we devote our attention. Whether it is laziness, fear or both, we go to great lengths to put off the lessons. Yet when we try to bypass the emptying process, eventually nature—or that aspect of God we call our Higher Self—helps us move through this process.

Nature may abhor a vacuum, but she is not fond of gluttony either. In an effort to restore balance, we will encounter episodes of loss in our lives. These losses, big or small, are symbolic of a higher purpose, which is to let go, to cleanse, and to empty. When we don't do this regularly, on our own, nature steps in to move us along. What are some examples of emptying in terms of loss? There are many: ending a relationship, losing a job, suffering a chronic disease, or being robbed of a possession. Each serves as a little reminder to "be in this world, but not of it." Remember, the dark night of the soul is only supposed to be a night, not an eternity. In the words of Winston Churchill, "If you're going through hell . . . keep going!"

At first, moments of loss seem like stressors; but in time they can turn into polished gemstones if we learn from the experience. To repeat the adage coined by author Richard Bach, "Every problem holds for you a gift in its hands. We seek problems, because we need their gifts."

Listening to a multitude of stories as well as reliving a few of my own, I have come to learn that it is the emptying process that takes center stage during a spiritual crisis or a moment of chaos. Whether it is an unmet expectation or the tragic death of a loved one, few people see a stressful episode as having any spiritual significance. Jung held the view that every crisis is spiritual in nature: "Even a happy life cannot be without a measure of darkness, and the word 'happiness' would lose its meaning if it were not balanced by sadness."[8]

Stressors are not so much a spiritual breakdown as opportunities for a spiritual breakthrough. Our moments of despair are the soul's attempt to take that first step into the void. According to Jung, these moments continue until we are ready to emerge from the dark night of the soul. As much as we would prefer life to be a bed of roses, the truth is that life is a blend and a balance of good and bad, happy and sad times. Perhaps nowhere can this be more eloquently stated than in Kahlil Gibran's book *The Prophet* where he described joy and sorrow as inseparable: "Your joy is your sorrow unmasked. . . . The deeper that sorrow carves into your being, the more joy you can contain."[9]

A client of mine named Aaron had been married for eighteen years to a woman he loved deeply. His love was so strong, so giving, that he was able to forgive two episodes of infidelity. One day he came home early to find his wife sitting comfortably in the arms of a close friend. Then came the news: She wanted a divorce. With three children and a mortgage, and without a circle of close friends for support, the security of a safe world came crumbling down rather hard. Although there were moments of pain, agony, and embarrassment, with hindsight, Aaron looks back and sees virtue where he once saw torment. He now admits without a trace of malice that his divorce was one of the greatest gifts he has ever received.

EMPTYING EXERCISE #1
_____

Quiet Internal Darkness

Engaging in the emptying process begins with a thought, in this case a thought to empty and cleanse the mind. There are several ways to enact this process, one of which is meditation combined with mental imagery. After having done some breathwork and centering, try this exercise to engage in the emptying process.

Begin by comfortably sitting or lying down. Using your imagination, visualize that you are suspended in the center of your own body. As you look around you, notice that surrounded by all your organs and fluids, it seems pretty tight and crowded where you are. Merely by thinking the thought, ask all the organs, tissues, fluids, and bones to symbolically leave your body so that all that remains is a hollow shell of skin. As you look around, you notice immediately how dark it is. You may even hear an echo of your breath. In the darkness you find a great deal of comfort. The quietness is calming.

Comfortably sit in the stillness of this dark, quiet space. This is the void, the place of unlimited possibilities. What appears to be nothing is actually the womb of everything possible. Taking a breath, you acknowledge this calmness and the potential it represents. Looking up, you now notice a spark of light suspended in the center of this hollow shell. You reach for it and hold it in your hands, watching the glow from the spark begin to radiate beyond your hands toward the perimeter of your once empty body. Rays of light emanate toward your legs and feet, up toward your shoulders and neck, down toward your arms and hands, and up to your head.

Feeling a sense of warmth from this light, you now call back, one by one, the organs, the tissues, the fluids, and bones. As each comes back into the shell of your body, every cell becomes bathed in the light. Soon you come to a full awareness that your whole body is filled with light, and you feel charged with the wisdom of new possibilities in your life.

As products of the American culture, so strongly influenced by the Puritan ethic, Judeo-Christian dogma, and the rising tide of victim consciousness, we rarely associate stress as a spiritual experience. Instead, when we think of spiritual moments, we are quickly drawn to what psychologist Abraham Maslow called the "peak" or "mystical moments"—the Disney World view of awesome sunsets, mountain vistas, angelic realms, and glorious bear hugs—where we truly feel a oneness with God. Conversely, stressful episodes are thought of as moments of "divine abandonment," with an ever-increasing chasm of separation. But in the realm of "All that is" (one common description of God), every experience is spiritual; we are never disconnected from God.

The separation we perceive is only a deception, often referred to as the veils of illusion, created by the defenses of the alter ego and fueled by the self-generated perceptions of fear. In the larger picture, the good, the bad, and the stressful are all part of the spiritual agenda, the true evolutionary process of the soul. Once again we are reminded of the words of Bolen—"We are not humans on a spiritual path. Rather, we are spirits on a human path"— and it is this path we walk on to smooth the rough edges of the soul by learning from our experiences.

SPIRITUAL CONSTIPATION

The human journey lends itself to many metaphors. One that comes to mind when reflecting on the emptying process is the aspect of shortcuts taken on the spiritual path, more commonly known as addictions. M. Scott Peck, expounding on this concept, once said, "You cannot slip into heaven through the back door." [10] He made this comment in reference to those people who connect to their divine essence through drugs or alcohol. (In England the word for alcohol is, in fact, *spirits*.) But in their effort to avoid the void, they circle in a whirlpool of addictive behavior. The attempts to regain the feeling of oneness or bliss with a host of chemical substances produces only a temporary fix—the state of artificial bliss. Frustration leads to further futile attempts to achieve the state of elation. Trying to fill the spiritual void with material means is like cramming a square peg into a round hole. Peck added that to complete the human journey, we must first visit the desert of the soul. In other words, empty ourselves.

There is a wonderful story told in some therapy circles of how Carl Jung played a very small but influential role in the start of AA (Alcoholics Anonymous). In a letter to Dr. Jung, Bill Wilson described how one of his colleagues, Roland H., a patient of Jung's and a chronic alcoholic, was advised that there was nothing more Jung could do for his condition. In a parting comment, Jung suggested that his client seek a "spiritual experience." Roland took this advice to heart and soon found himself praying to God. In what can only be called divine intervention, the compulsion to drink ended. In a letter to Jung, Bill W. wrote:

> Because of your conviction that man is something more than intellect, emotion, and two dollars' worth of chemicals, you have especially endeared yourself to us. Please be certain that your place in the affection, and in the history of our Fellowship is like no other.

In a letter dated January 30, 1961, Jung replied:

> Roland's craving for alcohol was the equivalent, on a low level, of the spiritual thirst of our being for wholeness, expressed in medieval language: the union of God. The only right and legitimate way to such an experience is that it happens to you in reality, and it can only happen to you when you walk on a path which leads you to a higher understanding. [11]

Just as birds fly south during the winter, the emptying process was never meant to be a permanent place of residence. Yet, there are many people who get stuck in this phase. They are spiritually constipated, not knowing how to exit gracefully from the darkness. For those individuals who book an overextended reservation in the void, we see them continually trying to fill themselves, rather than enjoying the profound yet brief freedom emptiness offers.

In her book *The Thirst for Wholeness*, Christina Grof refers to the addict as a spiritual seeker—someone who tries to quench the universal thirst for wholeness, yet goes about it with the wrong means.[12] Faced with the fear of loneliness, a common feeling as we approach and enter the void, some people become dependent on substances, behavior, or people. Undeniably, it is a journey that can only be traveled alone.

The success of programs like Alcoholics Anonymous, built on the foundation of a higher power, has become the hallmark for nearly every self-help and 12-Step recovery program.

To cleanse the soul, to empty it so that it may once again be filled, strongly resonates with the Taoist philosophy of yin and yang, where wholeness is composed of the union of opposites—light and dark, soft and hard, male and female, fast and slow. Stress is also composed of opposites. Good stress and distress are within the order of natural laws to give both highs and lows, joy and sorrow to make us whole. When we understand and appreciate the balance, we can see how necessary the emptying process is to becoming whole.

As winter turns to spring, the emptying process gives way to the grounding process—a time of gathering insights and cultivating divine wisdom—all of which serve to guide us on the spiritual path. Instead of perceiving the void as nothingness, we should see it for what it really is: a host of infinite possibilities, the womb of all creation. The void is not a dead end, it's a realm of unlimited choices combined with the freedom to move toward those choices. We need only step through the illusions of fear. After centering ourselves, after stripping away the walls of the ego, after the F.O.G. (Fear of

God) has lifted from the mirror, we are left standing in naked consciousness before our divine reflection. Remember that we are both the student and teacher. In the words of Gibran, "No man can reveal to you ought but that which lies half asleep in the dawning of your knowledge." [13]

Readiness is a process of centering and emptying. The naked consciousness in the reflection is the divine essence that connects us all.

INITIATING THE EMPTYING PROCESS

You don't have to leave your spouse, quit a job, or sell your house to initiate the emptying process. It can be done quite simply through meditation, writing, exercise, fasting, moments of silence, or any quality time dedicated to clearing the mind. In fact, there are many ways to embrace the emptying process. Although there is no preferred method to engage in this aspect of spiritual health, it is highly recommended that the path taken be one where our emotions can be detached from our thoughts. In other words, where the baggage of the alter ego is left far behind. When we make a regular practice of emptying, we will find it not haunting, but as refreshing as a cold shower on a hot summer day.

For years I have kept a journal. Journal writing allows a flow of thoughts and feelings quite literally out of head and on to paper, removing what is known in the field of health psychology as toxic thoughts. Studies by James Pennebaker at the University of Texas in Austin have shown that by getting your thoughts and feelings down on paper, you engage in more than just a cathartic effect; it actually enhances the integrity of the immune system. [14]

Meditation is a great way to initiate the emptying process. To make this a habit in your daily routine, first find a quiet place to relax and center yourself. Close your eyes and concentrate on your breathing. If you find your mind wandering, as you most likely will, allow each thought to leave your mind freely as you exhale your next breath. Repeat this for as long as you are comfortable, starting with five to ten minutes and building up to fifteen to twenty minutes. If you find your mind focused on some unresolved issue, imagine that you step outside yourself and watch yourself thinking this thought. At times boredom may overcome you, but stay with it. Boredom is a sign that the last veil is ready to be lifted. When the mind is clear of thought, it is more receptive to new insights, intuition, divine wisdom, and new ways of dealing with unresolved problems. Remember the adage, "Meditation—it's not what you think!"

Giving talks on the topic of stress and spirituality over the past decade, I learned to allocate special time for the emptying process, because I feel that this is where most people get stuck on the spiritual path. Perhaps more than any other aspect of all my presentations, I receive the most comments and accolades regarding the emptying process. It's almost as if hearing this topic in this context empowers people; it sets people free.

The emptying process may seem like a dark void, but true to the cliché of the tunnel, there is light at the end, a glorious light. The following Native American song reminds us of the promise of the void. [15]

> *All winter long*
> *behind every thunder*
> *guess what we heard!*
> *behind every thunder*
> *the song of a bird*
> *a trumpeting bird.*
> *All winter long*
> *beneath every snowing*
> *guess what we saw!*

beneath every snowing
a thaw
and a growing
a greening and growing
Where did we run
beyond gate and guardsman?
Guess if you can
All winter long
we ran to the sun
the dance of the sun!

THE GROUNDING PROCESS

One night at a friend's house for dinner, the conversation turned toward the direction of the spiritual. After exhausting the topic of near-death experiences, my friend Alan told us that a mutual acquaintance had held a conversation with God.

"She said God actually spoke to her," he said. "Has God ever spoken to you?"

Before I could reply, Alan exclaimed, "He's never spoken to me."

His wife replied, "Yes, he has! But you never shut up long enough to listen!"

God talks to me. On occasion, God whispers. Once in a blue moon God yells, but more often than not, I am simply aware of the subtle yet divine pantomimes that accompany every aspect of my life. Judging from my conversations with friends, acquaintances, and even strangers, I know I am not alone. Although many people feel this way, few will share their thoughts on this topic. They don't want to sound silly or crazy. I am reminded of comedienne Lily Tomlin's line, "Why is it that when we talk to God it's called praying, but when God talks to us, it's called schizophrenia?" [16]

The grounding process is an empowering reminder of our basic connection to the divine source we call God. There is no room for fear in this relationship with our higher self.

God talks to me, but on occasion, like everyone else, I shut God out. And there are times when I am left suspended in doubt, not wanting to listen to what I may have heard, envisioned, thought, felt, or known at some profound level (denial is a powerful tool of the ego!). More often than not, though, I am in constant communication with some aspect of universal consciousness, listening to those insights and aspects of wisdom that I know are not my own creation. Without exception, God communicates with each and every one of us, if we only take the time to listen! Listening at this level requires a unique receptivity to hear, to learn, to open up, and, perhaps most important, to not be afraid of the wisdom we might encounter. When the walls of the ego are lowered, we are the most receptive to divine whispers, insights, creative ideas, intuitive thoughts, and ageless wisdom. When these moments occur, you want to reach your hands up in the sky and shout "Yes!"

SEEKING A VISION

Stressors beg for resolution. While the alter ego tries desperately to defend its territory and hold its ground, our spiritual side strives for balance. In academic circles, the grounding process is more commonly known as a time of harnessing our inner resources to face the challenges of adversity. It is a time to sharpen our coping skills to a point where we can manage stressful encounters with some degree of integrity and satisfaction.

These same theorists will tell you that one of the most common coping skills for dealing with stress is called "information seeking"— a time when we search for clues to help us deal with our problems. The grounding process works much the same way. It answers problems by tapping into our inner wisdom. Even when solutions become evident from outside sources, our internal resources support the resolution of the problem.

In every culture there are occasions to seek the counsel of our higher self. It is most simply stated by the Native American culture in the ritual called the "vision quest." Typically a rite of passage from adolescence to adulthood, the vision quest can be initiated whenever there is a need to seek divine wisdom or spiritual guidance.

Going into the depths of nature, one travels alone to a solitary spot, usually for three or four days, to seek a vision from the Great Mystery (God). The vision quest begins with an intense period of centering, turning within to address the soul. Coupled with the emptying process, where no food is eaten, little clothing is worn, and sleep is not an option, the vision quest is an intense period of searching the mind to connect with the divine source. The ultimate mission is knowledge of the meaning of life. What is referred to as a moment of enlightenment in the Eastern culture, or a revelation to Christians, is synonymous with the power of a vision in the Native American culture.

Although a vision quest can prove to be a unique and powerful experience, you don't have to strip naked and wander through groves of tall pine trees for an insight. Sometimes, in seeking divine insight, we sit back awaiting the "messenger on a cloud" approach, only to miss the most silent of all whispers. Divine messages—which are all around us—are more subtle than dynamic. The words of God are not complex. They are simple and uncomplicated, and at the same time profound. For this reason, divine whispers always resonate deeply at the soul level.

How does the source of inner wisdom make itself known? Here is one example. Despite six years of trying, Bryce considered himself a novice in the art of meditation. An advertising executive, Bryce's professional life was in a rut. Disenchanted with his job and frustrated with life in general, he began to meditate on his career options. One morning in the midst of stillness, an image came to him. He was teaching in a classroom. He ignored the vision, thinking it was a distraction, and continued with a breathing exercise. Then while closing out his meditation with a mental imagery exercise, the words, "Quit your job and move to Seattle," came into his head as if they were whispered in his ear. He laughed. *Why Seattle?*

The thought stayed with him through the next week. Again in meditation, the vision of teaching came into his head. A few months later a friend called to offer him a job on the West Coast. Bryce already knew the specifics, a teaching job in Seattle, and he's had no regrets about his decision to take it.

GROUNDING EXERCISE #1
_____

Crystal Cave Meditation

Seeking advice from your intuition, the collective unconscious, or your higher self is not a complicated process. The following exercise can be used when trying to gain clarity on an issue or become more grounded with any decision-making process. This visualization, perhaps more than any other, has been a tremendous asset to my students and workshop participants. Begin by concentrating on your breathing or any other technique that you find helpful to engage in the centering and emptying process.

1. Imagine that you are standing at the bottom of a short set of stairs. At the bottom it is dark, but at the top of the stairs you see a radiant light.
2. You feel compelled to walk up the stairs toward the light, but you find that you can only take one step at a time. As you walk up the first step, you begin to feel a sense of inner peace within yourself.

On the second step, you feel an inner peace between you and your family members. On the third step, you gain a sense of peace and resolution with friends and acquaintances. The fourth step brings a sense of calm and serenity with your higher self. As you continue up the stairs you become lighter, more relaxed—as though you are floating toward the top.

3. At the top step you are surrounded by a brilliant white light. You float into the light, and each cell in your body radiates this brilliant, loving light. After a moment you cannot distinguish yourself from the light, and you feel an incredible sense of love, support, and nurturing from this glow.

4. You feel yourself floating down a hall of crystal glass, and rainbows appear everywhere. The colors of these rainbows make you smile in wonder and awe.

5. As you continue to float through this hall of crystal glass, you come upon a room of crystal glass prisms. As various colors of the rainbow filter through the room, you see an area that has a sunken floor, and you soon find yourself sitting on a comfortable step. As you look around, you notice the beauty of this room, like a charming living room, comfortable and cozy. Sitting next to you is a wise sage. It may be someone you recognize, or it may be someone you have never seen before. You feel a sense of comfort and compassion coming from within this person.

6. If there is a question you would like to ask, feel free to do so now. "Think" the question and your voice will be heard. Listen carefully for the answer. It will come as one of your own thoughts, but at a deep level you will know that this insight has come from a place beyond your conscious mind.

7. When you feel ready, thank this person, and as you do, you will float back through the hall of prism glass with multicolored rainbows, through the passage of brilliant white light, to where you now sit or lie. Take a deep breath and relax, contemplating the message you have received.

Sometimes we get clearer messages when we are asleep. Such was the case with Andrea, whose story begins in the kitchen. Cottage industries are often started on kitchen tables, which is where Andy began hers. As a health educator, Andy started the Spiritual Wellness Network, a focus group for health educators across the country. Andy, who refers to herself as the "network weaver," began a doctoral program at the University of Wisconsin. After her preliminary exams, Andy felt overwhelmed, particularly with the Spiritual Network. She knew it was time to end this project, but in her heart she couldn't let go.

One night she went to bed more exhausted than usual. With her eyes wide open, she whispered, "God, give me a dream." And she got one!

"I can recall the dream vividly, and the message was loud and clear," she exclaimed. "I dreamed I was an Amish woman, married and living in some rural setting. It was a very simple life. You know what the message was? Live a simple life! I have made my life too complex." At that point she knew the business had to go. The decision was made.

Dreams are a major vehicle for information. History flows with examples of scientists and inventors who went to sleep with a problem on their minds only to wake up with an answer. In many cases the dream led to an idea that provided the missing piece of information or synthesis toward a landmark discovery, as was the case with the nineteenth-century German chemist Friedrich Kekulé, who dreamed of a snake eating its tail—which he later interpreted to be the structure of the benzene ring. [17] There are countless others, all of which support the premise of this vehicle of the grounding process.

Sometimes we become the vehicle for the message of dreams so that the information may reach others who may need to hear it. Once on a trip to Sedona, Arizona, I was invited to spend the night with an acquaintance whom I had met through a mutual friend. Over dinner I explained that the purpose of my trip was to participate in a planning session, specifically, to organize a retreat for hospital board directors to learn about the concept of wellness and complementary medicine. My host, Carolyn, was a nurse who expressed a strong interest in our efforts.

That night Carolyn pointed to a group of family portraits in the hallway. Through the photographs she introduced her family, her husband and her two grown children. Asleep on the living room couch, I had a dream. In the dream I walked into the kitchen to get a glass of water. Standing by the refrigerator was a tall man about thirty years old with long brown hair, brown eyes, and handsome face. He introduced himself to me as Larry and said he was Carolyn's son. He asked me to give her a message "that everything was all right, in fact that everything was great!"

The next morning I awoke to hear Carolyn making breakfast and suddenly remembered the dream. After telling her about it, I added, "It's funny, he doesn't look anything like his photograph on the wall." Carolyn's eyes grew wide. She took a deep breath and then gave me a broad smile.

"Wow! There is no way you could have even known this. Larry was my first son," she explained. "He died of sudden infant death syndrome (SIDS). He had dark hair and brown eyes, and he would have been about thirty years old, had he lived." Then she added, "I guess I shut myself off from him, and he communicated through you to speak to me."

"There is one more thing he asked me to tell you," I said. "He said that he loved you very much. That we come and go from this earthly existence, but love never dies."

THE DOORS OF RECEPTIVITY

Preparation for the grounding process may take some discipline, and there is no guarantee that fasting the mind and starving the body will bring quick results. Receptivity is a process, not an immediate outcome. Many monks have sat patiently in silence for days, just as scores of Native Americans have perched on mountain precipices awaiting divine guidance, only to walk home empty-handed. This is not to say that access of universal consciousness has been denied, nor the summons of a heavenly presence neglected. Time, a fixed entity in this third-dimensional world, is unbound in universal consciousness. Just as you cannot push water uphill, you cannot demand enlightenment. Discipline and patience are essential in the grounding process.

Artists and writers will tell you that when the doors of receptivity are open, the most amazing thoughts surface. Whether doing laundry, taking a shower, driving a car, or lying awake late at night, one must be receptive. Observance of divine insight is groomed, not only through stillness of your mind, but also through the cultivation of thoughts, perceptions, and attitudes, and the domestication of the ego. Although the flow of consciousness cannot be forced, it can be enticed. Relaxation is the key! Relaxing the mind, in some cases, may mean shifting gears in the mind.

Years ago, while investigating ways to lessen the severity of grand mal seizures in epileptic patients, a researcher named Roger W. Sperry came upon a unique discovery leading to a greater understanding of how the brain functions as an organ for the mind.[18] In an effort to contain the seizure to one hemisphere, Sperry cut the corpus callosum, a bridge between the two cerebral hemispheres, in four of his patients. He soon discovered that not only did the seizures lessen with intensity and frequency, but upon subsequent observation, each hemisphere seemed responsible for specific cognitive functions.

Years of research into the field of brain lateralization have generated an excess of data leading to the current household expressions "right-brain" and "left-brain" thinking. The conclusion is that left-brained functions are more suited to judgment, analysis, linear progression, and time consciousness. The right hemisphere of the brain is noted for intuition, imagination, holographic consciousness, and receptivity.

There is a connection between left-brain cognitive functions and the thought processes associated with stress, judgment, and analysis. Left-brain thoughts, produced by stress, repeatedly eclipse those of the right brain, causing an imbalance. Any activity that favors right-brain thinking (meditation, exercise, listening to music) is more suited to opening the doors of receptivity. A relaxed mind is an alert mind— one that is ready for the seeds planted in the grounding process.

SOWING THE SEEDS OF CREATIVITY FOR HARVEST

There is a unique aspect of the grounding process that artists relish. It is the opportunity to tap into the unlimited reservoir of ideas from which to create. It is no coincidence how similar the concepts of the void and the womb are in likeness and promise. For what appears to be a dark vacuum is the supply of ideas, insights, intuitive thoughts, inspiration, and imagination. Deepak Chopra describes it this way: "The void is the source of infinite possibilities." [19]

If you were to engage several artists in honest conversation about their work, from Paul McCartney to Georgia O'Keeffe, they would admit their ideas are not solely their own. They are cocreators, or partners, in the creation process. We are all invited to the universal reservoir of ideas. Those who do not make a routine pilgrimage to the cache of ideas are ill-prepared to deal with the issues, concerns, and problems encountered daily. There is a strong spiritual aspect to the creative process, as noted by Julia Cameron in her book *The Artist's Way*. She writes:

> *The heart of creativity is an experience of the mystical union; the heart of the mystical union is an experience of creativity. Those who speak in spiritual terms routinely refer to God as the creator, but seldom see creator as the literal term for artist.* [20]

Although the word creativity is often used in the arts and entertainment industry, artists don't have a monopoly on this resource, nor is creativity a gift for a chosen few. It is a birthright of every individual. Nevertheless, we often take a passive role in the creative process, letting others be creative for us, while we just sit and watch. By letting our creative skills rust, we claim the role of the victim. Creativity is a way to make order out of chaos; it can be used by anyone trying to solve a problem. Necessity, the mother of invention, can serve as a wonderful stimulation to the creative process.

Our creativity skills are the best resource for dealing with the stressors of our constantly changing world. It is interesting to note that years after formulating his theory of self-actualization, psychologist Abraham Maslow was convinced that the ability to access and implement one's imagination and creativity was paramount in achieving self-actualization—the highest pinnacle of human potential.

MOMENTS OF SYNCHRONICITY

Although moments of insight, wisdom, and intuition usually come when the mind is open or receptive, there are rare occasions when, in the divine order of things, the message must get through at all costs. That's when it hits us like a hammer—a wake-up call to steer our lives in the right direction. When the message must get through, information is often given in the form of coincidence, or as Jung says, "moments of synchronicity," where two events may hold no specific meaning by themselves, but when coupled together they hold a special message.

In her book *The Tao of Psychology*, Jean Shinoda Bolen shares several stories of coincidences that point to a higher order of events that cannot be ignored. Synchronistic moments serve as a voice to remind us of this higher order. Jung explained synchronicity as "a meaningful coincidence with no rational explanation; a link that cannot be explained by cause and effect."[21] In his practice, Jung observed too many of these coincidences to disregard them. This string of cosmic moments led him to coin the term "synchronicity"—where all things, animate and inanimate, are inextricably linked. Examples of synchronicity range from dreams, to a fortuitous change of airline seats, to accurate premonitions of a sick family member. Bolen writes:

> *If we personally realize that synchronicity is at work in our lives, we feel connected, rather than isolated and estranged from others; we feel ourselves part of a divine dynamic interrelated universe.* [22]

The Tao Bolen describes is a name given to a dynamic concept that cannot fully be known in words. Although many have tried to define it—the Source, the Cosmic Mother, the Principle of Life, or the One—the Tao can only be appreciated. In appreciating our divine connection, we actively engage in the grounding process. Dr. Bernie Siegel, author of *Love, Medicine, and Miracles*, says coincidences are merely God's way of remaining anonymous. I think he's right! Case in point: An old college friend now living in Boston called me one night, and we talked for hours. Katy was engaged to a guy named Stanley. As she continued to describe her relationship, I could tell there was a shadow of doubt about this guy, but with love being blind, I could sense Katy was unaware of her reservation. So, we made plans to get together for a visit. Katy felt she needed some clarity about the relationship. She mentioned to Stanley she was going away, yet neglected to mention where. He, in turn, said he was headed to England on business.

Katy came to see me in Washington, D.C., the next week, and she was excited. Unfortunately, after her arrival, I discovered I had a tight deadline on a project that had to be finished. I planned to meet her downtown after she toured the museums, but I was very late. Katy was not amused! In fact, she was downright furious. As it turned out, however, I wasn't the focus of her anger.

To appreciate what happened, a little background on the Metro subway system would help. Each Metro train has about ten to twenty cars, with two doors on each side. Trains come and go every few minutes with hundreds of people coming and going. The chances of what happened are a zillion to one.

Katy was waiting for a train to come. When it stopped in front of her, the doors opened and out stepped Stanley—with another woman. Their eyes met in disbelief. In less than a nanosecond, Stanley yelled out, "What are you doing here?" Then, as if the imposition was too much to handle, he quickly walked away with his lady friend in tow.

After hearing Katy's story and letting her decompress, I said, "Wow! I think God is trying to tell you something here." Once outside in the fresh air, it didn't take long for her to realize the meaning of the coincidence. Later she confided that intuitively she felt he was seeing other women, but she wasn't ready to admit it. Now she had the proof—loud and clear.

As Sophy Burnham eloquently suggests in her acclaimed bestseller *A Book of Angels*, the voice of God has many mouths. [23] Insights, inspirations, and revelations can come from relatives, friends, and even strangers. I am reminded of a story told to me by a close friend of Elisabeth Kübler-Ross that again reveals the beauty of the grounding process and the amazing mystery of synchronicity.

In his last days, Elisabeth's former husband, Manny, and their daughter Barbara talked about various aspects of life and death. When questioned about life after death, Manny was adamant that no such thing existed. However, on the off chance that he was wrong, he made a secret agreement with his daughter. If life continued on, he would give her a sign. Father and daughter talked for hours about what the sign should be. It must be a sign of undeniable truth that only the two of them would recognize. On a hot Arizona afternoon, they finally came up with an answer. Elisabeth, who loved roses, would bend down and pick up several red flowers symbolic of love—in the snow! Since snow was uncommon, Manny was convinced it was the perfect sign. He soon grew weary and felt the conversation was for naught. Barbara, on the hand, was delighted. The promise was sealed.

Soon after his death, Manny's body was flown to Chicago for the funeral. That weekend, as the body was en route, Chicago braced itself for a large snowstorm. Despite the weather, the funeral and burial went as planned. Elisabeth, leading the way, took note of several roses lying on the snow and stopped to pick them up. When she handed one to her daughter, Barbara could only giggle with delight. It wasn't until later that day that she could share with her mother the source of the laughter, and the message passed on through the roses.

I myself have had far too many moments of synchronicity to deny a higher order to life. Even so, occasional periods of doubt cast their shadow in my direction. I have also had more than a handful of experiences that defy normal explanation. It is upon reflecting about these times when I remind myself of an experience that left me forever changed.

Early in my career, the concept of the grounding process was only theoretical. Then one day I had an experience that can only be described as a cosmic moment, where I was transposed from doubt to certainty. Years ago I was meditating when I noticed that I was stark naked, surrounded by a brick cylinder. I thought to myself, *Freud would have a field day analyzing this!* But it became obvious that I was trapped. There was no way out. As I pondered my dilemma, I realized my thoughts were keeping me hostage; I had to think my way out. As I surveyed the wall, I noticed that each brick was inscribed with some issue I had feared. The way out was by resolving the issues at hand. Eventually, the walls began to dissolve with each problem and issue conquered.

Soon I found myself standing in front of what looked like a wall of flames. As I walked backwards, the wall of light drew me in and surrounded me. Instantly, I was overcome with an incredible rush of love and compassion. I found myself floating in this brilliant light and soon noticed that I could not distinguish myself from the light. A profound message of unconditional love was given to me. I remember thinking how great it would be to feel this all the time, at which point I was instantly back in my room sitting calmly against a wall. What was real? The experience or the room?

Back in 1974, out-of-body experiences were rarely discussed, so it took me a while to understand this phenomenon. What became clear, however, was that I had somehow crossed the threshold to a dimension where insight and wisdom were abundant.

"To stand like mountain" is a profound yet simple reminder that we are deeply rooted in our own being. Mountains serve as a symbol of strength and stability. We, too, become strong, stable, and resilient to the stressors in our lives when we listen to the deep-seated wisdom of the soul. The image of mountains towering above the clouds conveys the mirror image of consciousness. As the mountain rises above the clouds, it also is connected to the very core of the Earth. To be grounded is an expression of security. To hear the voice of God, to receive a sign, a vision, a long-awaited insight, an epiphany, or a revelation, reconnects us to that part of our divine essence that provides a sense of security, a sense of stability on the human journey.

But the connection doesn't stop there! Just as the vision quest is not complete until a return has been made back to the village to share the insights and wonders gleaned from the experience, the grounding process is just one more step in the yearning to become whole.

One day over lunch, I found myself describing the seasons of the soul to a friend who was going through a tough time. As I began to explain the grounding process, he smiled.

"I call this the remembering stage," he said, "where we reacquaint ourselves with that knowledge that lies deep in our subconscious." He added that the word remember (re-member) means to unite with those people in our family and community of friends.

"Yes," I said, "and that leads me to the connecting process."

THE CONNECTING PROCESS

All life is relationship. Our interactions with family, friends, colleagues, acquaintances, and even strangers are a small fraction of the elaborate network of universal life. We are connected to everything and everybody—even when we are unaware of this profound association. Just as our interdependence to all humanity cannot be denied, neither can our inherent relationship to the natural world. The spirit of life flows freely through all things.

Perhaps this delicate balance of nature, and our humble place in it, was stated most eloquently by Chief Seattle in a letter to President Franklin Pierce regarding land acquisitions in 1854. "All things connect. Man did not weave the web of life, he is merely a strand in it. Whatever he does to the web he does to himself."[24]

All things connect. There may appear to be distance and separation, but as the wisdom of the soul knows, all is one. In the words of John Donne, "No man is an island, entire of itself; every man is a piece of the continent, a part of the main." We must do our best to nurture the ties that bind, rather than let them wither with fear, apathy or indifference.

The African proverb, "It takes a village to raise a child," speaks to the heart of the connection process. Even the apostle Paul recognized this when he wrote that we are cells in the body of Christ. From the wisdom of Taoism we also learn that nothing is separate. Based on the ancient writings of Chinese philosopher Lao-tzu, the idea of connection is referred to as the Principle of Oneness: "The Tao person embraces the One and lives in peace by its pattern."[25] The Principle of

Oneness reveals that we are an integral part of the holographic whole, connected through a dynamic network of universal energy. We are part of nature, not above or apart from it. This Taoist perspective encourages us to transcend our thoughts and perceptions and become one with the universe. From a Taoist perspective, when we see ourselves as separate from the whole, we not only distance ourselves from nature, we isolate ourselves from other people as well. In turn, this distance weakens our spiritual health and suffocates our very essence. The nature of the Tao reminds us that there is strength in numbers and also strength in oneness.

THE HOLOGRAPHIC UNIVERSE

Reductionism, the scientific model forged by the philosophical beliefs of René Descartes, is slowly shifting toward a more holistic view, where the subtle and dynamic aspects of life unite to reveal "a dynamic web of interrelated events."[26] The concept of connection began when Albert Einstein searched for answers to his unified field theory. Einstein was convinced that there was some common thread that tied the various forces of energy (gravity, nuclear, and electromagnetic) together. He often gazed into the heavens for answers. Exploring the smallest of particles known to man, Einstein discovered that atoms contain virtually nothing but vast amounts of space in which infinitely small particles of energy move around. Further explorations led him to the realization that all objects are composed of energy; through the fields of energy, everything connects.

Jung, intrigued with Einstein's theory of relativity (where, at the speed of light, space and time play by different rules), once discussed his theory with him. The exchange of ideas led Jung to substantiate his theory of the collective unconscious, which states that there exists a common level of wisdom that also reflects the elements of time and space differently than the conscious mind. According to Jung, through the universal mind, we are all connected—a term some refer to as "divine consciousness."

In his autobiography, *Memories, Dreams, Reflections*, Jung wrote, "Hence, I prefer the term 'the unconscious,' knowing that I might equally well speak of God."[27]

The concept of connection is seen in the field of medicine as well. To think that the mind (consciousness) has an ability to *heal* the body is anathema to the Cartesian principle of mind-body dualism where the mind and body are separate entities and have no relationship with one another. In the past decade, however, scores of studies support the holistic theory of mind-body-spirit unity. Data continues to show that innate healing is far more complex than we can understand through the Cartesian mind-set. All things do connect, and what makes this time in history so appealing is that the connection process is becoming very real indeed.

FULFILLING OUR LIFE PURPOSE

To know that our planet is home to more than 6 billion people may understate our uniqueness, but nothing could be further from the truth. We are born to fulfill a specific purpose. To deny our life purpose is to undermine the integrity of the universe. In his much-acclaimed book *The Seven Spiritual Laws of Success*, Deepak Chopra discusses the Hindu concept of Dharma, or life mission.[28] The Law of Dharma states that everyone has a unique purpose in life, which is manifested through those inner resources that compose our spiritual essence. Universal in nature, this message can also be found in the words of Jesus of Nazareth when he said, "I come to serve, not to be served."

When we utilize these gifts and share the fruits of our work, we fulfill the divine will of the universe. In turn, we experience the ecstasy and exhilaration of our own spirit. That, too, is worthy of sharing. So our life purpose must neither be concealed nor confined to a chosen few, but nurtured, utilized, and shared openly with all who may benefit from our best efforts and achievements.

There is a parable in the New Testament that speaks to the nature of utilizing such gifts and talents:

A rich man called three of his finest workers to meet with him before his trip to a land far away. Each was given a large sum of money with directions to plan wisely so that upon his return, he would reap the benefits of their investments. After entrusting each servant with a third of his fortune, he reminded them each would have to account for their deeds.

Upon his return, the three men were summoned individually into private consultation. In a short time he learned that two of the three men invested wisely and revealed a fourfold profit. The third servant, perhaps acting out of fear, buried his cash for safekeeping, and thus earned no interest on the capital. The master furiously admonished his servant, and then imprisoned him for his foolishness.

I have to admit that whenever I heard this passage, I found myself empathizing with the gentleman who buried the money, perhaps because I was so incensed with the greed of his master. Furthermore, I thought, why was the Church advocating long-term financial investments? Does this have something to do with the collection plate? My thoughts on this issue closely parallel those of the late Joseph Campbell, who once said that we need to get rid of all banking terms when we discuss issues of spirituality. It wasn't until years later that I learned the words "money" and "talents" were often used interchangeably in biblical translations. The version of the New Testament I was exposed to obviously opted for the banking metaphor.

Reflecting on this story now, the true message becomes crystal clear. The moral of this tale suggests that security comes from using our talents to their greatest potential; this means sharing them with others. As far as the grounding process is concerned, if we conceal those mystical insights, those creative thoughts, or that wisdom of divine consciousness, then we continue to remain locked into the confines of fear-based thinking. Ultimately, the perpetual stress feeds upon itself.

FROM GROUNDING TO CONNECTING

Balance is gained from both receiving and giving. The philosopher Buckminster Fuller said:

> *You belong to the universe. The significance of you will forever remain obscure to you, but you may assume that you are fulfilling your significance if you apply yourself to converting all your experience to the highest advantage of others.*[29]

As a concentration camp survivor who saw many fellow prisoners perish, psychologist Viktor Frankl wrote in his memoir, *Man's Search for Meaning*: "We had to learn from ourselves and we had to teach disparaging men that it did not matter what we expected from life, but rather what life expected from us."[30]

The idea of community is universal; so is the notion of our contribution to the whole. If the emptying process is akin to the long, dark months of winter, then the connecting process is like the glorious, warm summer. In the connecting process we reach out to others to make our presence known and our compassion felt. Peck's term, *mystic-communal* (described in Chapter Two), underscores the significance of the connecting process. As one of four developmental stages Peck highlights on the human path of spirituality, the mystic-communal individual is someone who continually searches for clues to the mystery of life. Striving to stay grounded, the mystic-communal is on a never-ending quest for clues and insights. Like pieces of a puzzle, each new piece not only gives more clarity, but it expands the perimeters of the puzzle.

These cosmic bread crumbs, as they are sometimes known, are divine reminders of a more universal perspective of life. Yet these mystical morsels cannot be hoarded or used for selfish means. Peck insists that the mystic-communal individual has an obligation to return to his or her community to share these cosmic bread crumbs with other members of their fellowship. People who are true to the nature of the mystic-communal maintain a sense of community by developing quality relationships based on acceptance, respect, and compassion.

CONNECTING EXERCISE #1

Open Heart Meditation

The connecting process begins with an intention. For the connection process to be genuine, the aim must come from the heart as well as the mind. We each have the ability to receive, share, and be an instrument for the attachment process. To open the heart chakra and hear its message, we must put into daily practice the following:

- Sit quietly for several minutes. Focus on your breathing. Feel the air come into your nose and down into your lungs. Feel your diaphragm expand. Exhale. Repeat this seven times, and as you let the air out, repeat this phrase: My body is calm and relaxed.
- After the seventh breath, focus your attention on the center of your upper chest, the area over your heart. If you desire, imagine a flower or heart or whatever you associate with love and compassion.
- For the next seven breaths, imagine that you are breathing air into your lungs and out through your symbolic heart.

- Using your imagination, picture someone whom you care about in front of you and allow yourself to picture a rainbow of light or a beam of light or some manifestation of your loving energy— from your heart to the heart of this person.
- Feel this loving energy in every cell of your body.
- Although it's hard, this can also be done with someone you do not like. The divine presence in them is a reflection of the divine presence in ourselves as well.
- Continue this meditation by refocusing on an image of a dear friend or family member with whom you wish to share a bond of compassion.
- Close with one final, slow, deep breath, sending a ray of loving light to yourself.

Poets tell us that love is the glue that holds the universe together. Healthcare practitioners acknowledge that love is the greatest healing energy. Ancient wisdom tells us that love is the true bond between all people, heart to heart and soul to soul. The connection process manifests itself through the power of unconditional love. Those people who engage fully in the connecting process, without the influence of judgment, greed, or fear, show an undeniable enthusiasm for life. They know that both passion and compassion combine to form the alchemy of unconditional love.

Connecting need not be difficult. Examples of connection range from the subtle to the dynamic, yet each contributes equally to the highest good of all concerned.

As a public speaker, Jay was dynamic. As an amateur nature photographer, he was remarkable. Photography was a passion that took him out of the confines of the city into nature. After taking thousands of photos, which sat unnoticed, Jay became increasingly concerned with the deteriorating state of the global environment. He wanted a way to introduce an environmental message during his seminars and workshops. One day during meditation the idea came to him: He could combine his digital images with his presentations. By superimposing text over his phenomenal slide images, he could convey information along with a message of environmental appreciation. Within weeks of his initial idea, Jay was traveling around the country with a dazzling slide presentation. Afterward he was surrounded by appreciative viewers inquiring about various scenes as well as the content of his presentation.

As we cycle through the seasons of the soul, the connecting process invites us to emerge from solitude and return to the fold of humanity. Like Moses who came down the mountain, we must be willing to share the message, insight, and fruits of creativity with all who wish to take part. Our mission is to build bridges, not walls; to offer a hand in guidance, rather than turn our backs with indifference. In the highest sense of connection, what we do for each other helps lift the spirits of all people. In reality, the connection between all people already exists, and the only request we are given, as we complete the grounding process, is to acknowledge, sustain, and honor this connection. Some day soon we may even discover with great clarity that the web of life reaches well beyond the planet Earth, far into the galactic universe.

CHAPTER FIVE

THE SEEDS OF CHANGE

God is not a noun,
God is a verb.

—Buckminster Fuller

Four gardens surround my house, three of which contain a multitude of bulbs, plants, shrubs, and herbs and, of course, all-too-often the uninvited weed. The fourth garden I designate each year as my wildflower garden and, by far, it's the one that gives me the greatest pleasure. With an annual purchase of a packet of wildflower seeds each spring, this garden grows to become a kaleidoscope of indescribable colors, with poppies, columbine, alpine asters, cosmos, hollyhocks, snapdragons, and quite often a few flowers whose seeds I know are clearly not included in the mix. Rather, these guests are carried by the westerly California winds or a careless bird snacking between meals. Sunflowers, lupines, foxgloves, delphiniums, Shasta daisies, and, once, a corn stalk have sprouted among the wildflower mix, adding an enchanting element to my version of the Garden of Eden, replete with monarch butterflies and ruby-throated hummingbirds.

I learned quickly that nature abhors a vacuum, and my wildflower garden was clearly an example of this data collection. Each year, the canister of wildflower seeds is packed with an overwhelming potential of delight. Yet I am convinced that it is more than just a can bursting with floral possibilities; it also serves as a metaphor for the potential that each of us holds. This metaphor surrounds us daily going far beyond flowers to the abundant foods we eat, each with a subtle reminder of human potential and the budding promise of the human spirit: sesame seeds, garbanzo beans, cherry pits, avocado seeds, tomato seeds, olive pits, grape seeds, poppy seeds, and watermelon seeds, to name but a few.

By and large, fruits and vegetables (and all the seeds they contain) are symbols of fertility: the prolific, creative abundance of nature. In a world of high-tech gadgets, from the iPod to the cell phone and wireless laptop, it's quite easy to forget our connection to the natural world, and our abundance of creativity. In fact, many people do forget or ignore this inherent connection and the human spirit suffers, followed by the body. Is it a coincidence that as we become more and more engrossed with the pleasures of technology, we also feel more stressed? Probably not!

Gardening as a hobby is a stress-management program unto itself. It is also a spiritual undertaking of the cocreative process. Today, I love spending time in my backyard, but it's an acquired interest—it wasn't always this way. As a child, I used to hate laboring untold hours in the family garden. I had more important things to occupy my time: searching for Sasquatch, building forts, and looking for buried treasure. Pulling up weeds seemed like a never-ending task and a chore that invaded my time to explore the forests beyond the backyard that called to me on a regular basis. One day, while pulling scores of dandelions and milk thistle, I noticed that alongside the marigolds my mother planted, stood a flower of unknown origin, with red flowering petals that defied any color in any palette I had ever seen. Rather than pulling it, I decided to let it stay. I asked, but no one seemed to know where it came from. But everyone welcomed this alien addition to the garden, including me. Perhaps equally intriguing to me were the butterflies and hummingbirds (angels of the garden world) that the mysterious flower attracted. Watching a tiger lily butterfly land on my hand one day, I realized that nature held many mysteries, all of which fascinated me, from the hummingbirds attracted to the mysterious red flower to the occasional acorn that beaned me on the head while mowing the lawn. As I grew older, I began to realize that like the small acorn that becomes the mighty oak tree, we too hold many mysteries, all of which beg to be given a chance to be revealed.

Over the past three decades I have taught stress-management classes to a wide range of people, from middle school adolescents and college students to healthcare professionals and corporate executives. People's reasons for taking these classes vary greatly, but if there is an underlying theme to their expectations, it is to alter the course of their lives so that they can flourish and, hence, achieve a greater sense of inner peace. In simplest terms, they are looking for answers to life's problems, but the answers alone are never enough. With these insights come an expectation to adapt and flourish in a world where anything is possible and nothing is certain. As previously mentioned, the words *stress* and *change* are now thought by many to be synonymous, but change doesn't have to bring with it a bad or negative connotation. Change also means growth, for without change we would be stifled and die. Even the tiny bonsai tree must be moved periodically to experience sunlight from all directions so it can grow evenly.

When one thinks of psychology, the works of Sigmund Freud and Carl Jung often come to mind for many, but as a student in the field of health psychology, I was far more interested in the mavericks in the field, like Abraham Maslow, Carl Rogers, and Fritz Pearls, who split off from the Freudian path to look beyond parental-induced neurosis to form what is now called the "human potential movement." In simple terms, the premise of this movement suggests that, like a seed, we hold a phenomenal potential for growth—in essence, to be the best that we can be. Not only is there a potential for growth, but there is an abundance of talent that resides within each and every one of us; talent that begs to be developed and nurtured. Perhaps Maslow, Rogers, and Pearls spent time outdoors in the forests or their respective gardens and observed the abundance of nature. Surely, the beauty of Big Sur, where their brilliant minds met at the famous Esalen retreat center, helped nurture the understanding of what human potential is.

While researching some articles for a textbook project, I came across an interesting fact: Before the days of corporate farming and television sets, the majority of Americans grew as much as 80 percent of their own fruits and vegetables in their own backyards. While perhaps not entirely self-sufficient, people, as countless generations before, were in touch with the cycles of Earth's seasons. Today, for many reasons, our relationship with the soil is as synthetic as the fertilizers and pesticides used on our foods. Many people don't even know (or care) which phase the Moon is in each night. Multinational corporations are now tinkering with the genetic wisdom of the seeds sold to farmers, changing the face of the landscape. But one thing nature reminds us of is that there is always hope.

Maple trees that release thousands of seeds each spring, dandelions that gift a multitude of offspring, and sunflowers that offer to feed the birds are just a fraction of examples of nature's proliferation. No tree or plant acts alone in this storyline of abundance. The forces of nature conspire together, with wind, rain, sunshine, moonlight, and aspects we may never fully understand to ensure the promise of this potential.

To paraphrase a now-famous line from the text of Chief Seattle, we are part of the web of life and it is a part of us. We must not only honor this connection. We must learn from it so we too can flourish. Our minds are a fertile field for growth, and the winds of change carry seeds of promise every day. It's time to till the soil so we can then reap the harvest of our human potential.

When I was a young boy, I took refuge in the local library as a means to escape the wicked temper of my alcoholic mother. Walking through the stacks of books was very similar to my other favorite pastime of exploring the miles of forest that surrounded my backyard. Books, like trees, hold great wisdom. While many books in the library stacks whispered to me, for some reason I was called to read biographies and autobiographies of renowned explorers, inventors, founding fathers, and various luminaries. I devoured books about the Wright brothers, Ben Franklin, Robert Fulton, Amelia Earhart, Harriet Tubman, Mark Twain, Florence Nightingale, Thomas Jefferson, Madame Curie, Abraham Lincoln, George Washington Carver, and Louis Pasteur, to name a handful. I wasn't intrigued by their notoriety as much as I was interested to know how they got to the point of achieving it. As if I had renowned mythologist Joseph Campbell peeking over my shoulder in the stacks whispering in my ear, I noticed a distinct pattern in the lives of my new collection of heroes. By and large, each individual overcame significant obstacles to achieve greatness. No one had a free ticket to success. The hero's journey is fraught with many potholes. Oddly enough, many of these inventors, discoverers, and luminaries credited events in their tumultuous lives as being the catalyst for discovery and their worldly contributions. They are not alone. In the course of my life, I have met many people who have made a trip to hell and back and done so gracefully. They may not make the headlines, nor have bestselling memoirs, but they are my heroes, nonetheless. They are also my teachers, for in the learning of the wisdom gained in their stories, I grow. I evolve my soul growth process and nurture the health of my human spirit. We all do, as these stories act like a compass to direct us "home."

Deep down inside everyone sees him or herself as an underdog. No doubt this is the work of the ego. Whether real or imagined, we perceive the odds are stacked against us, sometimes occasionally, sometimes constantly. Oftentimes hearing other people's stories serves as an inspiration for us to move farther along our own journey. With this in mind, using the metaphor of the mighty seed and the wisdom of Joseph Campbell's hero's journey, the following people and their stories have proven to be a mighty inspiration for me in allowing me to stand like mountain, flow like water. It is my wish that they inspire you too.

THE MUSTARD SEED: THE SEED OF FAITH

In my hand I hold a tiny mustard seed. I received it in church one day, several years ago. On that particular day, the sermon was based on the parable of the mustard seed, the point of which was that it doesn't take much faith to accomplish a goal or bear a hardship. In fact, a tiny amount will do just fine. To illustrate the point of how powerful faith really can be, the priest ceremoniously distributed a mustard seed to each of his parishioners. After the scripture reading he requested that each person bring the seed back to church four weeks hence. Drawing upon the metaphors of the seed and our minds like earthen soil, he gave us fair warning: Some of us would lose our seeds. Some would forget where we put them. Still others would carelessly toss the seed away. Yet there would be those who would indeed bring their cared-for seed back, symbolizing one's faith. The inherent message was that we are the metaphorical soil for these seeds of faith to take root. Implied was the question, do our actions support our faith or detract from it? Time would surely tell.

As I walked out of church I heard one guy say "Gee, I thought mustard was for hotdogs and hamburgers." I made a mental note that most likely this guy would not have the goods in hand the following month. The fact is though, he's right. Most people think of mustard as a condiment and not much else. There was a time long ago when mustard seeds were a prized commodity. As if peeking into the future, the priest's prophecy was to come true a month later when less than half of those attending the service could produce the seed that was provided just four weeks earlier. His point was that faith, like the mustard seed, must be cared for and cultivated. Once it takes root, it will grow to become a durable plant. Faith, however, like everything else, needs nurturing.

Faith, it is said, can move mountains, heal the sick, and serve as the catalyst for what we often call miracles. There is an intangible aspect of faith that goes well beyond any religion. Faith is more than a willingness to believe in something greater than yourself. Faith is the knowledge that we never stand alone. Nelson Mandala, who served over twenty-six years in prison for his political beliefs, once said, "Faith is not belief without proof, it's trust without reservation." Many people claim to have faith, but their faith can best be described as hope; wishing rather than knowing. As the saying goes, hope is a quick snack, but it's a lousy meal. For some, faith makes up the majority of their spiritual calories, including Julia "Taylor" Hyman.

Picture this: You are forty-eight years old and in perfect health. You are married to a loving husband, and the proud mother of two teenage children. Your career as a nurse is fulfilling. You have run sixteen marathons and several triathlons. Life is a bowl of cherries! On this particular day, you are out riding your bike. The sun is shining on this warm July morning and unbeknownst to you, within seconds your life is about to change dramatically. You hit a car, flip over your bike and after this moment of insanity, lying flat on the ground, you cannot get up. In fact, you cannot feel your legs or arms, and despite your best effort to move them, they clearly do not respond when called upon to do so.

My first encounter with Taylor was a phone conversation in the summer of 2005. She called to register for a workshop I was facilitating for a group of Duke Medical Center nurses that fall. At the end of the phone conversation she happened to mention that she would be the participant in the wheelchair. Our next encounter was in November when she entered the hotel conference room with a motorized wheelchair, wearing a smile as wide as the Atlantic Ocean.

"Hi, I'm Taylor," she said. Taylor's voice was jubilant but contained a hint of tension. She maneuvered her wheelchair among the other chairs positioned in a circle. Once all the participants arrived and took their seats, each person introduced themselves to the group. When it came Taylor's turn, she began by describing herself as a nurse. She added that she was an athlete who loved to swim.

"Despite my accident, I am still able to swim," she said. "One of these days, I will get back to walking. My goal is to compete in triathlons again. With the grace of God, I will."

One of the segments of the workshop included a session in art therapy where the participants drew a variety of pictures ranging from self-portraits to dreamscapes. Taylor's artwork was breathtaking: It featured a mermaid with long, flowing, blonde hair.

In the next few days I was to learn of Taylor's accident in finer detail and her determination to become self-mobile, if not walk again. Here is her story:

It was a Saturday at 7:15 AM The weather was 75 degrees with a light northeastern wind, a bright sunshiny day with puffy white clouds and blue skies. The water along Bogue Sound was calm and I felt like I was in heaven. I was so blessed to be living in such a beautiful place. Not only was I enjoying the beautiful morning and excited about jumping into the Sound after my bike ride in my new purple Speedo bathing suit, but I had a lot on my mind in dealing with my mother's death in May 2004. I was hurrying to get my exercise completed and to get on the road to Crisp, North Carolina, my hometown. I was to meet with my siblings to divide up household items. All week long I had thought to myself (and even told my husband, Sonny) I did not want to go home. So with all of this on my mind, I was looking at the beautiful calm of the water, yearning to dive in.

Suddenly I slammed right into the side-view mirror of a parked car. There was nothing I could do to avoid the collision. I fell on the right side of my head and neck, smack on the pavement. I tried to get up, but my legs would not move, my arms were pinned beneath me. I turned my head to the left and saw my watch and read the time, 7:15 AM I turned my head and put my forehead on the pavement and prayed to God that someone would find me soon. People are always walking in the early mornings up and down Evans Street, so I hoped it would not be long before someone came.

A man, I still do not know his name, stopped his car and asked if I was all right. I told him I had broken my neck and needed to be airlifted to Pitt Memorial Hospital in Greenville (about an hour and a half away). He asked if there was anyone he could call and I said yes, my husband, Sonny. This angel called both the ambulance and my husband, waited for the ambulance to arrive and then disappeared.

I was frightened when I could not move my extremities and then when the ambulance tech stated "Get the bike off of her," and I knew I couldn't feel the bike on me, I was really frightened. In the local hospital ER, I remembered them saying they had to cut my rings off and my new bathing suit and then I was out during all the X-rays and helicopter flight. In the trauma unit at Pitt Hospital I remember having difficulty breathing after surgery. I refused to be intubated and put on a ventilator. It wasn't that I was afraid to die. I don't fear death. After all, I had worked at Duke University and Pitt Hospital in the neurological intensive care units and knew the worst outcomes that could be from spinal cord injuries. Life, I have learned, can be more challenging than death.

It was two weeks into rehab that the effects of the spinal cord injury actually hit me. It was like an emotional tsunami. Interestingly, at the same time there was a hurricane in the vicinity so water was flowing inside (meaning me) and outside with the weather. I could not believe I couldn't move and was having to ask for everything I needed. As a nurse, to become completely reliant on others was extremely difficult at first.

As Taylor spoke I not only heard her story but witnessed the faith that sustained her through the injury and rehab. Nelson Mandela would be as proud as I to know Taylor.

I left Durham to return to Boulder upon completion of the workshop but promised to keep in touch with Taylor. Through e-mails and phone calls she kept me updated on her remarkable progress. The highlight was being accepted as a patient to the Shepherd Center in Atlanta (a "catastrophic care" hospital) in the spring of 2006 where, as she described it, she was pushed to the limits of her potential.

Though not able to walk yet, Taylor swims and works out on a stationary bike. She is now able to increase her independence with a non-motorized wheelchair and practices fine motor movements with her fingers.

"Sonny and I went blueberry picking the other day and I really practiced my fine motor skills. And what I couldn't pick with my fingers I ate with my lips. I looked like a deer out there in the bushes," she said with genuine laughter.

When I asked Taylor to share her thoughts about her faith, she answered:

I have always believed in God, the universe, light and love, and always felt that I was a special gift. I know my work is a conduit of light and love for others to help find themselves and heal themselves.

I always felt there are no coincidences, and things happen for a reason. I always felt the angels have been with me and always looked for signs and messages to lead me on my path for this journey of life. I knew I was being used according to God's plan for some reason, but not being able to move and be independent was so hard for me, for I loved life so much and was so free in the wind exercising or sharing with my family, friends, or students.

What keeps me going each day? My love for life and knowing I have God's divine plan to follow and striving to reach my highest potential by exercising my mind, body, spirit, and emotions in a positive way. My personal goals this year are to get stronger mentally, physically, spiritually, and emotionally every day. I want to return to teaching again. In the short term I need to increase my stability, stamina, fine motor and gross motor skills, and physical abilities. My ultimate goal is to walk and to return to the community with expertise and knowledge to serve in an educational way. There are many things this experience has taught me: patience, tolerance, forgiveness of self and others, to really be in tune to my body, mind, spirit, and emotions. I feel thankfulness for loving others genuinely and giving of myself from the heart, for these same gifts have come back threefold.

I know you talk about heroes and my hero is Sonny, my husband, for standing by me, coaching me, encouraging me, showing me unconditional love, and wiping my tears without leaving me.

The common denominator of all life is love, of which faith is a part. We all need it, we all want it, and it's just who we choose to give it to and receive it from. I have learned that before the accident I was a gift of love created by God and I have been loving to so many people throughout my life and therefore I have created a circle of love around me. The circle continues to evolve to encompass many other people of diversity. I have a view of nursing from both sides of the arena (nurse and patient), and I understand the meaning of loss to a greater degree and being physically diverse.

Taylor concluded by explaining to me that she loved the parable of the mustard seed: with faith all things are possible.

THE DAFFODIL BULB: THE SEED OF MIRTH

Picture this: It's the end of March, and cabin fever is making itself known painfully once again. Despite the threats of global warming, the temperature outside indicates otherwise. In fact, the Weather Channel has just announced a winter storm moving up the coast, headed in your direction. Initial predictions suggest three to four feet of snow. You feel another rush of Seasonal Affective Disorder coming on. As you walk outside to retrieve the mail before the storm begins, your mood suddenly changes . . . for the better! There, bursting out of the ground, is one of the first signs of spring, the lovely daffodil. Several of them, in fact. Against all odds of producing a flower in what seems like the end of winter, the daffodils prove otherwise, and you break out a smile, followed by a giggle. Nature in all her glory has a sense of humor, and it quickly becomes infectious.

If there is a seed, bean, or bulb of any type associated with mirth, surely the daffodil is it. Even the golden petals symbolize a message of goodwill from the sun to raise the spirits. Humor is to the mind, what the flower's petals are to this plant: a pleasant distraction. And given the unpredictable weather, like a well-seasoned comic, its timing is perfect.

It has been said that one attribute that separates humans from the rest of the animal kingdom is our ability to laugh, sometimes at ourselves, sometimes at others, but most likely at the incongruities, ironies, and absurdities of life. Humor, ultimately, is said to be a right-brain function, for the setup of any joke begins in the analytical left brain, but the punchline quickly jumps the tracks, veering in a sharp turn to the right hemisphere. Perhaps the reason why humor and laughter are so complex is because the mind that processes amusing stimuli is also incredibly complex. As you no doubt have experienced, two people can laugh at the same joke for entirely different reasons. And some people don't laugh at all. To parody the wisdom of Confucius, "He who laughs last, didn't get the joke." Humor is also spiritual. Many call humor a gift from God.

When Sigmund Freud coined the term "defense mechanisms" to describe how people cope with stress, along with rationalization, projection, and denial, he included humor as one of the tools in the mind's treasure chest. He said that the overriding purpose of defense mechanisms was to either decrease pain or increase pleasure. What he liked about humor was that this attribute gives the most bang for the buck. Moreover, unlike the other ego-driven defense mechanisms, humor does both at the same time. In terms of moving mountains, humor has a lot of leverage, because it's not only a muscle, but a (funny) bone as well. Humor has been studied since ancient Greece when Plato gathered his students around and told lawyer jokes. It's no less complex now than it was then. Humor and the laughter it elicits might seem simple on appearance but upon closer inspection, it is nothing less than profound. Humor has been dissected up and down in the efforts to understand what it is exactly that makes people laugh, how it works, and perhaps most important, why it works. The preliminary answers are anything but conclusive. Rather than finding one thing, researchers found many aspects of humor that trigger giggles and guffaws. First and foremost we know that humor itself isn't a mood, but rather a perception that under the best conditions can elicit a mood, hopefully a happy one.

Years ago I received some notoriety in Washington, D.C., while on the faculty of the American University for teaching a course called "Humor and Health." Somehow the word got out before the semester was over that I was teaching this course, and I was invited to speak at Johns Hopkins University Medical School on the "Healing Power of Humor." The talk went so well they invited me back again the following spring, which in turn led to several other speaking engagements, including one for the local chapter of the American Cancer Society. College students can be a rather tough audience, but nothing prepared me for people with terminal cancer. I knew I was in trouble when I walked in the auditorium and was practically accosted by a woman with a blue turban, who said emphatically, "There is nothing funny about cancer!"

As I set up my laptop projector, I heard similar rumblings, but just passed it off. Somehow, I naively misread the signs. Now, if the truth be told, I am not a comedian, but having given this talk many times, I have pulled together a fair amount of humorous material that really works. I know it works because people laugh, and they laugh a lot. After the host introduced me, I walked up on stage and proceeded with the presentation. The first fifteen minutes were grueling. Nobody laughed. But then something magical happened and by the end of the hour, people were roaring in the aisles.

As I packed up my laptop and LCD projector, the woman with the blue turban walked up to me, shook my hand, and asked for a business card. I fumbled around in my pocket to find one and handed it to her. She gave a faint smile and walked away. Usually when this happens I never hear from the person again, however, this was not to be the case.

About six months later I received a phone call. It was the lady with the blue turban. Her name was Barbara. She asked if she could meet me for lunch. We set a date for the following week at a local restaurant. I walked in and took a deep breath not really knowing what to expect. I had no difficulty finding her. Gone was the blue turban, but the clown nose was a dead giveaway. She walked up and gave me a hug, and we sat down at the nearest booth.

Barbara began the conversation by telling me she was a breast cancer survivor. "I don't care for the word *survivor*. I prefer the word *victor*," she confided. "That day I met you I had been going through a year of chemotherapy treatment. Did you know that chemotherapy is a derivative of mustard gas? I prefer mayonnaise," she said with a grin. "Anyway, I was fighting a losing battle, because it had progressed into my lungs and bones. I was scheduled for a bone marrow transplant, which is a very serious operation, and the rate of success is not great. I have two children. My eldest son will graduate from high school this spring and plans to attend the University of Maryland. I would like to be there at his graduation. My young son wants to be an actor. I intend to live long enough to see his dreams come true." She paused for a bit and then continued.

"Terminal cancer can morph into a huge guilt trip if you let it—and I did. A premature death reminds you of all the things you never did in life, yet wanted to do. You end up staring your regrets in the face. I have many regrets. But I have decided to view breast cancer as a chronic disease, not a life sentence. I have begun to live. I don't know what brought me to your presentation. I was angry at the world that day. Perhaps I have been angry my whole life. I was certainly angry with you too, for making fun of cancer. That was before I heard you speak." Barbara paused to take a sip of water. "But you didn't make fun of us, you opened our hearts and minds and that made all the difference.

"Something magical happened that day. I laughed for the first time in over a year. It was then I realized how important humor was and how much it had been missing in my life. I also stopped feeling sorry for myself and that released me from a bondage of sorts. I also took your invitation to create a tickler notebook. It's been my saving grace. It's amazing what is funny out there if you set your mind to it. I ended up going for the operation, and, boy, did I have fun in the hospital. Those people at MD Anderson Cancer Center never knew what hit them."

"Can you give me an example?" I asked with a smile.

"Well, you know the box of rubber gloves they keep in the room of patients who are quarantined to prevent infection? One night while on the way to the bathroom I grabbed the box and tied the gloves end to end then stuffed them back into the box. When the doctor came by to check on me, he pulled a glove out, and the next, and the next, and the next. It was so funny. I had the whole floor laughing. The nurses are still talking about it."

Barbara went on to tell me how humor had become her saving grace. Apparently at my presentation she took voracious notes filled with all kinds of suggestions and used it as her personal humor prescription. "I made a humor notebook, like you said, and brought it into the hospital. It was the hit of the oncology ward. It took me four days to get it back. I never thought I would say this, but I think that breast cancer was the best thing that ever happened to me. I felt like Ebenezer Scrooge after all the ghosts finished touring him around. I thought if laughter could help me, perhaps it can help others. So now I volunteer some time each week as a clown at the oncology ward in my local hospital.

"Do you know what I learned about humor?" she asked. "I learned that humor diffuses anger and dissolves fear. And that's not all! It lightens the heart. Now I am not going to say that humor cured me of cancer, but it has been a big part of my healing journey," she said with a huge smile—punctuated with a clown nose.

THE COLUMBINE SEED: THE SEED OF COMPASSION

Hiking along one of the thousands of alpine trails in the Colorado Rockies is an experience that takes your breath away, literally and metaphorically. But if you only keep your eyes directed upward toward the majestic peaks, you'll miss one of the smaller, but sublime earthly delights: the Colorado columbine, the edelweiss of the Rocky Mountains. Five long lavender petals surround five small white petals to form a stunning double star-shaped face that beams a ray of enchantment in all directions. Rarely does one flower bloom alone. Rather, several buds collude together, perhaps just to get your attention, and synchronistically they open to the endless sky. Sometimes they bloom under the lip of a rock, protected from the harsh elements of the occasional summer snowstorm. Still other times you can spot a carpet of lavender and white moving gently in the breeze as you approach the crest of a hill, and that too, takes your breath away. What looks so simple as the face of a small flower is nothing less than a miracle at high altitude. The science of genetic propagation now offers choices in the color of the columbine flower and today in flower beds you can find yellow, red, blue, and deep purple blossoms that are equally beautiful.

The decay of the columbine flower is an illusion of sorts; it's really a metamorphosis. As the exterior petals begin to lose their color and drop to the ground, inside the pockets of the petals are ripening its seeds. If you were to place your hand under the remains of the columbine bloom and gently tap on the brown dried-out petals, several tiny, round, black seeds would tumble into your palm. About twice the size of a poppy seed, the coat is black, hard, and shiny; the three things they need to survive a long cold winter before the germination process begins, once the snow and ice have melted.

Lately, the Colorado columbine has taken on a special meaning, not just in Colorado, but all over the world. On April 20, 1999, two seniors walked into their high school and killed twelve of their fellow students and one teacher, as well as wounding twenty-four others. They then turned the guns on themselves in what has become known as one of the deadliest school massacres in U.S. history. Columbine High School, named after the state flower, became the focus of international news. Years later, questions still arise about how kids so young could do the unfathomable. If you drive anywhere in the state of Colorado, you might notice that some license plates are adorned with the Colorado columbine, with the words, "Respect Life, not only in remembrance, but as an expression of compassion."

Love is not only defined by what it is, but often by what it's not, specifically the absence of fear. Unlike fear where one's energy is contracted, love's energy expands, in an effort to reach others in the most positive way. While there are many ways in which love can be expressed, compassion is perhaps best described as selfless or unconditional love: a giving without the slightest hint of reciprocation. Compassion is a special kind of love. It is a form of service without any expectations of reciprocation. Compassion is love in action. From random acts of kindness and unabashed generosity to lifelong missions of service, compassion is unconditional love made manifest. People who engage in acts of compassion are often called angels. They seem to appear out of nowhere and once the deed is done, they seem to disappear again. That's because they don't wait around for a thank you. The acknowledgement is in the giving. Love, it is said, is the one thing that you can give away and still have plenty left when you are done. People who make themselves available for service are not rich in material wealth; they are rich in spiritual abundance. They do not give out of pity or shame; their generosity is unselfish and genuine. It's altruism at its finest!

There is an old Hebrew expression, *tikkun olam*, which translates as, "Repair the world." It is an expression that Judith Jenya has taken much to heart. There are those who talk about changing the world for the better, and there are those who take the next step and exalt the soul. Judith is clearly in the second group. While there are a great many words to describe her works of charity, the word *compassion* clearly tops the list.

"I was born much too young to know the horrors of the Nazi concentration camps, but I was taught and grew up with the belief that the Holocaust would never happen again. As we all know it has," she said.

Like so many Americans, Judith was appalled at the atrocities making the headline news in 1992 regarding the war in Bosnia and the practice of "ethnic cleansing." Inspired to take a trip to the war-torn country in 1993, Judith was heartbroken to see the greatest casualty of the war, the children, many of whom witnessed firsthand the cruel death of their parents, their houses torched or bombed, and their friends brutally murdered. Not a day went by on this trip that the phrase, tikkun olam, didn't go through her mind, and before she walked on board a plane back to the States, Judith was already working on a way to rebuild this corner of the world. Her vision was to restore the precious moments of youth that these children had been denied. In her vision she saw a summer camp on an island in the Adriatic Sea where war-torn children could take a respite from the aches of war and recapture moments of happiness, joy, and perhaps even some innocence.

In 1994 Judith quit her law practice in Hawaii and started the Global Children's Organization, a nonprofit agency dedicated to allowing children to escape the trauma of war and recapture some essence of their youth by attending summer camp. Within four months of this vision, seventy children from Bosnia, duffel bags and knapsacks in hand, landed on a tiny island in the Adriatic just as she had envisioned it for swimming, dancing, creative arts, and sports, an event that was nothing less than magical. No less magical was the subtle influence of nonviolent solutions to conflict. Bosnia is a better place because of the Global Children's Organization, but Judith soon took the idea to Northern Ireland and replicated the results there as well. And efforts are underway for a similar experience closer to home in Los Angeles, where racial fighting and gang-related deaths are a common event in neighborhoods like Watts.

Compassion in action typically brings to mind an image of Mother Teresa, but Judith has a bit of Tom Sawyer in her too. She has a knack for enlisting people to volunteer their efforts as camp counselors to make each child feel safe and loved, and the metaphorical white picket fence around the perimeter of each camp is not finished being painted, as volunteers are always needed. I know because she asked me.

I first met Judith in the summer of 2001 in Palm Springs, California, at a conference titled "Spirit Rising," sponsored by the Institute of Noetic Sciences. Judith had just flown from Bosnia to receive the Temple Award for Creative Altruism. Her story brought tears of empathy to everyone in the audience, including me.

"I never heard of the expression 'compassion in action' but I like it," she said, as we stood by a water fountain pausing to enjoy its mist in the oppressive heat. "Each person can make a difference."

Perhaps what most brings a sense of wonder to one's mind when one sees a columbine flower is the combination of beauty and delicateness. Compassion is much the same way. When love is expressed unconditionally, it is nothing less than beautiful. Yet love is delicate. It must be nurtured so that it may perpetuate itself.

THE ACORN: THE SEED OF WILLPOWER

A typical acorn seed is about half an inch long and nearly an inch wide. Its characteristic trademark is the top, which resembles a French beret. It's the "beret" that attaches to the tree branch, and it's usually the autumn winds that helps release the seed, once the tiny branch becomes too brittle to hang on to. One might think that the size of the acorn and the height from which it drops would give it a gravitational edge as it aims for the ground. Watching many squirrels snacking on these seeds may prove otherwise. The acorn seed offers the squirrel a nutrient-dense, daily allowance of carbohydrates, protein, and fats so that he may make it through the winter. But nature's plan is clever, if not divine. Many squirrels bury their treasure for a later date, only to find that what was once a buffet is now a small forest. Given the chance to fulfill its mission, the acorn seed will send a root deep into the earth before shooting up into the skies—a surge of stability for uncertain days ahead.

The acorn seed is soft and round. It offers only a hint of what it is to become, a monolith of strength when fully realized as the mighty oak tree. As one of the most notable hardwoods, oak is a symbol of strength and fortitude, the signature of sheer willpower. Willpower is one of the most important muscles of the soul, yet it is a muscle that fails to be fully exercised on a regular basis.

I'll never know why dentists and dental hygienists try to hold conversations with us, their patients, while our mouths are stretched wide open unable to articulate a response to anything said. Nonetheless, I enjoy the one-sided conversations. On one particular visit my dentist, Stan, asked me if I had read the book *The Long Walk*. From the back of my throat came a noise that resembled no.

"I just finished it," Stan said, "Here, take my copy and enjoy. I think you'll really like it."

Stan wasn't the first person to mention this book to me. A week earlier I had encountered the same book title through another friend. So I walked out of the dental office with a new toothbrush in one hand and a new book to read in the other. To say I could not put the book down once I started reading is an understatement. Within the pages of Slavomir Rawicz's *The Long Walk* is the story of survival, the epitome of willpower, and the embodiment of the classic hero's journey.

You could say that Slav was in the wrong place at the wrong time when he was picked up by the Russian soldiers at the start of World

War II. A cavalry soldier for Poland stationed in Pinsk, he was first detained without so much as a word to his bride of several weeks, then was hauled off to Moscow for what appeared to be an undetermined amount of time. Claiming innocence to the trumped-up charges of spying, Slav naively thought the authorities would ultimately see the truth. Instead, he languished in jail for nearly a year, when not being repeatedly interrogated by a tribunal of Communist officials. As if nearly starving and physical torment weren't enough, his first demonstration of willpower came during his four-day trial as he repeatedly denied any wrongdoing, to no avail.

Instead of being found innocent, he was found guilty and sentenced to ten years in a labor camp in Siberia. The train ride alone was torture, as many men suffering similar fates perished on the three-thousand-mile trek across the barren land of Russia's northern provinces. To ensure that no men would escape, all five-thousand prisoners on the train were given pants with enormous waist sizes and no belts, thus forcing them to have only one hand free at a time. The grueling train ride was only superseded in anguish by an unending marathon hike in the snow, chained to fellow prisoners. If someone died along the way, his body had to be carried or dragged by the guy behind him till the next official stop.

Their destination was a crude labor camp, #303, with housing quarters yet to be built. The prisoners' first task upon arriving there was to chop down trees and build a set of barracks. What makes all of this even harder to understand is that the three-thousand-mile train ride, fifty-mile hike, and construction was only fueled by a day's rations of a piece of bread and a cup of low-grade coffee.

To say that Slav had escape on his mind was an understatement. Escape was on the minds of all the soldiers, but there were obvious deterrents, including armed Russian soldiers and the obligatory fences. The biggest deterrent was the sheer remoteness of the concentration camp. It might as well have been the moon. Prisoners who did try to escape starved, and those who were caught were merely killed and made examples for the others. One man couldn't go it alone; only a small group of able-bodied men would have a chance of survival. Under conditions where trust among prisoners was always in question, Slav befriended a handful of six people he knew he could trust as he developed an escape plan, a plan that would prove timely and workable.

There is an old proverb that says that luck is when experience meets opportunity, and luck landed at Slav's feet through the good graces of an officer's wife. It was she who, out of pity, passed along a few simple tools (a small ax blade and knife) and enough information about guards' whereabouts to make an escape possible. Once they had a week's worth of food stored, they made their way in the midst of a huge snowstorm, as a way to cover their tracks so as not to be found.

What impressed me the most from Slav's story next was not only the sheer will to survive an escape to India on foot that would take more than a year to complete, but the unbelievable resourcefulness of each of the group's members: hunting without weapons, cooking without utensils, making clothes from the hides of hunted animals, navigating without a compass, negotiating with vagabond Mongolians, Tibetans, and Chinese, and trauma care without medicine. Granted, these men weren't couch potatoes to begin with, but they weren't cavemen either. Their survival story not only mocks, but puts to shame, any reality TV show of a similar nature. I venture to say that few if any Americans today could survive a week, let alone a year of what these prisoners of war endured.

The four-thousand-mile trek to freedom was not without its perils, and there were many. The most incredible was an eight-day migration through the Gobi desert without water and a choice of food that might turn anyone's stomach. This was followed by a tortuous trek through the Himalayan Mountains, the highest mountains in the world. Every day of their journey they were haunted by memories of brutality and punishment, and taunted by the taste of freedom. Every page of Slav's memoir is a testament to his sheer willpower to survive.

By the time they reached India, British troops, and ultimate freedom in 1942, they looked like cavemen, with long matted hair, beards down to their waists, and threads for clothing. They were emaciated, dehydrated, and forlorn, but alive. What was it that kept him and his band of friends alive? It might have been the love he held for his wife, whom he was never to find again. It most certainly included a disdain for the Russian soldiers whose cruelty and torture were incomprehensible. But what kept Slav alive with the fortitude to continue, day after day, was the thirst for freedom and the willpower to ensure that he would indeed die a free man. No words can adequately describe the remarkable endurance of the human spirit as depicted in this book.

Upon finishing the book, I looked up Slavomir Rawicz on the Internet in the hopes that he might still be alive, but I was sad to learn that he had passed away in 2004 at the ripe old age of eighty-eight.

In a day and age where healthy boundaries regarding eating habits, spending habits, and relationship fidelity are often in question due to lack of willpower, Slavomir's example of this muscle of the soul is not only refreshing, it's invigorating to the human spirit.

Like the packet of wildflower seeds I sow in my garden, we each contain a bounty of seeds that holds the potential of our spiritual growth. Planting the seeds, of course, is not enough. These seeds and the plants they become need nurturing as well so that they can endure the winds of change that blow often and from all directions. You have a unique packet of wildflower seeds within the confines of your heart. Each of these seeds holds the potential to accomplish mighty deeds and reveal our real beauty. Each of these seeds holds the promise to weather the winds of change and in doing so, we become the seeds of change for a better world. Before you cast these seeds to the wind, first you must ask yourself: in what condition is the soil for these to take root? Do the negative thoughts in your mind deplete the rich soil of its nutrients? Do ego-based or fear-based thoughts, like weeds, crowd out the intended plants you wish to nurture? What does the garden of your soul look like? These are questions we must ask ourselves regularly for it is in the answers that we find the strength to continue life's journey with grace and dignity.

CHAPTER SIX

WORDS OF MERCY, WORDS OF GRACE

*God is a sphere whose center
is everywhere,
and whose circumference
is nowhere.*

—Hermes Trismegistus

Oh God!" is a common expression of both fear and surprise. Although this may not seem like a prayer, these two words definitely qualify. In times of stress we invoke help from a higher source through the power of prayer. Prayer knows no one style nor a special order of words to get God's attention.

I once thought prayers were special poems repeated in church, recited before meals or at funerals. I now know words of mercy and grace are used for a multitude of reasons. Prayer is the hotline to God, from your mouth to God's ear. And if God isn't home, there is an entire directory of options from which to choose—starting with angels and saints and working your way down to a host of dead relatives.

During my adolescence I discovered that prayer was the currency of divine forgiveness, employed to remove the stains of sin on the soul. But perhaps most important, prayer was the ultimate lifeline in times of trouble. On those occasions when divine intervention was sought, prayer could be used. There are no special incantations, no mystical eloquence, no magical words to get God's attention. All prayers offered in sincerity are equal to the ears of divine consciousness. In simplest terms, *all* thought is prayer.

We summon God's attention and solicit divine inspiration during moments of personal crisis—a human need as old as history. As many

nonsecular surveys reveal, the popularity of prayer as a coping technique to deal with stress has never wavered. If anything, the interest in
prayer has increased over the years, particularly in the field of alternative medicine, where complementary modes of healing have brought
new light to the ageless wisdom and power of prayer.

THE DYNAMICS OF PRAYER

In 1985 a remarkable study by Randolph Byrd, M.D., was published
in the *Southern Medical Journal* titled "Positive Therapeutic Effects of
Intercessory Prayer in a Coronary Care Unit."[1] The study investigated
the possible outcomes of prayer as a form of bona fide healing. Over
a ten-month period, 393 cardiac patients admitted to San Francisco
General Hospital were randomly assigned to either a treatment or
control group. Those in the treatment group were remembered in
prayer by groups of people across the country. According to Byrd,
patients in the treatment group had between five to seven people
praying on their behalf, without their knowledge. Those in the control
group simply received standard medical care with no known prayer
support. The findings were remarkable. The cardiac patients in the
treatment group fared better statistically—with reduced need of
antibiotics, fewer cases of pulmonary edema, no cases of endotracheal
intubation—and fewer patients died.

Initially, the remarkable findings made international headlines, but
their significance fell off the radar screen. (As of 2006 several attempts
to duplicate the Byrd study have been attempted with varying results,
suggesting that it is hard to design a controlled, double-blind study
involving the nature of God.)

The idea that prayer was used as a medical intervention technique,
not to mention that this double-blind designed study was conducted
in a hospital setting, did not go entirely unnoticed. Dr. Larry Dossey

was so fascinated by the implications of this research that he began a ten-year search for more data on this topic. He learned that Byrd's analysis was neither the first nor the most prominent. There were well over 130 studies addressing the topic of intercessory prayer in what Dossey termed "credible science methodology." He also found several case studies that poked significant holes in the mechanistic world view so prevalent in Western society.

In Dossey's words, "The wheels are falling off the machine we call reality." [2] As a Western-trained physician with a specialty in internal medicine, Dossey admits he was skeptical at first. Repeated encounters with unexplainable factors in medicine lured him to explore a more holistic approach, not only regarding health and prayer, but the universe itself. His review and commentary on the topic of prayer can be found in the celebrated book *Healing Words*, an insightful synthesis of medicine, physics, and metaphysics. Dossey has since written several other popular books on prayer, intentionality, and the growing field of complementary medicine, and has become one of the most respected voices in the science of spirituality.

To best understand the significance of these findings, we must first examine the larger context of human consciousness, of which prayer plays such a significant role.

The scientific study of consciousness began in the 1960s as an off-shoot of psychedelic drug experimentation.[3] Inquiring minds like those of Charles Tart, Stanislov Groff, and Ram Dass were curious to pinpoint a more accurate definition of reality. Their conclusions were based on case histories of clinical exposures to LSD and other hallucinogens. Just as the microscope enhanced sight, various drugs enhanced the perception of reality. As Tart explained in a keynote address given at the third annual conference of the Institute of Noetic Sciences on the topic of consciousness, "You can say what you want about drugs of this nature, but the truth of the matter is that they opened the door to a new understanding of human consciousness."[4] And in his book *Beyond the Brain*, Stan Groff wrote:

> *While the traditional model of psychiatry and psychoanalysis is strictly personalistic and biographical, modern consciousness research has added new levels, realms, and dimensions and shows the human psyche as being essentially commensurate with the whole universe and all of existence.*[5]

In the 1960s Elmer and Alyce Green, researchers at the Menninger Clinic in Topeka, Kansas, conducted experiments in the emerging field of psycho-physiology and biofeedback—a means of self-regulation through the amplification of machine frequencies that measured various physiological parameters. The purpose of their work was to help define the link between mind and body, particularly in the fields of stress and disease. Their explorations led them to Asia, where they studied several Hindu yogis, each of whom possessed the uncanny ability to control autonomic nervous functions—breathing, heart rate, blood pressure, and blood flow. These findings left them scratching their heads because Western thought said these functions were largely unaffected by human consciousness. Fasten your seat belts, please, we are now entering the turbulence of a new paradigm of reality!

What emerged from these and several related investigations on near-death experiences, spontaneous remissions, clairvoyancy, therapeutic touch (TT), visualization, and shamanistic healing was a radical new set of theories. The consensus of findings indicates that the mind is just one aspect of consciousness that uses the brain as its primary organ of choice. In effect, we are not a mind in a body, we are a body in a mind.

Dossey, who also explored mind-body healing, decided that this larger aspect of consciousness needed a name, one that would be accepted in the scientific medical community. So he coined the phrase "nonlocal mind." The term nonlocal, borrowed from the field of quantum physics, refers to a field that cannot be represented or measured in the typical space-time continuum. Dossey explained that the human mind is an extension of the nonlocal mind—which is not simply localized in the body.

The Byrd study mentioned at the beginning of this section nicely illustrates the concept of nonlocality, since the people praying for the sick patients were not located in the vicinity of the hospital housing the patients. Instead, they were scattered across the country in several time zones. Grounded in quantum physics, the concept of the non-local mind has much in common with Jung's theory of the collective unconscious. Jung believed that if we travel deep beneath the layers of the personal unconscious mind, we begin to explore that aspect of divine consciousness that unites all of humanity. Jung rediscovered a simple truth: All things connect. In fact, we are never disconnected from anything. The eloquent words of Chief Seattle bear repeating until their meaning is fully understood: "All things connect. Man did not weave the web of life. He is merely a strand in it. Whatever he does to the web, he does to himself."

Decades after Chief Seattle's eloquent reply to the U.S. government's effort to purchase land in the Pacific Northwest, Albert Einstein was driven to prove his unified field theory. This theory describes a force or energy that is responsible for uniting the fields of nuclear, gravitational, and electromagnetic energy. Although best known for his theory of relativity, Einstein is also respected as a first-class philosopher on the nature of the universe. "I want to know the thoughts of God," Einstein once said. "All the rest are details." In fact, the seeds he sowed to germinate the field of quantum physics have led many to pursue the thoughts of God. The field of quantum physics has inspired an acceptable name for divine consciousness—

the nonlocal mind. But if we look to science to prove the existence
of God, we give our power away. In the words of Gregory Bateson,
"Science probes, it does not prove." [6]

Despite a longstanding feud between science and religion, it all
boils down to one word—energy. Energy unites us all. It has even
inspired a common language among scientists, mystics, and healers. I
was exposed to this language when I attended the second annual
meeting of the International Society for the Study of Subtle Energy
and Energy Medicine (ISSSEEM). This organization, started by Elmer
and Alyce Green in 1989 as a spinoff from the groundbreaking Council
Grove conference, brought together some of the greatest minds in
science and clinical medicine with those who practice the ancient art
of energy medicine. [7]

ISSSEEM sees as its mission the reunification of scientific and
esoteric wisdom. The direction of unity, however, is not toward the
religious but the spiritual—transcending the dogma, politics, and
confines of religion. As it turns out, the nonlocal mind shows no
religious preference whatsoever. The mind of God is open to all.

Energy is not only the raw material of the cosmos but the glue that
holds it together. Thoughts, perceptions, beliefs, and attitudes are no
different. They are also included in this prototype of defined energy.
In the mind of physicist David Bohm, consciousness in the form of
thought is itself a type of energy. As such, thoughts vibrate at a different frequency than chairs, books, or food. Energy in a thought form
can transcend the space-time continuum and travel across the country to heal cardiac patients. It can cross a continent in a dream form
in a frequency still unmeasurable by today's technology. Yet, as Dossey
warns, don't be too quick to abandon ideas that don't fit so nicely into
the mechanistic world view.

The notion that prayer is energy is not unfamiliar to those of the
Hindu culture. Ancient Sanskrit writings show the power of the

spoken word—the resonance that words reverberate. The mystical word *om* is believed to carry a vibration that resonates with the frequency of the planet Earth. To chant "om" brings one in harmony with the universe, leading many to assume that being one with nature is no longer merely a poetic expression, but a practice of good health. Prayers may be spoken or sung. Music therapist and composer Steven Halpern notes that the sounds of chants typically employ vowels, offering a soft healing resonance. Sound is audible energy.

The question still remains: Is prayer as thought really energy? Dossey doesn't think so. He states that if prayer is a conventional form of energy, subject to the law of inverse square, it would weaken over distance. Yet research studies tell us this is not the case. The message gets through regardless of the limits of space or time! Consider these examples:

- Caroline Myss is a clinical intuitive who, by means of the human energy field, can sense symptoms of disease and illness in patients. According to her colleague and associate Norman Shealy, M.D., she has an accuracy rate of 93 percent. What makes this extraordinary is that the distance between where Caroline lives and where Norm practices medicine is over 500 miles.[8]
- From her home in Baltimore, Maryland, renowned healer Olga Worell sent healing energy to a cloud chamber in Atlanta, Georgia, 600 miles away. Studies conducted by Dr. Robert Miller were designed so that all motion in the cloud chamber was videotaped. Wave motions observed in the cloud chamber corresponded to identical motions made by Worell at the same time at her home in Maryland.[9]
- Mietek and Margaret Wirkus practice and teach a healing technique where bio-energy is sent through the layers of subtle energy by viewing and sensing the energy in photographs of patients with

specific ailments. One example is that of a young woman who was diagnosed with lupus. Healing vibrations sent via the energy of photographs was observed to significantly decrease the symptoms of the disease.[10]

- Studies designed by physicist Helmut Schmidt of the Mind Science Foundation in San Antonio, Texas, have shown that intention of thought can actually change the results produced by a random event generator (REG), affecting the order of zeros and ones.[11]

- Studies designed by Elizabeth Targ, M.D., and colleagues looked at the effects of nonlocal prayers, energy, and intention for AIDS patients to reveal the efficacy of these modalities.

It may seem like prayer goes from sender through the godhead to receiver, but Dossey suggests that words of mercy don't go anywhere— they are present everywhere, always. Prayer, a creation of the human mind, instantaneously becomes one with the nonlocal mind. Nonlocal means to be anywhere and everywhere at the same time—infinite in space and time. Whereas time and space do not influence the power of prayer, case studies show that the most important part of healing, including prayer, is unconditional love. The nonlocal mind, Dossey suggests, is similar to the three traits of divine consciousness: omnipresence, omniscience, and omnipotence. By association, the nonlocal mind is what he calls "direct evidence for the soul."

Dossey's theory made sense long before I ever heard him speak of it. This understanding came to me as a young boy as I lay on a grassy field observing the formation of clouds. All thought became suspended upon watching a jet fly across the sky. Within seconds the ground shook as it broke through the sound barrier. I found myself in a vision—traveling as fast, then faster than the speed of light. Like the jet, I broke through. Suddenly in my vision, I entered a dimension where brilliant light was everywhere; the radiance was blinding. I imagine the nonlocal mind to be much the same way.

THOUGHTS THAT INQUIRE, WORDS THAT HEAL

How do we access the nonlocal mind? By keeping our hearts open and our thoughts clear.

As Dossey eloquently expressed in *Healing Words*, we do not have to re-establish or re-create the connection to the divine because it already exists. Prayer is not a means to cross the abyss from human consciousness to divine enlightenment. Instead, it is a process of remembering our true (divine) nature and our connection to the universe. The kingdom of God is within. When intention is merged with love, it is another form of remembering. Although the dynamics of prayer are far more complex than words can ever explain or science unravel, we can still enjoy the mystery.

Words of grace will come to us in many ways: through dreams, meditation, moments of synchronicity, or the words and actions of others. God is not only multilingual but is extremely creative in the selection of vehicles used to respond to our call. Those who meditate will tell you that messages do get through. As explained in the previous chapter, the centering process is a means of clearing the mind to make way for direct access to the higher self. There are countless stories of people who have heard divine whispers when they stop the incessant chatter of the alter ego. Several friends, colleagues, and acquaintances have confided that hearing the voice of God is no strange occurrence, nor is the serendipity of synchronistic events a series of bizarre coincidences.

A friend who has meditated for years once shared with me this thought: "When we pray, we talk to God. When we meditate, God talks to us."

Dreams are also a vehicle for divine whispers. History is loaded with stories of people—from Pontius Pilate's wife to astronaut Jim Lovell—who awoke from a dream with a message conveyed, a problem solved, or an insight conceived. As Jung asserted from five decades of dream research, we are all privy to divine thoughts expressed through dreams.

One night during the second week of December 1995, I awoke from a dream about my godmother, Pat O'Connor. Although extremely close in spirit, we had not seen each other in over two years. Her visit in my dream seemed peculiar, since I had never dreamed of her before. In my memory, she gave me a kiss on the cheek. Immediately I awoke. Although I had such good intentions to call her that day, I put off the call until Christmas Day. When the connection was made, Caleb, her husband, informed me that Pat was in the hospital, the result of a stroke that occurred two weeks earlier—the night of my dream.

In his landmark book *The Road Less Traveled*, M. Scott Peck began with these three words: "Life is difficult." Anyone involved in a relationship knows the potential this expression carries. Hal was no different. A highly successful engineer, Hal's romantic life was not as fortunate. Relationships with women didn't last more than a few years. At age forty Hal was forced to take a closer look at the direction of his life; the forecast was not appealing. He asked for help through prayer and told himself he was ready for a change.

A short time later, Hal told me of a dream he'd had in which he met a woman. He knew she was his soul mate, and he awoke knowing that they would meet shortly. Amazingly, they did. She is now his new wife. Dreams of this nature are not uncommon; it is our cultural beliefs that prevent us from fully accepting them without reservation.

Words of grace are not solely manifested through the will of God; they can germinate in our hearts when we seek assistance for others in distress. Stories abound of people who have prayed on behalf of a loved one, only to experience remarkable results. In her book *The*

Trapp Family Singers, Maria Von Trapp describes several occasions where prayers were solicited for her family in times of insurmountable strife—and the prayers were answered. [12]

We relish the stories where God comes to the rescue, but our faith wanes considerably when prayers seem to go unanswered. On those occasions our faith is pushed to the point of spiritual exhaustion. The impression is that even almighty God is fallible. Do prayers for the people in strife-torn lands fall on deaf ears? Is God listening to prayers for cancer victims? Does God only work from nine to five? Are there no second shifts when it comes to divine consciousness?

Surely free will, unconscious desires, and the dimension of time, as we know it, all play a role. However, it appears that the complete answer lies outside the realm of human comprehension. When prayers seem to go unanswered, we must remind ourselves that there is a higher order to the universe. We must relinquish control, trust the process, and give in to this higher order.

When one begins to grasp even the slightest inkling of the dynamics of the universal mind, it becomes a bit easier to appreciate some of life's mysteries. The universal mind not only receives vibrations of thought, it has the ability to transmit as well. An Australian physician lived in the depths of the outback. Because of the rough terrain of the land and the great distances between ranches and towns, the vehicle of choice is a plane. On a summer morning in 1972, Burk Vaughn, known affectionately as "the flying doctor," was making plans to load up and fly out to the next ranch station. As he loaded his last bag behind the cockpit, he looked up to see an aborigine standing near the right wing.

The native introduced himself and asked if he might hitch a ride. It was an emergency, he said, and he needed transportation right away. Although surprised, Burk quickly obliged. Not long after the plane was airborne, Burk asked his fellow traveler the nature of the emergency. There was a sudden death in the family, and his presence was required for the mourning ceremony, he answered. Burk asked how he knew about the death without access to phone or radio. The aborigine smiled and explained that he received a message from his family by way of the mind.

"How did you know I was leaving today for this ranch?" asked Burk.

"The same way," he replied.

As the plane made its descent to the makeshift runway, Burk noticed several people standing alongside the road waiting.

"That's my family," the passenger said.

Pulling up to the small crowd, Burk asked, "How did they know that you'd be landing right now?"

"I sent them a message—through my mind."[13]

INVOKING WORDS OF MERCY

There are numerous ways to cope with stress. We rarely use only one skill or technique. Because stressors are perceived as the enemy, we arm ourselves with several coping skills to attack our problems from all sides. There are, of course, occasions when our dilemmas seem so overwhelming that nothing seems to work. Cornered by the opposition, we must bring in the reinforcements.

Prayer is repeatedly used as a coping technique, no matter what size the stressor. In times of frustration, turmoil, or insurmountable odds, we find ourselves gazing toward the heavens in a desperate plea for help. When we invoke the power of prayer, we consciously invite the subtle mystery of providence to gently guide us on the human journey.

As a coping technique, the power of prayer is undeniable. Prayer works. It has been substantiated in countless stories. However, we yearn for additional proof that the mystery of prayer still delivers. For this reason, we find that stories of miracles renew our faith. When our fears evaporate, the power of prayer is revealed.

In an effort to deal with stress, prayer is used throughout the entire life cycle. But it's interesting to note that the bigger the challenge, the more likely we are to solicit divine intervention. Researchers have found that middle-aged to senior adults seem to employ prayer as the primary intervention tool to deal with stress—particularly as they approach the end of their lives. Fear of death and dying can bring out the most holy of behaviors. And whether it is fear of our own death or merely the death of an unmet expectation, fear has often proved to be a significant motivator to fold one's hands and bow one's head in prayer. What starts with fear, however, must transform into love if the dynamics of prayer are to be set in motion.

Whereas individual styles certainly vary, prayer typically falls into one of two categories: goal-oriented prayer and open-ended prayer. As he explored various research endeavors regarding the force of prayer, one of Dossey's discoveries was an organization in Salem, Oregon, called Spindrift. At Spindrift the effect of directed prayer (the desire for specific outcomes) was compared with the effect of nondirected prayer. Although both appear to see results, Dossey reports that: "The nondirected prayer appeared quantitatively more effective, frequently yielding results that were twice as great or more when compared to the direct approach." If there is a message we can glean from these results, it is that although we play an active role in the prayer process, we certainly do not control the outcome.[14]

By permission of Johnny Hart and Creators Syndicate, Inc.

As a coping technique, prayer can act like a double-edged sword. When used to empower ourselves—like a surge of energy to recharge our batteries—prayer can direct our efforts toward a peaceful resolution of any stressor. The nondirect approach of prayer used by the Spindrift studies calls to mind the word *surrender*. Surrender does not mean to give in or give up. "Surrender to the will of God" is an invitation to work with, rather than in opposition to, the divine game plan. Think of surrender as flowing with the current.

Although we can petition our needs in times of stress, we cannot force the will of God. To flow with the current serves as a potent reminder that surrendering to the divine plan is better than swimming upstream, only to get swept back against the rocks of hardship. Surrendering to the will of God is a recurring lesson in humility, patience, and faith, where one's inner resources are put to the test. However, surrendering the ego in times of trouble does not mean abandoning the ship. When the power of prayer is kept outside ourselves, we are no better off than if we chose not to pray at all. In the words of Sri Ramakrishna, "The winds of grace are blowing perpetually. We only need raise our sails." [15]

A friend once said, "I don't like the word *surrender*. It makes me feel powerless. So instead I use the word *release,* as in, 'I release my ego and align myself with the divine will.'" The word *surrender* is synonymous with detachment, letting go, moving on. But to truly align yourself with your Higher Power, you must truly surrender.

Despite our spiritual maturation, stress has a way of bringing out the worst in all of us. It can reduce faith to a shadow and replace confidence and personal integrity with negative vibrations and a mind-set of punishments. Petitioning an external God is an act of giving away your power. It closes the channel of divine energy and sets the stage for repeated encounters with those things we find stressful. Words of mercy, as expressed in prayer, are most clearly "received" when our hearts are open and our inner resources are called to action.

This fable describes that part of the human spirit that is always connected to the divine consciousness:

> *When the gods had finished creating the heavens and all creatures on Earth, they focused their attention on the creation of humanity.*
>
> *"Where should we put the soul?" the first asked. "Where does the spirit go?"*
>
> *The second replied, "We cannot put it in the depths of the oceans, for one day they will likely build a craft to explore the fathoms and they will surely find it."*
>
> *The third replied, "We cannot place it in the heavens above, for one day they will likely build a craft to explore miles above Earth and they will surely find it as well."*
>
> *"Then we shall place it within the heart of each person," the first said, "for they will never think to look there." They all agreed.*

Inner resources are intangible aspects of the human condition that reside within us. Faith, love, patience, courage, and optimism are the means by which the human spirit manifests itself. Prayer is as much a conduit to these inner resources as it is an extension to the universal mind. Should the embers of the soul's fire fade in darkness, prayer, like a gentle wind, helps to rekindle these embers. In times of trouble we should remind ourselves of this simple wisdom: The winds of grace are blowing perpetually. We only need raise our sails.

Messages from Water

Listed on the conference schedule were several speakers for the 4 PM session, one of which caught my eye: Doug Boyd, sharing stories from Native Americans. Being a person who loves to hear a good story, I quickly headed down the hall from the grand ballroom to the conference room hoping to get a decent seat. As I entered the room, the first thing I noticed was that there was not a chair to be seen anywhere. The second thing I observed was that there was a big glass bowl in the center of the room. People filed in quickly and sat in a large circle around the glass bowl. I, too, took my spot in the circle. The once empty room was now filled with eager participants. Each person was given a cup filled with water and was told to hold it, but not drink it.

Doug is not a Native American, but he has written several books about Native Americans including *Rolling Thunder* and *Mad Bear*, two noteworthy biographies of contemporary indigenous healers. He began his talk by giving rich context to the philosophy of the Native American medicine wheel. He then shared several personal stories of his time spent with several Native American healers. All the while we patiently held our cups of water. Water served as more than a metaphor for Doug's stories. The water in our cups *was* the story. In the mind of indigenous healers, all thought is prayer. Long before the book *Messages from Water* by Masaru Emoto hit the shelves or became well known through the movie *What the Bleep Do We Know!?*, indigenous tribes all over the planet spoke of water's ability to carry messages. Imprinted with an intention, water becomes a vehicle for prayer of any kind. Catholics are reminded of this every time they enter a church and bless themselves with holy water. Buddhists, as an offering, hold a similar respect for this liquid. So do Hindus. Most likely all cultures hold water in great reverence. Like wind, water serves as a profound metaphor for the divine. Like a stream meandering through a forest, water was the theme that tied all of Doug's stories together.

Focusing our attention to the water we held in our hands, Doug instructed us to hold a positive intention in our thoughts and then send this intention directly to the water contained in each cup. The intention, he explained, should be simple and heartfelt. The words love, healing, peace, or compassion were all we needed to focus on. Like an eyedropper releasing a drop of blue liquid, we telepathically sent the intention into the cup of water to have it permeate the entire volume.

He then directed us to take a moment to ponder where this water came from. He continued by speaking of clouds filled with moisture, raindrops that fell to the Earth, streams, of water that filtered through miles of earth to form aquifers, mountain streams, and lakes. He then asked us to perceive the water through our five senses: to hear the water, to see it, to smell it, to dip the tip of one finger in and touch it, then finally to taste it. As we lifted the cups to our lips, we were reminded to not only let the water pass over our tongues and mouths, but to absorb the healing intention that we dissolved into the water. Once in our bodies, this water and the message it held would travel to every cell in our bodies. In closing, Doug invited us to pour the remaining water from our cups into the glass bowl. This water, in turn, was later brought outside and poured over the earth in a gesture of goodwill for the planet—something we all agreed was necessary given the state of global environmental concerns. A step-by-step description of the healing water meditation can be found in the back of this book (Appendix 1).

To gaze through a book of Masaru Emoto's photographs of frozen water crystals (or better yet, view his video) will surely take your breath away. Perhaps what is equally astonishing is the notion of what our own thoughts do to the water, the element that constitutes over 80 percent of our bodies. If ill intentions can block the natural formation of water crystals or turn a mixture of water and rice sour, the question begs to be asked, what impact do our thoughts have on our health? Once again Doug's voice echoed in my ears: All thoughts are prayer, and we must direct our thoughts wisely.

In the past two decades science has turned an inquisitive eye toward the healing power of prayer, more specifically the power of intention. As might be expected, the results are a bit mixed. Whereas some prayer studies show remarkable results, others don't. (How do you control for the impact of friends and family who pray but are not part of the study?) Perhaps trying to measure God through the limitations of the scientific method is nothing more than eating soup with a fork. Personally, I find the most remarkable stories to be firsthand accounts that reveal more to life than that perceived through the five senses. One recurring theme I have encountered in my study of the healing power of prayer is the collaboration of both the conscious and unconscious minds and the effects of a mixed message. It is well documented in hundreds of case studies in which a conscious intention to heal is often sabotaged by the unconscious resistance (the subpersonalities of the unconscious mind that refuse to relinquish control). In other words, if both minds are not working in unison for the common good, the results will indeed, be compromised.

Mark is a close friend who, through no small nudging on my part, had begun to explore the mystical side of life with gusto. It was Dr. Wayne Dyer's book, *The Power of Intention*, that helped Mark begin to control his lower back pain.[16] "The power of intention has become a staple in my stream of consciousness. I have found it gives balance to my life where I now have learned to live in the present moment."

HOW TO PRAY

Betty Eadie is someone who is quite familiar with the prayer process. On the evening of November 18, 1973, Betty experienced an episode of internal bleeding that soon led to shock—and her death. Once free from the confines of her physical body, her spirit soared toward the bright light. In a remarkable journey that has been described as "the most profound and complete near-death experience recorded," Betty was guided to view several unique visions, which she recorded in the book *Embraced by the Light*.[17] About prayer she writes:

> *I saw many lights shooting up from the Earth, like beacons. Some were very broad and charged into heaven like broad laser beams. Others resembled the illumination of small pen lights, and some were mere sparks. I was surprised to learn that these beams of power were the prayers of people on Earth.*[18]

In this brief, mystical voyage that others might call a visit to the afterlife, Betty said that her understanding of prayer changed. She observed that those prayers represented by obscure sparks emanating from the planet were generated by what she called "insincere prayers of repetition." Prayers of this nature often go unnoticed in the higher realms. The prayers that got immediate attention were those offered with an open heart and a detached outcome.

Insincere prayers are not uncommon, even in moments of stress. Once, while talking to a priest about various world issues, the topic of prayer came up—the rosary, to be specific. As a priest with a great many duties, he felt the undue pressure to support a congregation. At times he felt stretched beyond human limits, which even God couldn't help. Marriages, funerals, baptisms, budgets, personnel problems, Sunday service, and more formed only the tip of the parish iceberg.

In this conversation, the tables turned as I assumed the role of listener in his half-apologetic confession of sins regarding his own time management. "I'll admit, when I'm in a rush, during morning prayers with my parishioners, I do an abbreviated version of the rosary. It saves me ten to fifteen minutes, which I need in order to get some other things done during the course of a day," he said.

"Don't these people catch on? Aren't they aware you are doing this?"

He explained that once the verbal momentum gets going, the crowd of ten to twenty people enters a trance-like state, mechanically repeating the prayers of the rosary. It's at this point where he slips in an edited version of the Hail Mary to move things along. "We are going through it so fast no one even notices. They get out early, I get out early, everybody's happy."

I sat for a moment until I heard the expression pop into my head, *caveat emptor*, but with a slight variation—*caveat orans*: Let the one who prays beware!

Prayer is prayer. Yet the quality of delivery is essential to having the message be heard. Prayer is a language with a communication style all its own. There are no secrets to prayer. Is there a right way to pray? It would be foolish to say absolutely yes. However, based on what little we do know of the universal mind, there are some things to consider that will contribute to a healthier relationship as we court the will of God.

In *A Book of Angels*, Sophy Burnham expounds on the concept of prayer.[18] Her explanation was very similar to that used to describe the practice of visualization—a mental training technique used in stress management therapy to promote relaxation or heal chronic illness. Burnham prefaces her observations on the dynamics of prayer this way: "How do we send our thought in such a way that it can best be received?" Her recommendations reflect the perennial wisdom of the sages, healers, and shamans throughout time. This inherent wisdom serves as a guide in our moment of need.

1. **Honor the present moment.** The universal mind only knows the present moment, for it has no concept of time. Unlike the human mind, which races from the past to the future with little time spent in the present, in divine consciousness there is only *now*. As hard as it may be to understand, the rules of space and time as we

know them do not apply to nonlocal consciousness. In other words, God's clock is not calibrated to the human mind. With this understood, requests and solicitations in the form of prayer are best addressed in the present tense, so "as if" becomes "as is."

2. **Accentuate the positive.** In the universal mind there is only positive energy. Through the will of divine grace, negative words such as not and don't are transformed in a positive light. Negative thoughts send a mixed message on the canopy of prayer. Fear, by means of negative thoughts, can dig its roots into our mind with doubt, until these roots crack the foundation of our faith. Burnham writes, "There is no absence or negative in the universe and, therefore, it deletes all but the active voice and positive words."

Celestial offerings through a negative voice reverberate and distort the true essence of any prayer. In fact, fear-based thoughts may attract that which we are trying so hard to avoid. So rather than say, "Please God, don't let me be late for this meeting," turn the negative thought into a positive and align your thoughts with the flow of universal consciousness. Instead, try "Please God, allow me to make this meeting on time." With this thought, you can also create an image in your mind to achieve the desired results. Should fear rear its illusionary head, acknowledge it, face it, turn it around, and focus your mind on the positive.

Mind-body healing expert Joan Borysenko tells a remarkable story of the importance of positive reframing. On a trip to Australia she met a man named Ian Gawler. As the result of cancer, he had lost his right leg. Months after surgery, he went in for a checkup only to learn that the cancer had spread; over twenty tumors resided in his body. As he sat there describing his story to her, he explained that he decided to think positively. His mantra became, "I will live! If I tell myself I am not going to die, the unconscious mind only understands positives and will interpret this as, 'I am going to die.' That was twenty years ago," he told her with a smile.[19]

3. **Send a clear transmission.** It is an injustice to compare the human mind to a machine. However, the comparison can offer insights to human consciousness that cannot be expressed in words. The mind is like a radio transmitter, sending and receiving messages. Some stations are easier to hear than others. Fear in the form of doubts, negativity, worry, or apprehension creates mental static that distorts messages of prayer. Through the law of universal attraction, like a self-fulfilling prophecy, energy directed toward our doubts will sabotage our best efforts if the transmission is not clear.

4. **Detach yourself.** There is an essential component of prayer that involves faith—a deep-seated knowledge that trusts the will of God, even if we don't understand how it works. Detachment means letting go of the outcome: "Thy will be done." If we got everything we asked for we would be in big trouble. As Oscar Wilde once said, "When the gods want to punish you, they answer your prayers."

According to author and physician Deepak Chopra, there are seven spiritual laws that govern the universe. The law of detachment is the corollary to the law of intention and desire. If we cling too tightly to our desires, we smother and kill them. Learning to let go is a big step in spiritual maturation and a lesson we must all learn.

I was traveling with Deepak one weekend, when he noticed he had lost a small suitcase. Several attempts were made to locate the missing luggage, but to no avail. Deepak turned to me and said, "I must detach and let it go. If it comes back, it was meant to be." Minutes before his scheduled presentation, a man walked up to us with the black case. The news brought a smile to Deepak's face. I smiled, too. The universe didn't miss a beat.

Detaching from the purpose of prayer is letting go. A student once shared a joke about detachment. It goes like this: An old man who had spent several years in a wheelchair prayed to God for a healing. In his dreams he heard a response. "Go to Lourdes. Go to Lourdes." So after securing some money and making some arrangements, he was on his way to the place of miracles. As he approached the water, a kind stranger pushed his chair into the center of the pool. There the man sat and prayed, begging for mercy, asking forgiveness, wishing for a healing. After an hour, he thought it best to wheel himself out. As he got to the edge, someone yelled out, "Look, a miracle! Your chair has new wheels!"

5. **Practice an attitude of gratitude.** Gratitude is an element of love. It is part of love's rainbow. Love is the energy that connects all things, but expressing thanks is not so easily done. We often fall victim to the reward and punishment mind-set of prayers, saying, "God, I've been good, please do this for me." The underlying intention says that to receive something we have to earn it. If prayers aren't answered, it is our fault. Nothing could be farther from the truth.

God's love is unconditional; there are no strings attached. This alone is reason to offer thanks. A prayer offered in gratitude is a reminder of the bond of unconditional love. Every prayer is answered, even if the answer is no. For this we must be grateful, too. I once heard a joke that reinforces this concept. One person said to another, "I incessantly pray to God, but he just doesn't answer me." To which the next person says, "Oh, God heard you. The answer was no!"

Burnham refers to gratitude as responding. Others call it the acknowledgment of trust. In the words of Brother David

Steindl-Rast, "Love wholeheartedly, be surprised, give thanks and praise. Then you will discover the fullness of your life." [20] Honoring the law of universal love requires a response from our hearts, most humbly said in the words, "Thank you."

WORDS OF GRATITUDE

At best, stress is an awakening. At worst, stress can be a devastating mess. For better or worse, stress is almost always an inconvenience. Moments of distress can leave one feeling anything but grateful. However, to beseech God in times of trouble without giving due thanks for the times of abundance undermines our attempt to walk in balance. To stand like mountain requires us to honor our divine essence in moments of peace as well as in moments of uncertainty. Prayer is one way this can be done. Just as we repeatedly teach our children to say thank you, we must remind ourselves to practice an attitude of gratitude.

During the last semester of my tenure on the faculty of American University, I invited a Native American healer to be a guest lecturer in my "Modern Theories of Health and Wellness" course. A Lakota Sioux named Harley Goodbear came to speak on the topic of Mother Earth spirituality. His appearance was scheduled to coincide with the course segment on human spirituality.

On the night of his visit, many students brought roommates and friends to class. Each brought a gift. The room, which normally seats twenty, was packed. I presented Harley with some tobacco, as was the custom, and introduced him to the students and guests. Harley opened a long, wooden box and pulled out several items: first a sage stick, then some sweet grass, followed by an eagle feather, corn, cedar, a peace pipe, an eagle bone whistle, and some pine needles. Lighting the sage, he held up the stick and waved it in the air, honoring the four directions: east, south, west, and north. (For those of you who have not smelled burning sage, it has an odor like marijuana. The smoke from the sage stick permeated the entire wing of the building, and with the aroma still lingering the next day, I had a lot of explaining to do.)

Harley held up the items and carefully explained each one's purpose and significance as it was introduced into the ceremony. Harley's presence, the resonance of his voice, and the ageless wisdom he shared mesmerized the students.

Harley placed the sweet grass in a tin can to burn, then softly said, "Now I would like to say a prayer. This is a prayer of thanks." He thanked Mother Earth, Father Sky, and the four directions. In a voice grounded in truth and poised with eloquence, Harley thanked the four-legged and winged creatures, and the creepy-crawlers. He thanked all the elements: wind, fire, metal, and water. He acknowledged the spirits of the forest and oceans. He expressed gratitude to all the world's races and the great many blessings bestowed on humanity. He thanked the smallest particle on the face of the earth and then extended thanks out to the entire universe. Uttering the words, *"Mitakuye oyasin"*—all my relations—he paused and looked around the room. Finally, he thanked the Great Mystery that created it all. Not a student stirred. He thanked everything by name, which took him almost an hour. If there was one thing my students learned that day, it was that not only is patience required for God's reply, but it's also a necessary requirement when offering a quality prayer of thanks.

Native Americans take prayers of gratitude seriously. No stone is left unturned when giving thanks. After the ceremony, Harley explained the nature of prayer through the eyes of the Lakota Sioux. "All thought is prayer," he said, "and all life is sacred. We talk to our brothers the trees, we talk to our brothers the animals. We constantly give thanks in our thoughts. To walk the Earth is a privilege, which I never take for granted, nor should you."

When Harley had answered the last question, the room filled with applause—perhaps a prayer of gratitude in its own way. Then, unrehearsed but well choreographed, the students formed a line and one by one approached Harley Goodbear with an offering: tobacco, corn, a pocket knife, candles, sage sticks, beads, leather straps. Reluctantly, the last student walked up and, with an air of apology, placed a can of baked beans in his hand. Harley just looked at me and winked. Holding up the can, he offered one last word of thanks.

The following is another prayer of thanks and remembering offered that night in the Lakota tradition: [21]

> *Where I sit is holy*
> *Holy is the ground*
> *Forest, mountain, river,*
> *Listen to the sacred sound.*
> *Oh great Spirit,*
> *Circle all around me.*

CHAPTER SEVEN

HEALTH OF THE HUMAN SPIRIT

That the birds fly overhead,
this you cannot stop.
That they build a nest in your hair,
this you can prevent.

—Chinese Proverb

225

A crimson sunset. A hot bath. A monarch butterfly. The reassuring voice of a good friend. These are gifts that nurture the soul. We yearn for and cherish these special moments to give balance to the harsh realities of life. These gifts—a type of divine energy—filter through our senses to invigorate the human spirit. It is the vibrancy of our inner resources that continually draws our attention toward these special moments. The unique alchemy of humanity and divinity allows us to cope with life's problems and sustain the health of the human spirit. It is also sound strategy for stress management because it acknowledges the critical importance of the spiritual dimension.

Stress and human spirituality are partners in the dance of life. Just as nervous tension can tighten muscle fibers to restrict the flow of oxygenated blood and nutrients to muscle tissues, repeated perceptions of fear and anger limit the flow of life force, thereby denying nourishment that is essential for physical well-being and spiritual growth. To repeat the words of Sri Ramakrishna, "The winds of grace are blowing perpetually. We only need raise our sails."

The word health comes to us from the Anglican word *hal*, meaning to be whole or holy. One cannot speak of health without understanding human spirituality, for spiritual fitness is inextricably linked to our mental, emotional, and physical health. Ensuring the well-being of the spirit is assuring all aspects of ourselves. Herein lies the thread that binds stress and spirituality together. As the daily pressures of life pile up, effective coping skills and relaxation techniques are essential for calming the body and quieting the mind. This allows the constant flow of divine energy—from the highest level of our being to our deepest body tissue—so we can find peace for mind, body, and soul.

Nurturing the health of the human spirit is an individual undertaking. There are no special guidelines, strategies, or formulas—only recommendations. The following suggestions have been passed down through the ages. Each points out the necessity of integration, balance, and harmony with all aspects of life—the three components to any successful stress-management program.

THE ART OF SELF-RENEWAL

Not long ago I purchased a cordless phone. While I appreciated the freedom of moving around without the restraint of a cord, there was a catch. The instructions warned: "This phone must be placed back in the cradle for a ten-hour period to recharge or it will not work properly." I will be the first to admit that comparing humans and machines is not wise, but in this case the link was undeniable.

Like the cordless phone, we must make the time to recharge our personal energy. The similarity stops there. We are not machines, and the human consequences are much more severe if we do not replenish the life force of our personal energy. Without recharging we become susceptible to the increased demands of stress, until we stop dead in our tracks.

Imagine that every thought, every concern, every feeling that you have toward your work, family, and friends is like a thin cable of energy. Constantly sending out vibrations through these lines will eventually lead to a depletion of strength. What happens to people who don't take time to recharge? Obvious signs of energy depletion become apparent in their behavior: They are less patient, more rude, less tolerant, more irritable, less humble, and more sarcastic. In essence, people who don't make time for themselves become even more overwhelmed, and their stress-prone behaviors attract more stress. Life is reduced to survival tactics. It becomes "every man for himself."

Take a moment to reflect on the concerns and issues in your life and it is easy to see just how emotionally draining they can be. Steps should be taken to re-energize. This is what self-renewal is all about—taking time to recharge.

Clinical intuitive Caroline Myss, author of *Anatomy of Spirit*, refers to these perceptions as tiny lifelines that constitute our source of power, also called personal energy.[1] As a rule, we extend ourselves through multiple lifelines that become permanently plugged in. That's why our energy is drained so easily.

Myss notes that if we want to recharge ourselves by balancing our personal needs with the needs of others, first we need to disconnect our lifelines from their point of attachment. Next we need to reconnect to our divine source. Under ideal situations, this is done in solitude or in a place where interruptions and distractions are kept to a minimum. By calling our spirits home, we begin to replenish the stores of our personal energy, which, in turn, will revitalize us. It's no secret that repeated self-sacrifice leads to energy depletion. Learning to take care of ourselves may mean letting go of behaviors and attitudes that impede the self-renewal process. We must teach ourselves to relax without feeling guilty or selfish for taking time out.

To constantly give to others without equally supporting our own needs may seem valiant and caring in the short term, but in the long run it becomes quite ineffective and ultimately serves no one. Too many people fail to take time to recharge their personal energy and thereby chronically run on empty. In the business world this is known as burnout. Research shows just how prevalent burnout is at the workplace, especially in the service-related professions. Sad to say that the most common coping techniques for burnout are nothing that remotely resembles self-renewal. Instead, people opt for quick fixes and stimulation through alcohol, drugs, and other addictive substances. Initially, these may look appealing; however, spiritual energy cannot be replaced through material means or physical substances. These only drain the human spirit through illusion and deception.

Self-renewal is a continual process, and we must constantly strive to replenish the energy of spirit. It is as important as breathing. To be present and attentive to those around us, to be strong for others in times of need, we must look after our own well-being first. Without strength and endurance, we run the risk of pulling everyone down with us when the pressures of life become overwhelming.

As a former Red Cross water-safety instructor, one of the first concepts I was taught to share with students is that in order to save another person's life, you must be strong enough to save your own. Before a lifeguard-in-training learns to throw a ring buoy or grab a shepherd's hook, first comes the practice of endurance swimming. Conversely, on the front line of spiritual growth, it is a blend of solitude and grace that fosters strength and endurance on the human path.

The principles of lifesaving are as appropriate at home and the office as they are at the beach or pool. We must attend to our own source of personal energy so that we may be available to others in times of need. At first this notion may seem to contradict the Christian ethic of placing others before yourself, but a closer look reveals there is no contradiction whatsoever. The Golden Rule reminds us to love others as ourselves. This equation of human conduct has become lopsided because most people, in placing others first, grow accustomed to ignoring their own needs. Cultural influences imply that taking time to love and honor ourselves is selfish, even sinful. But by neglecting our own needs, we pave the way for feelings of frustration and victimization.

The art of self-renewal is neither selfish nor ego-enhancing. Instead, it gives us permission to appreciate and love ourselves. When we feel good about ourselves we have something of quality to give, instead of offering empty gestures, insincere actions, or conditional love. Author Leo Buscaglia emphasized this point when he wrote the following words:

> *When you love yourself, you will love others. And to the depth and extent to which you can love yourself, only to that depth and extent will you be able to love others.*[2]

The concept of self-renewal is the basic premise of holidays and vacations. Whereas a two-week vacation may be a reprieve from fifty weeks of work, the art of self-renewal is a habitual routine of making personal time, however long or short in duration, on a daily basis. Meditation may be the most popular method of self-renewal, but it's not the only recourse. Going for walks in the woods, taking a warm bubble bath, listening to a special piece of music, or cooking a favorite recipe all qualify. In fact, consciously engaging in almost any hobby fulfills this need to recharge, provided there is no feeling of guilt. Guilt is an energy drainer, and self-renewal must be guilt-free.

Any secretary knows how frenzied work can be. More often than not, it's a thankless job trying to meet the expectations of several people who have little sympathy for anyone who cannot make their lives easier. Secretarial work is synonymous with stress, especially when several people think their work has the highest priority. Stressed-out secretaries feel they have no sense of control; Sharon is one such secretary.

Sharon has high blood pressure. "My doctor says it's caused by stress," she said. I explained the importance of relaxation and making time to re-energize. It was not a foreign concept to Sharon, but one she never put into play. She thought quiet time came after all her other obligations were met. Unfortunately, her chores were never completed, which meant there was no time for herself. It took the red flag of hypertension to dramatically change Sharon's perspective. We worked out a time in the evening where she could sit undisturbed for a period of five to ten minutes and practice a breathing meditation exercise. This has become her time for self-renewal. She calls it her salvation.

Self-renewal typically begins with some aspect of the centering process, a time to go within. It continues in whatever way feels most appropriate. The most essential aspect of self-renewal is preparing a quiet space to be alone—to calm the waters of the soul. There is no one way to do this, only a way that is best for you.

Recharging our personal reservoir of energy is equal in importance to that which we give to others but not necessarily equal in the amount of time spent. In other words, you can spend eight hours at work or fifteen hours a day caring for the kids, but you can recharge in only ten minutes! There are two keys for self-renewal: time management and high self-esteem.

TIME SHIFTING

The premise of time management is not finding more time to finish all the things left undone by the end of the day, but using time most effectively. This includes time for yourself. For most people time management should be an exercise in eliminating things that steal time away, such as watching television or marathon phone calls. We are prone to adding, not subtracting, more chores and duties.

Working a twelve-hour day may be considered a status symbol to some, but not to Stephan Rechtschaffen, M.D. In his popular bestselling book *Timeshifting*, Rechtschaffen explains that being over-productive is not a symbol of pride but an index of stress. A fast-paced rhythm leads to dysfunction of the mind-body-spirit model.[3] Rechtschaffen declares that the rhythm of society itself is increasing; many people are unaware that they are caught up in it. He states that people who work in a rhythm that he calls hyper-productivity will show impressive short-term results. But the long-term effects are devastating to one's health. Rechtschaffen, the founder of the Omega Institute for Holistic Studies in Rhinebeck, New York, suggests that we learn to slow down from the high-paced lifestyle of work and society by consciously changing the rhythm of our activity. The key is enjoying the present moment. Time shifting is an easy concept to understand, but a hard one to act upon.

When describing this concept of self-renewal, it is not uncommon to hear people say that although the idea of re-energizing is very attractive, they just don't have time to sit and meditate, read a book, or take a long walk. The combination of family obligations and work responsibilities is a recipe for exhaustion, leaving room for nothing else. A closer look reveals that where there is no time for self-renewal, there are poor personal boundaries. As such, any personal time is invaded or freely abandoned, but most likely it's given away to children, colleagues, or friends. What are your time robbers? What prevents you from taking time for yourself? Reflect on this for a moment and start a list here:

1. _____

2. _____

3. _____

4. _____

5. _____

Once you have identified the significant time robbers in your life, decide what steps you can take to minimize these habits, then do them. Next, pinpoint a time each day that you can allocate for personal time to recharge yourself. Start small. Even though you may feel like you need hours to rejuvenate, the thought of that much time may become a barrier to actually doing it. Start with a period of five to ten minutes of uninterrupted time. Set your boundaries, and hold them hard and fast without a trace of remorse or guilt. If you desire some quiet time and don't want to be disturbed, you need to communicate this to those around you. Ask them to respect your boundaries.

As the saying goes, "If you don't do it for yourself, no one else is going to do it for you."

SELF-ESTEEM

It is not enough to want time for yourself; you must realize that you deserve time for personal rejuvenation. Honoring yourself with the practice of self-renewal requires a belief that you are worthy of this time to recharge, that it's neither selfish nor egotistical. It's essential!

The link between poor self-esteem and stress is undeniable. When self-esteem is low, you become a bull's-eye for stress by attracting negative influences, which only perpetuate more stress. Conversely, when self-esteem is high, things just seem to roll off your back. The question becomes, How can I elevate my self-esteem to an optimal level?

Raising your level of self-esteem begins by disarming the negative critic, the tape-recorded message in your head that constantly tells you that you are not good enough. The negative critic is the fear-based voice that whispers in your ear, "You'll get nothing done if you take any personal time, so don't even think about it." Stated simply, the negative critic is the voice of the ego, which preys on your insecurities through guilt. The truth is that taking several moments to re-energize will not only keep you grounded during stressful encounters, it will significantly add to the quality of what you are doing.[4]

One effective way to disarm the negative critic is to offset the negative talk with positive feedback and affirmations. The most successful athletes, actors, and business people do this regularly; once learned it becomes second nature. I have found that it is best to learn and practice positive affirmations when you are calm and relaxed—when the mind is most receptive to these suggestions. Positive affirmations can be done at any time to boost self-esteem, but they are particularly useful when stress knocks at your door. Examples of positive affirmations are as varied as the reasons for using them, such as losing weight, increasing performance, and boosting confidence before a public speech. Like prayer, positive affirmations have specific attributes that support their effectiveness. The first and most obvious is that they are stated in a positive manner. Second, they are stated in the present tense (I am, rather than I will be).

The following are some examples of positive affirmation statements:

- I am a lovable person.
- I am worthy of taking personal time to re-energize my life.
- I am deserving of my personal time.
- I am responsible for my own happiness.
- I am the source of my own security.

Stop and listen to the dialogue in your mind, and you will discover that negative thoughts are common and plentiful. In fact, they may completely dominate your thinking patterns. This is not to say that negative thoughts are entirely bad, as long as they don't become self-defeating and influence everything you do. The use of positive affirmations is not a display of arrogance. It is an exercise in balancing the negative thoughts with positive feedback so that your mind stays focused in a forward direction.

It is not often that we are asked to comment on our positive attributes, but for purposes of enhancing self-esteem, we need to constantly remind ourselves that we do have many. Take a moment to identify and list five of your most significant attributes. If you have a hard time coming up with five, then ask a few close friends what they consider to be your most redeeming qualities. Remember, when the chips are down, these are the aspects you need to focus on to get you through a tough day.

1. _____

2. _____

3. _____

4. _____

5. _____

Life is not a tightrope on which we teeter endlessly from day to day. Life is a journey. The practice of self-renewal is an exercise in walking in balance. No matter who you are, you deserve it.

THE ART OF SACRED RITUALS

All life is sacred. There are no exceptions. Perhaps because we are constantly surrounded by the hollowness of life, it is common to take its sacredness for granted. Some aspects of life appear more sacred than others; others may seem sacrilegious. To balance the sublime with the ridiculous, to remind ourselves of the divine in everyday life, we engage in the practice of sacred rituals. These temporarily lift the veils of earthly illusion and remind us of our divine nature. In simplest terms, sacred rituals act as a compass on the human path; they direct our thoughts toward God.

We all have rituals, called habits, routines, even idiosyncrasies; they fill our day with behaviors that compose our lives. If all life is sacred, does that mean then that all acts, behaviors, and habits are sacred? Not necessarily. One must remember that it is not the act of doing something that makes it special or mystical, but the conscious awareness of the holiness we attribute to the ritual that makes it sacred. Driving to work or walking the dog can be either a mundane act or a mystical ritual, depending on the significance you attribute to it. And walking the dog can be as spiritual and sacred as any blessed sacrament, if you attribute this meaning to it. The sacredness of life is the very premise of the Native American concept, Mother Earth spirituality, where all life is deemed sacred and honored as such.

Like life itself, even the most sacred rituals can be taken for granted. Too many people adopt rituals they deem sacred, only to find that in time they lose their magic; the mechanical gestures become plain boring. Stress will certainly arise when one realizes that what was once considered sacred holds little or no meaning. It was this observation that became the focus of concentration-camp survivor Viktor Frankl, whose theory of *logotherapy* speaks to the very nature of meaning, purpose, and the vacuum that arises when meaning evaporates.

Boredom and lack of meaning are reasons commonly cited as to why people become disenchanted with rituals performed in religious institutions. Meditation is another example in which the ritual can lose its edge and become flat. It is not the act or ritual itself that is sacred. It is the meaning we give to it that makes it holy. When rituals become boring, it is time to adopt a new rite to bring back the awareness of life's sacredness.

Years ago I belonged to a group of holistic healthcare practitioners in Burlington, Vermont. Work schedules varied considerably, but we would congregate one morning each week for a regular staff meeting. It was a common practice to honor the sacredness at each meeting;

however, to stave off the boredom of repetitiveness, the opening was never the same from week to week. In fact, one never quite knew what to expect.

A common fallacy is the notion that sacred rituals are synonymous with religious practices such as reading the Talmud, genuflecting in front of the altar, or kneeling to the east on a prayer rug. While one cannot deny the holiness of religious practices, it should be noted that these rituals are not exclusive to religious rites and sanctuaries. If this fallacy is accepted as fact, the total sacredness of life becomes relegated to one day of the week or to one specific location and denies the individual the full appreciation found in all of life.

A friend of mine invited me to her church to pray for a mutual friend who was dying of cancer. As she parked the car, she told me she felt this was the only place she could pray because she was taught as a young girl that this was God's house—as if to say this was the only place in which to communicate with her deity. Chagrined, she admitted this was rather silly, but old habits die hard and she couldn't talk to God anywhere else.

Some people find God in stained glass windows, others seek the divine in incense and burning candles. My grandmother discovered providence at her birdfeeder, and this quickly became her sacred ritual every morning. Partially immobilized by an arthritic hip, she was prevented from honoring a previous, more structured routine, but she adapted quickly to a chair and binoculars by the kitchen window in the early morning hours. "Hear that song," she would say with the excitement of a six-year-old. "That's a cardinal." After watching her for a few mornings, I became convinced that the comings and goings of chickadees, woodpeckers, hummingbirds, and finches were as fulfilling to her spiritual thirst for the divine as anything she had done. One morning I found her sitting at the kitchen windowsill, the window wide open, and her arm outstretched. To my surprise, a chickadee was perched on her fingertip, eating shelled sunflower seeds from her palm; she was elated.

Several friends read Shakespeare sonnets in the bathroom every morning, write postcards to dear friends every week, make cookies for the homeless, meet in monthly men's and women's groups, play charades with their children once a week, or sit on the beach to watch the sunrise every day. These are their sacred rituals, each serving as a constant reminder that we are always connected to the divine. The human spirit stays healthy not through sterile routines and heady theory, but through direct, personal experience. Indeed, this is the only way we will every truly realize the source of our divine connection. The art of sacred rituals invites us to take off our shoes and run through the field of grass like an uninhibited child.

Take a moment to list those rituals you consider sacred in your life. Next to each one, cite the location where each one is performed and how frequently you engage in it. If you find that your list is lacking in either quantity or quality, begin with a new list of those things that you always wanted to do but for some reason never found a way of doing.

Ritual Location	Frequency
1. _____	
2. _____	
3. _____	
4. _____	
5. _____	

Sacred rituals are like musical instruments—they only sustain their blessing when life is breathed into them. If you find that your revered practices have become lifeless, and participating is more akin to CPR, then it is time to abandon that which is hollow for that which is hallowed. The true art of sacred rituals is keeping them pious. This happens through the heart, not the head.

Sweet Forgiveness

Every act of forgiveness is an act of unconditional love. If unresolved anger is a toxin to the spirit, forgiveness is the antidote. Where anger is a roadblock, forgiveness is a way to drive around and transcend the experience. For forgiveness to be unconditional, one must be willing to let go of all feelings of anger, resentment, and animosity. Sweet forgiveness cannot hold any taste of bitterness; the two are mutually exclusive. When feelings of anger are released, the spirit once held captive by anger is free to journey again.

Why is it so hard to forgive? The answer may be tied directly to the strength or weakness of the ego. Equally painful to the ego is the recognition of our own shortcomings. So the ego hangs on to anger because the illusion of control is strong and appealing. Initially anger may serve as a fuel for fight or flight, but over time the emotional pollution can suffocate the spirit. Unresolved anger becomes a corrosive agent.

It is a common and perhaps unconscious belief that forgiving someone who has violated us is equivalent to being victimized again; first you are wronged, then you are wronged a second time when forgiveness is extended. The result is perceived to be the equivalent to ego-bashing, which in itself is quite painful. So the alter ego settles for the illusion of control, by maintaining some degree of anger in the form of resentment or contempt. Turning the other cheek is admirable and even encouraged, but not at the risk of losing self-esteem. So again the word balance comes to mind. How do you release feelings of anger and resentment while maintaining a sense of strong self-esteem?

Sweet forgiveness is a process of letting go. As the expression goes, "To err is human, to forgive, divine." In the words of John F. Kennedy, "God's work must truly be our own." Those who are familiar with the Lord's Prayer and who take those words "as we forgive those who trespass against us" to heart, know that forgiveness is not only part of God's work, but also part of our own. Forgiveness is a human trait known throughout all cultures, practiced by all races, and advocated in all religions.

In Chapter 1, we learned that the average person becomes angry fifteen times per day, usually as a result of an unmet expectation. Every occurrence of uncontrolled anger is a control issue. We may not give a second thought to the little aggravations that upset us, like a rude driver or a cranky store clerk, but assaults to our identity are more difficult to release.

The bigger the breach of the ego, the longer the grudge will take to resolve. As difficult as it may be, large-scale ego-bashing encounters offer the best occasions to practice forgiveness. In the words of Joseph Campbell, "Jesus said, 'Love your enemies.' He didn't say, 'Don't have any.'"[5]

Forgiveness means more than condoning someone's inappropriate behavior and excusing personal violations. It means letting go of the feelings of denial, anger, and indignation, and moving on with your life. Forgiveness is a healing process where the wounds of injustice are allowed to fully mend by going from controlling others to empowering yourself. To paraphrase the words of psychologist Sidney Simon, forgiveness is not something you do for someone else; it is something you do for yourself. Forgiveness sets you free again.[6]

The words *I hate you* leave a terrible sting. The pain is even more damaging when these words are directed at you from your own child. Such was the case with Susan, the mother of two children, who escaped an abusive marriage only to feel repercussions from her daughter for the next decade. The mother-daughter relationship has tension built into it from the start, but as Susan tells it, this went beyond any Greek tragedy.

"I gave this child everything, but what she wanted was my death certificate," said Susan. "Oh God, do those words hurt, more so than anything I have ever gone through." Moving through the hurt and verbal abuse toward the precipice of forgiveness was a daily chore, but Susan held strong. Time was on her side. She let those words go through her, not reside in her. "Because," she said, "I knew one day she would come around. As hard as it was, I had to keep myself above her anger, not get caught up in it. Faith in a relationship means you are willing to work through it. I am convinced that anyone who is capable of feeling hurt or anger is also capable of forgiveness."

Susan will tell you forgiveness isn't a one-shot deal; it's a process and an investment that has paid off considerably. Today Susan and her daughter are the best of friends. Those harsh words of years ago have been replaced with the words *I love you.*

Processing your anger is the first step in any act of forgiveness. This requires time. The greater the sense of violation, the longer the preparation time. To do this, ask yourself: Why do I feel violated? Why am I harboring a grudge?

The second step of forgiveness involves some aspect of grieving as we come to terms with our loss, whatever it may be. The range of emotions in the grieving process spans the continuum from anger to depression. Many people fail to get past this stage, endlessly spinning their wheels in the rut of victimization. To get a little, you have to give a little. In some cases, this may mean offering an apology where appropriate, even if it's to yourself.

The third step is a detachment from the feelings of anger and resentment—in essence, separating yourself from the emotions associated with the nature of the incident. Detachment doesn't mean indifference, it means liberation. Climbing upward toward a point of objectivity enables you to gain a sense of focus, clearing the path of resolution.

This step leads to the fourth step—a declaration of independence— where emotional inertia transforms into inspiration, enabling you to move forward and get on with your life.

The adage "forgive and forget" reveals two faces of unconditional forgiveness. But is it really possible to forget? And should we? When forgiveness is unconditional, you may be hard-pressed to remember what offended you in the first place. Time not only heals wounds, it has a habit of promoting amnesia. Sweet forgiveness is not solely an external expression toward others. Like all aspects of love, the hand of forgiveness must be extended within as well. The expression "I can never forgive myself" becomes a life sentence in hell if we lock ourselves up in the confines of guilt and shame. As spirits on a human path, we are prone to make mistakes, including several costly ones. No one is exempt from this experience because life isn't perfect. But each mistake contains a pearl of wisdom if we take the time to learn from our experiences. Self-forgiveness is a practice in the acknowledgment of our human limitations, and it is as essential to spiritual growth as self-love.

Some of the most remarkable stories of self-forgiveness come to us from the collection of near-death experiences. The overriding evidence indicates that only we judge our lives, with the criterion being how great was our capacity to love. Many people who return from a near-death experience recount a host of similar episodes. In observing their "life review," self-forgiveness was essential to returning to the earthly plane.

What can we learn from their experiences? For one, holding ourselves in contempt for our past behavior is no better than refusing to forgive those who trespass against us. Second, each moment of true forgiveness is an act of unconditional love. Every encounter with anger, no matter how small or grand, is a lesson in forgiveness. Every act of forgiveness is a lesson in empowerment. True empowerment is the alignment of our humanity with our divinity; this is how we reach our greatest human potential.

EMBRACING THE SHADOW

It is commonly said that the image of God can be seen in the face of others. With the exception of young children, we rarely see the image of God imprinted on each face, in a smile and the twinkle of an eye. Instead, we are quick to point out the features that we don't like. Judgment quickly turns to annoyance and prejudice. It has also been said that each face we gaze upon is a reflection of ourselves, slightly camouflaged through the ego's censor. Cast in this light, we quickly notice the faults of others but rarely recognize our own. Nobel prize-winning author Hermann Hesse put it this way: "Whenever we hate someone, we are hating some part of ourselves that we see in that person. We don't get worked up about anything that is not in ourselves."[7]

The father of modern psychology, Sigmund Freud, was quick to point out the human trait of projection—the assignment of negative qualities to others as a self-defense tactic. But it was Carl Jung who proposed the idea that the shadow was meant to be acknowledged, not to be feared. To be whole, Jung argued, we must learn to embrace the shadow and bring light where there is darkness, promote acceptance where there is fear, and instill understanding where there is ignorance. Turning our back on the shadow only begets more darkness. He used these words to describe his insight of this aspect of the human condition:

That I feed the hungry, forgive an insult, and love my enemy, these are great virtues. But what if I should discover that the poorest of the beggars and most imprudent of offenders are all within me, and I stand in need of the alms of my own kindness; that I, myself, am the enemy who must be loved—what then?[8]

Wherever there is light, there are shadows. In this three-dimensional world, we are bound by these natural laws. The human shadow is both symbolic and tangible, and every bit as real as the mind-body that it stands behind. If you have an ego, you have a shadow. No exceptions!

The elements of shadow manifest themselves as prejudice, greed, laziness, or rudeness. These are rooted in the human emotion of fear. Those people who seem to be at peace with various aspects of their shadow are the ones who have taken the time to confront specific fears. In doing so, they have brought light to that side of darkness. Or, in Jung's words, "the shadow has been embraced."

Todd is a self-described Christian who admits to seeing issues in terms of black and white. His shadow side was the color gray. He consulted me about a problem with his son. Todd was extremely proud of his son's achievements as captain of the football team and member of the honor society. In his third year at college, Todd's son came home for a vacation and nervously broke the news that he was gay. Todd was stunned. Forced to deal with an issue that he once considered repugnant and morally wrong, Todd was now torn between a son he loved and an issue he despised. It took Todd months to come to terms with it. He readily admitted to his feelings of dread; homosexuality conflicted with his religious beliefs. For years Todd had kept the gay issue away from his comfort zone. But it was impossible to avoid now since it involved his son, whom he loved and admired. The shadow had to be confronted.

Through a series of conversations with his son, Todd learned what it meant to be gay in a straight and often hostile world. Todd began to confront his black-and-white vision. The bear hug of acceptance that he finally gave his son became his own personal embracing of his shadow.

Our trip on the human path frequently requires judgment regarding opportunities and people, especially when critical life decisions are at stake. To be used effectively, judgment must be balanced with acceptance; analysis and assessment must be balanced with receptivity. We err when we judge people at random or those who seem to threaten our ego. Judgment is a double-edged sword that causes harm when used incorrectly. Many mistakes have been made when decisions were motivated by fear rather than loving kindness.

So when is a good time to use judgment? Only when you have surveyed every conceivable piece of information and questioned your perceptions so that they are grounded in wisdom and not seduced by the voice of fear.

The shadow and the critic often share the same voice. The whispers that say we are not worthy and that find fault with others all come from the same source—the ego. However offensive these thoughts may be, they are common to all minds. At first it appears to be an issue of good thoughts versus bad thoughts, but this, too, involves judgment. The question is, how can we make peace between ego and soul and rise above the duality of opposites?

Embracing the shadow means to acknowledge these thoughts and accept that part of you where these ideas originate. Over time you will find it becomes easier to respond to these thoughts with loving kindness. As the shadow becomes trained, fewer negative thoughts will surface. The source that fuels them is minimized by a greater comfort level and is less likely to react to perceived threats in that fashion.

With every stressor we are given a choice to confront the fear that it stems from or avoid it altogether. Avoidance is no guarantee that the fear won't reappear. In fact, when we turn our backs on our problems, they will continue to reappear until we meet them head-on. We will encounter several dynamics that we have no control over and many factors we cannot change. Such is the nature of life. On these occasions, embracing the shadow means accepting how things are, not how we would like them to be for our convenience. It may require forgiveness as well as compassion. Just as there are several ways to design an unfinished basement, there are many ways to embrace the shadow.

One final word about shadows. Embracing the shadow is not the same thing as exploiting it. Embracing means to acknowledge those aspects that may appear to be less than desirable and to accept them. Try to minimize the behavior associated with them. Getting in touch with your "inner bitch" or "inner bastard" may be a cute play on words of the inner child, but calling upon the negative aspects of our dark side is nothing more than exploitation. This does nothing to evolve the soul. It only perpetuates stress. Eventually we reap what we sow.

KEEP THE FAITH

At the young age of twenty-eight, Mary Jane was diagnosed with endometriosis. Newly married and wanting to have a family, her dream seemed to evaporate as she listened to the test results. The news was traumatic but not devastating. Mary Jane is a woman of great faith. Weeks later, upon her doctor's suggestion, she underwent surgery for a hysterectomy.

"When God closes a door, a window is opened," she has told me on more than one occasion. She knows from experience; her confidence has been tested many times. Never one to lose faith, Mary Jane and her husband, John, examined their options for creating a family. The most logical choice was adoption, but their efforts in this direction had proved quite complex and legally challenging. As Mary Jane explained it, "Our mean combined age made us ineligible as candidates for adoption."

Years passed before anything possible began to materialize. Mary Jane told me her faith waned at times, but never vanished. With the help of a special church organization suited to match couples like themselves with newborn babies for adoption, she and John became the recipients of a beautiful baby boy named Eric, nine months to the day after they completed the adoption papers. Mary Jane smiles. Faith delivers!

Sarah's story is different, but the theme of faith remains the same. Sarah would often describe her marriage as close to perfect. She and Tony were an ideal couple. To look at them, one would think they had no stress because they communicated so well and supported each other's careers and personal interests. With the birth of their first and second sons, things only got better.

"Then," Sarah explained, "came Tony's midlife crisis the week he turned forty; all hell broke loose." For Sarah, life didn't slowly crumble—the earth shook beneath her feet.

"At first I told myself, it just didn't make sense. He has a successful career, a successful marriage, a wonderful family. It was very puzzling. But I kept telling myself it would all work out," Sarah said. "It took an incredible amount of faith to endure the angst as Tony reassembled the perceptions of his life." As Sarah noted, there are many couples who travel through the turbulence of a midlife crisis and end up going their separate ways. She was determined not to become one of them. So she prayed in silence, she listened to Tony's fears, she took the boys for long walks, and she put her trust in God that it would all work out. The crisis lasted just under a year, and Sarah held strong to her faith that once again her safe and happy marriage would resume. It did. Faith delivers!

The components of faith are puzzle pieces made up of faith, optimism, confidence, wisdom, patience, and love, with a sprinkling of mystery for good measure. On the surface it may seem like faith is composed of several inner resources. But faith is unique unto itself. We think of faith as having the ability to move mountains, but the power of faith is as subtle as it is dynamic. Not all mountains are made of earth and clay, and not all problems can be pushed through. Some must be transcended.

Does faith have limits? Not really. There is, however, a limit to how we use this resource. To put all our problems in the hands of God is to avoid our own responsibility. We cannot have the dynamic force of the universe live our lives for us; this defeats the purpose of our earthly existence. Conversely, to think we can handle every problem on our own without any help, divine or otherwise, is naive and foolish. The power of faith requires balance.

There is an old saying that reminds us, "We are given no task too great to bear." To this we can add, "Everything we do prepares us for everything we are going to do." Faith guides us through the moments of turbulence. In the spirit of Chief Seattle (Mother Earth spirituality), Albert Einstein (the unified field theory), Carl Jung (the collective unconscious), John Donne (no man is an island) and everyone else who understands the notion of life's integration, each and every aspect of life is connected—even if we cannot see what holds it in place.

Faith is a realization of this connection process. If what we seek is in the best interest of our soul's development, then with faith it will surely come to pass. A friend once told me, "God doesn't test faith, but instead continually provides the opportunity to exercise it, which is a good thing, because we all need exercise."

OF FAITH AND HOPE

I know many people who use the terms faith and hope interchangeably, but the two are not the same. There is a significant difference between them. As it was once explained to me, faith is a house made of brick with a cornerstone of confidence—a deep knowing from past experiences that everything will work out all right. Faith is more than a perception or a belief; it is a sense of trust you feel in your gut that everything will be okay.

Whereas faith comes from a place of strength, hope can be described as a house of cards built on a foundation of fear. As the expression goes, "Hope is faith that hasn't said its prayers." Whereas hope is expressed for those things that seem out of reach, faith is acknowledged for those that are already there. Deepak Chopra once described hope in the following way: "Hope really stems from the seat of fear and doubt. It may not seem as potent as anxiety and at times is even appealing, but hope comes from the same source."[9]

Perhaps this is the basis for the expression "false hope"—that which is based on fear. Fear wears many faces, the most benign being the expression of hope. "I hope this doesn't happen," "I hope that you make it home okay," or "I hope I get that contract" are expressions and thoughts that come from a place of fear. Hope is quickly yanked back by fear. So rather than saying, "I hope this works out," or "I hope you do well," reframe your words from a place of confidence, from your reservoir of faith: "I trust this will work out," "I have faith you will get the best job," "I wish you the best."

BLIND FAITH

If there is such a thing as blind faith, the blind spot comes from ignorance. Faith requires knowledge, independent from intuition and past experience. Faith gives us a better perspective on the problem at hand. In the field of stress management this is called "information seeking," where one copes with stress initially by learning about the current problem. A prime example is Lorenzo Odone, whose parents, Augusto and Michaela, helped discover an oil to halt the progression of adrenoleukodystrophy (ALD), which was killing their son. Their remarkable story was made into the movie *Lorenzo's Oil*.

Most stressors require some insight as to why they surface and how each is best resolved. They may also require some homework to find out more about the nature of each stressor's origin. So we seek clues and ask questions that will provide some answers. With this under way, the power of faith is harnessed and released. If hope is faith that has not said its prayers, blind faith is faith that has not done its homework. Seldom if ever does faith alone move mountains. Faith combines forces with us in an active partnership to face adversity and overcome life's obstacles.

At some point in our lives we realize that we are not the center of the universe; there is a much greater whole of which we are a part. Faith is not only a reminder of that connection, but the realization of it. Big or small, faith moves mountains for one and all.

LIVE YOUR JOY

To see the look of wonder or the twinkle in a child's eye is to know the meaning of joy. Stroll lazily down the street with a youngster and enjoy the chance to explore new territory. There is a whole world to explore in a field of grass, an entire universe waiting to be discovered in the crack of a sidewalk.

Children live in the moment. And what joy there is to be found there! With maturation we quickly outgrow the magic that once kept us suspended in curiosity and awe. It is no secret that the demands of adulthood narrow our attention so that our view of life becomes intensely myopic—focused almost entirely on past events or future possibilities, with little or no time for the present.

There is much truth to the expression that all work and no play promotes a dull life. However, life is anything but dull. Whether we are feeling overwhelmed or bored with our day-to-day existence, we alone must take full responsibility for our perceptions. Sadly, some people cannot live their joy, while others cannot even identify with life's simple pleasures.

A massage therapist once explained to me that the stress and tension of everyday life quickly manifests as stiffness and knots in people's muscles. "When I massage people who hold that rigidity in their neck, shoulders, and lower back, I ask them to name their joy," she said. "Many people can't even do this."

Living your joy is not just an expression, it's a philosophy that reminds us to seek and appreciate life's beautiful side. Don't just acknowledge it, participate fully. Walk barefoot on a lawn, lick a spoon with frosting, smell fresh-cut flowers. Living our joy reminds us to be in the present instead of being immobilized in the past or worried about the future. There is no denying that life certainly has its stressful moments. However, living your joy means balancing moments of pleasure with pain, joy with sorrow, laughter with tears. When the focus of life becomes derailed by the demands of work, cheer as expressed through humor, creativity, curiosity, and wonder are the means to get back on track and start moving again.

THE TAHITI FACTOR

Stress is a perception. So is joy. Which do you choose to perceive? The question then becomes, like a rose that has both beautiful petals and sharp thorns, where do you choose to place your attention?

If you choose to focus on the thorns (stress), that is exactly what you will find. In fact, most likely you will begin to attract more stress to you. Conversely, if you choose to focus on happiness, fun, and bliss, your eyes and heart will gravitate toward those things that support this perception (the self-fulfilling prophecy). This is not to say that we must deny our other feelings. Instead, being happy means using gaiety as both a compass and the fuel to direct your life, rather

THE FAMILY CIRCUS By Bil Keane

"Yesterday's the past, tomorrow's the future, but today is a GIFT.
That's why it's called the present."

Reprinted with special permission of King Features Syndicate.

than wallowing in a rut of pity and frustration. As the saying goes, "Every situation has a good side and a bad side; each moment you decide." Choices made with a positive attitude attract similar opportunities.

The semester before I finished my doctoral studies, I took a six-week trip to the South Pacific. Originally I had intended to go to Australia and New Zealand. But my travel agent said, "Your plane stops in Tahiti to refuel. Do you want to get off for a few days and check it out?"

Something about the word Tahiti put an immediate smile on my face and I said, "Sure, let's do it." In all honesty, I really had no clue where Tahiti was, but I was scheduled to stop over for three wonderful days.

The minute I walked out of the travel agency, I was inundated with things about Tahiti. I saw ads in magazines I had never noticed before. By chance, I encountered people who had just returned from Tahiti. I even got a postcard from a friend who had just returned from the island of Bora Bora, one of the Tahitian islands. Where was Tahiti before I decided to go there? The same place it has always been, only now my attention was clearly focused on it, and Tahiti drew me toward it like a magnet.

You don't have to take a trip to Tahiti to discover the law of attraction. If you have ever been in the market for a car, you know that the moment you decide on a specific model and color, you start seeing that same car everywhere, as if it were the only car on the road. I call this the "Tahiti Factor," but this is only my name to signify the concept of selected awareness—that on which we focus our attention.

The voice of the critic has a tendency to distract our attention toward the negative side of life. Living your joy is a reminder to focus your attention on that which provides fun and pleasure in your life.

Following your bliss doesn't mean abandoning your adult responsibilities; it does mean engaging in healthy pleasures—those things that give a rush of endorphins without additional calories, credit card bills, or latent guilt. In the book *Healthy Pleasures*, authors Robert Ornstein and David Sobel address this very issue of how bringing joy, mirth, and bliss back into our lives is essential for healthy living.[10]

Can you name your joy? What is it that brings you happiness? Regarding the health of your human spirit, what things give you pleasure that you haven't done for ages? They don't have to be complex fantasies. In fact, healthy pleasures are quite simple. To get your mind focused in this direction, to enact the Tahiti Factor, start by listing those things that qualify as healthy pleasures to you.

1. _____

2. _____

3. _____

4. _____

5. _____

6. _____

7. _____

8. _____

9. _____

10. _____

After you have completed this list, select a time and a place when you can do each one. Copy them down and place this list on the refrigerator, the bathroom mirror, or any place where you will be reminded to do them. Your list will become a treasure map of sorts. Soon you may find that you don't need a list anymore because your outlook on life simply draws you toward these healthy pleasures. You don't have to be an optimist to attract and live your joy, but it helps. In his book, *Learned Optimism*, Martin Seligman states that optimism is a trait found in everyone. Regardless of where you are, optimism can be enhanced in each and every one of us. [11]

Optimism is an inner resource that, when exercised, draws your attention to positive things. If your cup is half empty, it's time to fill it up!

Can healthy pleasures become unhealthy? Sure they can! Life is filled with attractions that can quickly become distractions. It is human to think, "If some is good, more is better." The end result, no matter what the situation, is an imbalance. Then we wish we had been a bit less greedy and a bit more conservative. Stopping to smell the roses is not the same thing as lying down in them and taking a four-hour nap. When we walk in balance, we must be mindful of the link between freedom and the responsibility. To live your joy you must first name it, be on the lookout for it, find it, engage in it, and then at some point, let it go. Life is a smorgasbord to be tasted and savored.

I THINK, THEREFORE, I AM CREATIVE!

Creativity isn't a gift for a chosen few. Like all inner resources, it is a birthright for everyone. If necessity is the mother of invention, then it only stands to reason that play assumes a paternal role in this relationship. The creative process, no matter what endeavor, is an exercise in play. Play and joy are mutually inclusive. For as many inventions that have resulted from need, an equal number have resulted from playing in the garage workshop—including the Apple computer.

Anyone who has wandered off to the garage or basement to mess around will tell you that time is not a fixed entity when the rules of leisure play are enacted. We become suspended in time. By our very nature we are creative beings. True happiness manifests itself when we are engrossed in the creative process, no matter what the outcome. Reflecting on the aspect of creativity, psychologist Abraham Maslow once said that it was this characteristic, more so than any other, that propelled one to the heights of self-actualization.

Recently, the creative process has been inspected, dissected, and reconnected to understand how we can best utilize this valuable inner resource. The answer comes none too soon. As stress becomes more potent, play becomes more important. Those who have studied the creative process agree that it engages a very spiritual quality.

Julia Cameron, author of *The Artist's Way*, writes:

> *Creativity is an experience—to my eye, a spiritual experience. It does not matter which way you think of it: creativity leading to spirituality or spirituality leading to creativity. In fact, I do not make a distinction between the two.*[12]

Roger von Oech, a creativity consultant in Menlo Park, California, describes the creative process in four stages:

1. The explorer (looking for ideas)
2. The artist (playing, manipulating, and refining the ideas)
3. The judge (separating the good ideas from the not-so-good)
4. The warrior (campaigning the best idea into reality)

In his book *A Kick in the Seat of the Pants,* von Oech reminds us that creativity and play are synonymous, especially when we start the creative process. There is much joy in being creative and much happiness in sharing the fruits of one's efforts.

STICKS, STONES, & FUNNY BONES

Laughter is a human magnet. Start telling a joke and people come out of the woodwork to hear the punchline. In those precious few moments of laughter, the bonds of unity are realized. Humorist Victor Borge once said, "Laughter is the shortest distance between two people." He's right.

It's no secret that giggles and chuckles can soften even the hardest of hearts. Stress (specifically, unresolved anger) will harden the heart if we repeatedly pull into ourselves with our problems. If the body requires vitamins and minerals for optimal functioning, the soul needs humor as an essential nutrient.

Humor therapy is ageless, as noted in the biblical passage of Proverbs 17:21: "A merry heart does good like medicine, but a broken spirit drieth the bones." Just how important is humor to the health of the human spirit? It's as essential as human touch is to a newborn baby.

Years ago, in a study published in *Psychology Today*, it was reported that on average, a person laughs fourteen times per day.[13] That number has become the official quota advocated by "humor therapists" in their efforts to balance the emotional scales between joy and sorrow. Sad to say, many people today never reach this quota. Instead, they wallow on the side of negative emotions. National surveys suggest that public morale and confidence have been on the decline for the past decade. If humor is used at all, it is often in the form of sarcasm—which literally means to tear flesh. Sarcasm, a latent form of anger, is the equivalent of sticks and stones hurled at the emotional body. *Ouch!*

Humor is most potent as a stress reducer when it acts as a diversion to some of life's bigger problems. Humor gently reminds us that we are neither perfect nor are we the center of the universe. It can also stem the tide of stress emotions, if only momentarily. This is the purpose of black humor and slapstick. From the memoirs of concentration camp survivors and prisoner-of-war camps, several stories have surfaced about how crucial humor was as a coping skill under the worst possible conditions. Comedy became a divine gift to get the victims through deeply troubled times. Hans Selye, the grandfather of stress management, advocated mirth and joy as well. In his book *Stress Without Distress* he wrote, "Nothing erases unpleasant thoughts more effectively than the concentration of pleasant ones." [14]

Laughter not only contributes to our mental, emotional, and spiritual health, it plays an important role in our physiological health as well. Various studies now substantiate what Norman Cousins discovered decades ago—humor heals. Research data compiled by William Fry, M.D., indicates that with each bout of laughter, muscle tension decreases, blood pressure decreases, ventilation increases, and various *neuropeptides* are released throughout the body. These chemical messengers, synthesized through the dynamics of emotional response, are the interface between the mind and body. In turn, they affect the function of various cell activity, with a specific focus of enhancing the integrity of the immune system. And it's not just laughter that causes this synthesis of opiates in the body's pharmacology. There appears to be a host of positive emotions associated with the feelings of joy, happiness, wonder, creativity, and love that all produce the same effect.

During my second year at the American University, I was asked to create a new course for our department. I designed a spin-off from my stress-management course and called it "Humor and Health." The class filled immediately. Not long after, I received a call from a student named Andrew who inquired about enrolling in the humor class. I told him the class limit was sealed at thirty students and thirty chairs.

Half an hour later, I heard a motorized buzz outside my office door. Soon there was a wheelchair in my office occupied by a young man about twenty years old. A smile greeted me. "Hi, I'm Andrew," he said. He proceeded to explain to me how humor therapy was an integral part of his recovery from a diving accident years earlier. He told a story of a nurse involved with his rehabilitation who would greet him each morning with a joke. The first few months Andrew simply ignored her. When that failed, he tried to thwart her mirthful attempts, but she persevered.

One day, she caught him with his guard down, and he found himself laughing. In his words, humor was his "saving grace." Laughter was a great stress reliever, he explained, with the voice of experience.

"Now I am a senior, and my life is very stressful. I could really use this class to help me cope with the complexities of my life in college. Is there any possible way for me to get in? And," he added, "I have my own chair."

Andrew ended up being more of a teacher in that course than a student. On the last day of class he made me promise that if I ever talked about humor therapy, no matter what the occasion, I would do my best to make people laugh. In Andrew's words, "People just don't laugh enough these days. They're way too serious." That day I made an oath to Andrew. So to honor my promise, here are a few jokes to share some joy and mirth. Enjoy!

The New CEO

A company, feeling it was time for a shake-up, hires a new CEO. This new boss was determined to rid the company of all slackers. On a tour of the facilities, the CEO notices a guy leaning on a wall. The room is full of workers, and he wants to let them know he means business!

The CEO walks up to the guy and asks, "And how much money do you make a week?"

Undaunted, the young fellow looks at him and replies, "I make $200 a week. Why?"

The CEO hands the guy $1,000 in cash and screams, "Here's a week's pay and a month's severance, now GET OUT and don't come back!"

Surprisingly, the guy takes the cash with a smile, says "Yes sir! Thank you, sir!" and leaves.

Feeling pretty good about his first firing, the CEO looks around the room and asks, "Does anyone want to tell me what that slacker did here?"

With a sheepish grin, one of the other workers mutters, "Pizza delivery guy from Domino's."

Once Again at the Pearly Gates

The time had come for St. Peter's annual two-week vacation, and Jesus offered to fill in for him at the Pearly Gates while he was gone.

"It's quite easy, actually," said Peter. "You sit at the registration desk, and when a person arrives, you inquire about his or her life. Smile, make them feel comfortable, and then send them to housekeeping to pick up their wings."

Early one morning on the third day, Jesus looked up to see a bewildered old man walking toward the desk.

"I'm a simple carpenter," the man said. "And once I had a son. He was born in a special way and was unlike anyone else in this world. He went through a great transformation despite the holes in his hands and feet. He was taken from me for a long time, but his spirit lives on forever. All over the world people tell his story." A tear rolled down the old man's cheek as he paused in silence.

Jesus stood up with his arms outstretched. He, too, had tears in his eyes and gave the old man a big bear hug. "Father," he cried out. "It's been such a long time!"

The old man peered over his bifocals, stared for a moment, and said, "Pinocchio?"

Humor is a gift; in some eyes, a gift from God. When we can laugh at ourselves without sacrificing self-esteem, when we can see the irony in everyday events and giggle at life's incongruities, when we learn not to take ourselves too seriously, God's gift of humor is honored. So when the black clouds begin to head in our direction, we need to remember to lighten up, play around, and use a smile as an umbrella when it rains on our parade. Life isn't a cosmic joke, although at times it may seem like it. Through it all, there are infinite ways to tickle the funny bone. Does God have a sense of humor? Many theologians think and hope so.

Living your joy may not constitute divine rapture, but it certainly has the potential to steer you in that direction. In doing so, it gives weight to the emotional scales, allowing a balance between the highs and lows that we all experience as we journey onward. I once heard Norman Cousins make a presentation shortly before he died. He said, "Many people misunderstood my message about humor. It wasn't humor that healed me. It was love. Humor is just a metaphor for love."

Decompression: Practicing the Art of Calm

Consider this: The mind craves stimulation. The threshold of stimulation is reached repeatedly each day through the use of sensory organs: eyes, ears, nose, mouth, and skin. By and large, we gather most information through our sense of sight, roughly 70 percent. We take in another 20 percent through the sense of hearing, leaving our skin, nose, and mouth with the remaining 10 percent. Cell phones, laptops, instant messaging, high-speed Internet access, TiVo, satellite radio, on-demand movies, and new technologies that have yet to hit the marketplace are all competing, if not screaming, for your attention; the vast majority are primarily targeting their messages to your eyes and ears. Collectively, they provide untold, if not ungodly, amounts of mental stimulation. Perhaps it's no surprise that an overstimulated mind is one of the precursors for insomnia.

When stress is added to the mix, the chances of getting a good night's sleep are greatly diminished. If the combined affects of this technology were a drug, the majority of Americans would be dead from a lethal overdose. Indeed, there is an addictive quality to this technology, particularly to cell phones and e-mail; perhaps you've noticed. To use another metaphor, these gadgets of technology, when left unguarded by consciousness, act like a boa constrictor that literally chokes the human spirit.

Yes, the mind craves mental stimulation, but the mind also requires solitude, a period of little or no stimulation. In essence, this is the mind's way of detoxing from all the unnecessary stimulation processed over the course of any given day. One might think this could happen during sleep, but don't be fooled. Even though the conscious mind shuts down during sleep, the unconscious mind is very active. The best way to calm the mind is meditation or mental stillness, a period of conscious and unconscious desensitization—while you are awake!

Think of this as decompression of the mind. Deep-sea divers decompress on their way to the earth's surface. Prisoners of war decompress when they are released. In this day of constant sensory bombardment, we all need to decompress! Think of mental decompression as essential as brushing your teeth or taking a shower. Think of this as recharging your personal energy. Once I was working with a group of middle-school teenagers on the topic of decompression and meditation, and one kid raised his hand and said, "I get it. Meditation is like deleting old e-mails." Touché! Dan Millman, author of *The Way of the Peaceful Warrior* and the recent movie based on his 1984 book, *The Peaceful Warrior*, was more blunt: Take out the trash![15]

Meditation goes by many names, including *centering, stillness,* and *quietude*. One friend of mine who leans toward fundamentalism confides in me that he doesn't like the word *meditation* but engages in the process daily.

"I just call it sitting," he says. No matter what you call it, it is the act of increased concentration that leads to increased awareness and inner peace. While some call meditation the Rosetta stone of consciousness, I like the expression that states, "Meditation; it's not what you think."

Whether speaking to groups of executives, physicians, schoolteachers, nurses, or college students, my advice for decompression is the same. I suggest carving out a minimum of five minutes in the course of each day to sit still, with no interruptions (unplugged!), to simply focus on your breathing. A focused concentration on your breathing cycle (inspiration and expiration) acts like a gentle wind that blows the clouds of thoughts away. Although this may seem similar to the art of self-renewal, clearing the mind goes beyond recharging your personal energy. It gives clarity and direction to your thoughts. Increased concentration leads to increased awareness.

Decompression not only involves designating a spot in the house or office where you can sit still, it also requires assertiveness to maintain the healthy boundaries necessary for no interruptions. A third requirement is willpower—to not only make the time to sit still, but to unplug and detach from the grips of technology that left unchecked can become a process addiction.

GET BACK TO NATURE

Over a century ago science-fiction writers foretold a day when planetary citizens would spend their entire day inside buildings and never have a ray of sunshine grace their skin. Their message wasn't so much a prophecy as a dire warning: Never lose touch with nature. Sadly for many people, that day is here now. Today it's easy to transport yourself from your home to your car to your office and never feel the warmth of sun on your face, nor have a gentle breeze caress your skin. In fact, experts now suggest that Americans are becoming deficient in the sunshine vitamin (vitamin D). Try as we might to avoid, even control nature, we cannot. We are a part of nature, and it is part of us. We are greatly affected by the seasons of the Earth and the circadian rhythms of a twenty-four-hour day. Despite the fact that Mother Earth is herself going through some growing pains, nature overall has a very calming presence. This is the reason why people take vacations at seaside resorts, lush tropical rainforests, and mountain cabins. Getting back to nature helps us put our problems into perspective, particularly when compared to miles of ocean or insurmountable mountain peaks.

Getting back to nature also means cultivating a healthy relationship with food. America is renowned for having the greatest varieties of foods in grocery stores, yet at the same time, providing the worst quality of food imaginable. Our food is processed with enough chemicals and preservatives to make any Egyptian mummy envious.[16] Sadly, it's processed enough to keep the pharmaceutical companies in business for millennia. Fast food, junk food, and processed foods greatly diminish our relationship with nature. It doesn't have to be this way, nor should it. In his landmark book *The Hundred-Year Lie*, investigative reporter Randall Fitzgerald highlights the derailed path Americans have taken and empowering steps we can take to get back on the road to healthy living. Similar revelations have been made by bestselling author Michael Pollan in his book *The Omnivore's Dilemma*.

Here are some suggestions to help you reacquaint yourself with the natural world once again:

1. Consider taking an early morning walk several times a week to watch the sunrise.
2. Locate the nearest park to your house, and stroll through the paths till you find a tree; then sit with your back and head against the trunk and meditate for five minutes.
3. Walk, bike, or drive to the nearest body of water (e.g., stream, pond, lake, ocean), and try to spot as many different types of birds as possible.
4. Check your calendar to find the phase of the Moon and head outside on a cloudless night to stargaze. The late winter and early spring are ideal months to observe the northern lights in many parts of the country, and August and December offer the best times for shooting stars.
5. Whenever possible, buy organic fruits and vegetables. Also remember it's best to purchase local fruits and vegetables and always buy fruits "in season." Try to avoid foods with hormones, antibiotics, and synthetic chemical compounds such as petroleum-based fertilizers, herbicides, fungicides, and pesticides.
6. If you live in a city where the ratio of concrete blocks to blades of grass is too sad to contemplate, consider buying some fresh-cut flowers, or better yet, a new house plant. Whenever possible take a side trip to a greenhouse and spend time with your nose buried in the roses for some real aromatherapy.

I was delighted, but not surprised, to learn that when several spiritual luminaries from Stephen Covey and Harold Kushner to Marianne Williamson were invited to contribute essays for the book *Handbook of the Soul* nearly everyone spoke to the healing power of nature and our essential need to reconnect to nature regularly. This sentiment was echoed once again in the Megatrends 2000 and 2010 book series. Perhaps more than ever as we are inundated with technology and 24/7 accessibility, it is incumbent upon us to voluntarily break these artificial ties and reunite regularly with our natural connection.

There is a reason why the expression Mother Earth is used to connote a sense of peace and harmony. When given the chance, nature provides an invaluable ability to heal mind, body, and spirit.

SEIZE THE DAY!

Do you have any regrets about things you wished you had done, but didn't do because fear held you back? If so, you are not alone. Fear has a subtle way of giving people something in common. Moreover, fear is perhaps the greatest deterrent to our human potential. At the root of every regret is fear. Even apathy is often masked as fear. Once while listening to National Public Radio, I heard a story about the number of Americans who travel abroad. The number was remarkably low, given the population of this country. Fewer than 15 percent of Americans hold passports. As a person who loves to travel, I found this fact astonishing. It's not just the lack of international travel that puzzles me. The same type of attitude can be found closer to home. I live in the outskirts of Boulder, Colorado. It's a well-known fact that about 80 percent of the state's population never venture west into the mountains. For those of us who do, this means smaller crowds, but truth be told, a lot of people are missing out on some great mountain scenery. A news article on the subject revealed that although many people move to Colorado because of the mountains, few make it up them because they tend to take them for granted, thinking they can always head up the next weekend. The next weekend syndrome has killed a lot of dreams.

Reality shows, blockbuster movies, personality magazines, and video games are just four of many examples that suggest people tend to live a passive rather than active lifestyle. Obesity is another. Fear is yet another. Fear, like anger, not only immobilizes us, it can literally choke the human spirit. As the expression goes, "Face your fear, and it will disappear." Not only will confronting one's fears get the heart pumping, ultimately (and when done correctly) it will invigorate the human spirit, through empowerment.

Sam is a friend of mine who has traded in his couch potato status for a *carpe diem* T-shirt. It might have been the fact that he was turning the big five-0. It might have been the fact that he was diagnosed with prostate cancer. It might be a few other factors that he has yet to mention, but one day over lunch Sam shared with me his intention to run a 26.2-mile race: the Marine Corps Marathon. Like someone who plans a vacation to the Greek isles, Sam went out and bought a few training books to get the lay of the land. As a means of motivation, he bought a pair of New Balance 992s. He even joined a jogging club. Within a few weeks he had sketched out a four-month training strategy. On October 30, 2005, Sam crossed the finished line in Arlington, Virginia, wearing a smile from ear to ear. After he caught his breath and drank in his success, I could have sworn I heard him utter the words ". . . Honolulu marathon . . ."

At dinner that night Sam shared with me that he sees life a little differently now. "I now realize that I have lived more years than I have left to live. I am not wasting time sitting around. I know this sounds like a cliché, but clichés are based on truth: The focus of my life now is to live each moment to the fullest and that's exactly what I intend to do," he said.

COMPASSION IN ACTION

There is a man who comes to the pool where I swim every day in the early morning hours. His name is Bob, but my hunch is that it's an alias. Not only does he bear a striking resemblance to Santa Claus (he even wears reindeer boxer shorts), but every now and then he will make a remark that makes me wonder who he really is.

Once his wife and I engaged in a conversation about travel as we paused at the deep end of the pool. After sharing some of my more recent adventures, she said without hesitation, "Oh, we've been to places you can't even imagine."

One day as I walked into the locker room, Bob greeted me with a hearty "Hello, son!" And with a pause that refreshes, he asked, "How's your love life?" Most of our conversations never got past the weather or the water temperature in the pool, so I was a bit taken aback.

"Really well," I said, as I explained the relationship with my girlfriend-turned-fiancée.

"No, I don't mean that love life," he said with a chuckle. "I mean your real love life. How open is your heart to compassion, your capacity to love?"

It was at that moment I realized his real identity: Santa Claus was alive and well and living in Boulder, Colorado.

There are a great many people who speak to the theoretical nature of love, but love is so much more than a theory. A theory without application has little merit. You cannot think love, you can only feel it. Confined to mere words, love evaporates. For love to be real, for love to be true, love must be put into action. Compassion in action asks the question, how is your love life? This question takes on new meaning when we realize there are many colors of love's rainbow. Compassion is one of the brightest. Compassion in action can be explained in one word: service. In a presentation made at the fourth annual conference for the Institute of Noetic Sciences, Dr. Rachel Naomi Remen shared some of her thoughts on this very topic. "Service," she explained, "is not the same thing as helping."

Helping is rooted in inequality; a type of superior/inferior relationship. Those being helped can feel this inequality. Helping infers a sense of debt. Service offers a dividend of love to all parties involved. Compassion includes empathy, the ability to feel another's pain, but it doesn't stop there. To engage in true compassion is to move with the feelings, which is why the expression "compassion in action" has so much more meaning than the word compassion itself. Compassion in action is service.

What makes service to others different from helping others? Service is based on the premise of equals, where an exchange is made in the offering. Helping involves a sense of judgment—an us-versus-them attitude—whereas service is given for the highest good of all concerned. In Rachel's words:

> I would go so far as to say that fixing and helping may be the work of the ego, and service is the work of the soul. . . . When you serve, you see life as whole. From the perspective of service we are all connected. The impulse to serve emerges naturally and inevitably from this way of seeing.

Compassion in action is nothing less than the manifestation of unconditional love. Insincere gestures influenced by guilt, resentment, or greed are conditional—there are strings attached, as if to say, "What's in it for me?" Service given with condition negates good intentions. Moreover, the reluctance to serve springs from anger and frustration. And resentment is a roadblock to putting compassion into action.

Compassion begins with ourselves. This is why the art of self-renewal is so important as a precursor to coming from a place of compassion. Compassion in action and the art of self-renewal are the actualization of loving your neighbor as yourself.

There is certainly an element of empathy in compassion, but there is no room for pity. When Ian O'Gorman's hair fell out he didn't want pity, and he didn't get it. Instead he got compassion in action. Just ten years old, Ian was diagnosed with cancer. He was warned that the ten weeks of chemotherapy might make his hair fall out. His doctors were right! It did. Strands of red hair left his head daily. Within weeks, he decided to simply shave his head and avoid the embarrassment of looking like a Cabbage Patch kid. When Ian was well enough to return to school, he walked into his fifth grade classroom one morning to find that the thirteen boys in his class, as well as his teacher, greeted him with huge smiles—each one resembling Ian with a shaved head. [17]

"Practice random acts of kindness and senseless acts of beauty" is a phrase Anne Herbert doodled on a napkin one day in a San Francisco restaurant. Faced with the general malaise of the country, increasing violence, and a demoralizing culture in which to raise children, she felt a need to spread the message of love. In Anne's mind, there is no such thing as a small act of kindness, for every act of kindness is an act of immeasurable love. Subtle words can have dynamic consequences; intuitively she knew that peace on Earth begins with goodwill toward men, women, and children everywhere.

The words that she wrote that day leaped off the napkin and spread like wildfire. Soon the expression "random acts of kindness" found itself printed on billboards, bumper stickers, and T-shirts across the country. These words had quite an impact because random acts of unconditional love began to manifest themselves everywhere; coins were placed in parking meters anonymously, polite store clerks smiled, and secret donations were made to charitable organizations. People who shared their goodwill gestures admitted that they received a euphoric uplift beyond any expression of words. This is what Rachel Naomi Remen refers to as service—an act of kindness where everyone benefits.

The unique aspect of service, where all who partake benefit, can be found in this story. An elderly woman died and found herself on a marble slab seated next to St. Peter (who, by the way, was back from vacation). "I will take you to your place in heaven, but first I would like to show you hell for the purpose of comparison," he said.

In the blink of an eye, the woman found herself in a very large room packed with people. As the woman looked around, she saw that bowls of delicious stew were placed before each person along with an extra-long spoon. For some reason they could not bend their elbows and, thus, they could not eat the stew. The cries of angst were deafening. The woman looked at St. Peter quite puzzled and asked to leave.

In what seemed like a nanosecond, she was in another room, but this time laughter could be heard everywhere. In fact, it seemed like a huge party. In front of each person was the same bowl of delicious stew and the same type of spoon. These people also had arms that were unable to bend at the elbow. But instead of being frustrated, each person used the long spoon to feed the individual directly across the table, thus allowing everyone to eat, drink, and be merry. Service benefits everyone!

Human beings have a remarkable ability to respond to the needs of others in times of crisis. One only need think of the Midwest floods of 1993, the Northridge earthquake of 1994, or the famines in Ethiopia and Somalia, all of which brought about an outpouring of financial and humanitarian support. But it's sad to say that in most cases it takes a crisis or catastrophe to bring out the best in people—as if we need a reason to act on the behalf of others. Compassion in action asks us to respond to the call on a daily basis, not just in times of crisis, catastrophe, or disaster.

Of compassion in action, noted author and lecturer Ram Dass writes:

> *Compassion is the basis of all truthful relationships: it means being present with love for ourselves and for all life, including animals, fish, birds, and trees. Compassion is bringing our deepest truth into our actions, no matter how much the world seems to resist, because that is ultimately what we have to give this world and one another.*[18]

If the course of humanity is ever going to change for the better, the change has to come from a place of love and compassion. There is no other way. In answer to the very sad state of world dynamics, the Dalai Lama imparted these words:

> *Love and compassion are necessities, not luxuries. Without them, humanity cannot survive. With them, we can make a joint effort to solve the problems of the whole of humankind.*[19]

Love is needed everywhere, please give today.

CHAPTER EIGHT

A SPIRITUAL RENAISSANCE

There will come a time when, after
harnessing the winds, the tides, and gravitation,
we shall harness for God the power of love.
And on that day, for the second time in the history
of the world, we shall have discovered fire.

—Pierre Teilhard de Chardin

S everal years ago, I was asked to give a presentation about the benefits of cardiovascular exercise at a conference for the American Holistic Medical Association. The concept of holistic medicine was novel in 1981. The keynote speaker was Dr. Elisabeth Kübler-Ross. Renowned for her work with dying cancer patients, she electrified the room with her energy as she masterfully spoke about holistic wellness and the integration of mind, body, spirit, and emotions for optimal well-being. As she spoke, I sensed a premonition of the magnitude of the changes yet to come.

After the applause faded, Kübler-Ross drew a circle on a flip chart. "This," she said, "is a symbol of health. To be healthy means to be whole—to be whole has a spiritual quality to it. One cannot speak of health and well-being without making reference to human spirituality. To focus on health we must acknowledge the human spirit. There is no other way."

She divided the circle into four equal parts and identified them as mind, body, spirit, and emotions. All four components are ever-present, she explained, but in successive progression each takes dominion in the human life cycle. The emotional quadrant enters the limelight in early childhood when we try on various moods and feelings like love, hate, joy, or sorrow.

The physical quadrant then takes center stage from the onset of puberty into adulthood. In essence we become our bodies, continually grooming everything from our muscles, teeth, and hair to the clothes we wear.

Next came the mental or intellectual phase of human development. She explained that the mind and all of our mental processing skills receive the majority of attention. The intellectual aspect comes into its own during the college years and lasts well into midlife. It is in this quadrant that we seek mental stimulation and often swing between sensory overload (stress) and sensory deprivation (boredom). Even though all other aspects of our being are present, the focus on our mental processes takes dominance over the other three.

Last was the spiritual quarter, the facet of life that deals with relationships, values, and purpose in life. She sadly acknowledged this area is virtually neglected so that we never get the attention we need to integrate, balance, and harmonize all aspects of our being. As a result, few people ever reach a state of wholeness before they die. She explained that her work with dying patients was her effort to help them fill this quadrant so the people she worked with could leave this world in peace.

Toward the end of her talk and hours afterward, my mind began to wander as I processed her message. Soon thereafter, a revelation came to me. Just as the microcosm is a part of the macrocosm, I saw the American society going through the same progression of conscious evolution as Kübler-Ross described. The vision that unfolded in my mind went like this: in the mid-1960s to early 1970s, the time of cultural revolution, America was in its emotional stage. We saw it in the list of bestselling books: Wayne Dyer's *Your Erroneous Zones*, Thomas Harris's *I'm OK, You're OK*, and *The Art of Loving* by Erich Fromm, to name a few. There were messages in the music too: Carole King ("You've Got a Friend"), James Taylor ("Fire and Rain"), and the

Beatles ("All You Need Is Love"). We were trying to make sense of our emotions and the ability to feel and express them. Group therapy was in; we learned to reach out and touch with our feelings.

Then *shazam!* The fitness boom came upon us like a surge of adolescent hormones. Aerobics classes, workout machinery, the running craze, and expensive athletic footwear became fashionable. In an effort to heal our hearts, we became our bodies. The fitness boom peaked by 1985, and although its presence can still be felt, the information age was ushered in. Through the magic of computer chips, a screen, keyboard, and electricity, anyone could have a world of information at their fingertips.

Although the fitness boom was in full swing during the time I heard Kübler-Ross's talk, the "information superhighway" was little more than a dirt road. IBM had just released the personal computer, Apple's Macintosh was still three years from its public debut, and the World Wide Web was not even close to becoming a part of the American lexicon. If her theory held correct, the age of information processing was just around the corner. But so was a spiritual awakening—if only we could maneuver around the roadblocks put in place by our own perceptions.

It occurred to me that the Western philosophy, dominated by left-brain cognitive skills (judgment, analysis, and critical thinking) and the scientific method that it supports, does little to encourage spiritual growth. This mode of thinking dates back to the early 1600s when we began to see ourselves as separate from nature instead of an integral part of it. And it went one step further by distancing us from our divine source—thus denying the spiritual essence of life.

In the search for truth, we drifted toward absolute science and the power of technology and came to the conclusion that we were dominant over nature. History shows that this view of reality became the prevailing pattern, especially after the rift between church leaders and scientists. It seemed the church, the seat of knowledge and power at that time, was reluctant to change its worldview of Earth's position in the solar system, despite scientific data proving otherwise.

A new way of scientific thinking prevailed. Reality needed to be substantiated through the five senses. Technology added such instruments as microscopes, microphones, and radar to extend the five senses, thus giving itself greater power. Many prominent scientists agreed: anything outside the realm of the five senses was deemed supernatural, immeasurable, and thus invalid. Several scientific discoveries, including the use of antibiotics and the automobile engine, provided them with a sense of power and security. They even supported the idea that perhaps we humans were above the laws of nature. This dominant cultural ideal turned from pride to arrogance as science began to further erode the awareness of our divinity. We became convinced that technology could solve all our problems.

Moreover, it seemed God had taken a hands-off approach. For all practical purposes, God rolled the dice of the universe, then turned about-face and went on vacation. The outcome was an implicit understanding that we are separate from, not connected to, all aspects of life. In other words, the divine factor was left out of the scientific equation.

As explained by one futurist whose voice speaks for many, "We were naive in our expectation that mechanistic science would explain the mysteries of life."[1] Those who were disenchanted with the mechanistic viewpoint explored other possibilities. Each led to the same conclusion—there is no separation in the divine universe; everything connects. Occasionally a reassuring voice would rise above the hum of the machines, yet too often the message was ignored by the mainstream, as our fascination with the discoveries of science, the power of technology, and the promise they held for a better, more comfortable life continued to grow.

Earlier this century, one voice in the field of quantum mechanics did make waves. It happened when Albert Einstein proposed his theory of relativity and his unified field theory. The latter suggests that all things are connected through an unknown form of energy. Einstein argued, "God doesn't play dice with the universe."

This thought began to resonate. Those who agree say there is a higher order to life and all things are connected. Not being able to measure it through the limitations of technology does not preclude its existence. Einstein foreshadowed this with these comments:

> A human being is part of the whole, called by us Universe, a part limited in time and space. He experiences himself, his thoughts, and feelings as something separated from the rest—a kind of optical delusion of his consciousness. This delusion is a kind of prison for us, restricting our personal desires and affections for a few persons nearest to us. Our task must be to free ourselves from this prison by widening our circle of compassion to embrace all living creatures and the whole of nature in its beauty. Nobody is able to achieve this completely, but the striving for such achievement is in itself a part of the liberation and a foundation for inner security.[2]

In 1981 it was quite uncommon to hear the word *spirituality* spoken in public, especially with regard to medicine. So I found Kübler-Ross's message reassuring. Based on the patterns emerging, I sensed that in the early to mid-1990s there would be a spiritual awakening. The winds of change were in the air. Reflecting on my interactions with Kübler-Ross, I heard the whispers of a revolution—an evolution of human consciousness—an awakening of the human soul. Indeed, there was an awakening, but only a few actually got up out of bed. The rest rolled over and went back to sleep, it seems. I had the opportunity to visit with Elisabeth before she died in 2004. She had offered to write a foreword for a textbook I was working on but insisted that

I fly down to her house in Arizona to take dictation. As it turns out, the stroke she suffered a few years earlier left her partially paralyzed. Among the many things we discussed, she reminded me that not only do we spend the majority of our time in the intellectual quadrant, but that the spiritual quadrant always take a little longer to step into, individually and collectively as humanity.

A Spiritual Calling

Half asleep with a book on my chest, my eyes opened to the sound of my telephone. It was a college friend, excited about a book she had just finished. "As a matter of fact, I am reading it right now," I said, picking up the book and holding it in my hand.

We proceeded to talk for hours on a host of topics like human spirituality, near-death experiences, mystic coincidences, mind-body healing, reincarnation, and soul mates. Back in our college days and well into her adult years, Jane's view of life was black and white. I could tell within the first few minutes of this phone call that something had dramatically shifted. Her voice was as excited as if she had just discovered the Holy Grail. As the conversation neared its end, I asked Jane what first sparked her interest in these matters.

"I know you have been into this for quite some time and I have to admit, I thought back then you were nuts," she replied. "I can't cite any one thing, but suddenly I was ready and, boom, a whole new world opened up."

At some point in life, each individual is beckoned by the call of his or her soul to fully awaken spiritually. It may be curiosity, an intuitive inclination, or a full-blown crisis. My friend Jane is one of many people who, as Kübler-Ross would say, has entered into her spiritual quadrant—someone who has begun to question the meaning of life and her relationship to the universe.

Some people walk gracefully into this stage, a few tip-toe, some stumble, still others immerse themselves. Because the territory is unfamiliar, however, the majority of people refuse to budge, thus denying any pursuit of the spiritual aspect of their lives.

This step into the spiritual quadrant is a natural and necessary progression in the life cycle, but one that most people are hesitant to make. One reason for this reluctance is that it requires a leap into the void. Fear holds them back. The emptying process of the soul is unavoidable, yet essential. No matter how you frame it—letting go, unlearning, detaching from, or cleansing—the spiritual phase of the life cycle demands it. Less than two decades ago, the trend was to give the topic of human spirituality only a silent nod, if that. Lately, it seems as if an invitation has been sent repeatedly to the masses to engage in this phase of human growth. In fact, it's accurate to say that at this point in time there is a universal wake-up call that beckons the spirit to arise and start anew. Wake up, get up, and show up.

Today, more than ever before, people feel the need to personally address matters of the heart and issues of the soul. Many people who are addicted to consumer goods are quick to learn that these material pleasures can never satisfy the spiritual hunger, nor contribute to the health of the human spirit. Instead, they block the life force. This spiritual calling is not only related to personal growth; it's a much larger issue.

The awareness of our cosmic connection and the significant problems on the world stage—acid rain, global warming, famine, wars, terrorism, AIDS—require critical choices. As these problems mount, our attention turns toward providence for assistance. Whether the problems are of a personal nature or a global threat, the answers are to be found within us, for it is true that God helps those who help themselves. In other words, we made this mess, and now we have to clean it up.

THE WINDS OF CHANGE AND GROWING PAINS

We are living in exciting times. Never before in history has every
culture, every population been so directly connected environmentally,
economically, and electronically. Likewise, never before has there
been such trouble and strife. Marshall McLuhan's phrase, "the global
village," is now a reality. An economic ripple in Japan, a natural disaster in Indonesia, a political coup in Africa, or an environmental disaster in Russia all send immediate vibrations around the world. Child
abuse, urban sprawl, alcoholism, depression, cancer, and rush-hour
traffic may seem like dilemmas in our personal world, but in truth,

they reflect the problems set on the global stage as well. Indeed, all things connect.

Take a look around you. It is easy to see the cracks in the cosmic egg. The frantic, addictive pace of life, coupled with today's rapid rate of change, makes the world seem like a chaotic place. While advances in technology once promised us more leisure time, in reality we feel pressured to do more. With less time at our disposal, the concept of leisure time has become an illusion. Time seems to be compressing while accelerating faster and faster with each passing day. As is so often heard these days, "Time is quickly flying by, even if you're not having fun."

The desire to do more is heightened by the realization that there just isn't enough time to accomplish everything.

More Growing Pains

Change has become synonymous with stress. It has reached epidemic proportions worldwide. At this time and place in humanity, let there be no doubt we are entering the spiritual quadrant of our collective being. We are encouraged, not required, to look at the spiritual aspect of our being—relationships, values, and purpose in life. In a sense, the soul of the world is going through an emptying process, whereby we are given a chance to pause, reflect, and emerge with a new understanding of who we are. We are learning the meaning of our collective purpose as planetary citizens. Vaclav Havel, president of the Czech Republic, articulated these thoughts dramatically in a speech made at Independence Hall, July 4, 1994, words that ring true even more so a decade later:

In short, we live in a postmodern world where everything is possible and nothing is certain. The abyss between the rational and spiritual, the external and internal, the objective and subjective, the technical and moral, the universal and unique, constantly grows ever deeper. In today's multicultural world, the truly reliable path to peaceful coexistence and creative cooperation must start from what is at the root of all cultures and what lies infinitely deeper in human hearts and minds than political opinion, convictions, antipathies, or sympathies; it must be rooted in self-transcendence. Transcendence as a hand reached out to those close to us, to foreigners, to the human community, to all living creatures, to nature, to the universe. Transcendence is the only real alternative to extinction.[3]

Simply stated, we need to put aside our political, religious, and cultural differences, rise above our prejudices, and come together as one people. Recently one of my colleagues shared this thought: "We need to change the expression from human race to human family. Race implies an inherent level of competition and separation at a time when what is most needed is collaboration."

There is much work to be done in the spiritual quadrant; it's not all fun and games. Although there are moments of joy (the connecting process), there are also valleys of darkness as we come to terms with our past fears and current dangers. In each case we must learn to let go and move on. Initially, it is in the letting go that we most readily feel the pain. Periods of growth typically result in pain at some level. Today this is happening collectively to the family of humanity, as it has for each individual. We label these times "growing pains"—those moments of awkwardness that push our limits of mental, emotional, and spiritual tolerance. We must remind ourselves that with each growing pain there is the promise that something better lies ahead. There is no way to stop the growing pains; we can only embrace them with love in whatever capacity that may be.

The Sky Isn't Falling, It's Expanding

Today the winds of change are blowing as our global village spirals into the new millennium. There are many who say we are in the midst of a global crisis. The predictions and prophecies are plentiful, and they are not pretty. For instance, the 2006 *Vital Signs* report compiled by the Worldwatch Institute announced global climate changes coupled with grain shortages, indicating a world out of balance. Severe water shortages are forecast for China and many African countries. Ozone holes in the atmosphere, deforestation, animal extinction, gang violence, overpopulation, drug addiction, changing weather patterns, and unconquerable infectious diseases are only a few of many factors that indicate a rising level of worldwide dysfunction.

Natural or man-made, each crisis is a wake-up call to transformation and evolution.

Pablo Picasso once said, "Every act of creation is first an act of destruction." This thought is not uncommon to those of the Hindu faith. Lord Shiva is their god of creation and destruction. He stands perched on one foot in a dance, with two sets of arms. As legend goes, when Lord Shiva puts his foot down, the end of the world, as we know it, is at hand. But destruction or chaos is always followed by creation—just as emptying is followed by grounding. According to the late Joseph Campbell, this theme is common to many cultures. For instance, it is depicted in the mythical fire that gives rise to the phoenix, as well as the crucifixion and resurrection of Jesus of Nazareth.

The word *renaissance* means rebirth, the emergence into light that typically follows a period of darkness. Just as the butterfly emerges from the cocoon, our spiritual awakening reflects this movement from dark to light. And while global crises look like destruction, they provide the opportunity to actively engage in the creative process of evolution through the healing power of love. However dismal it may appear, we are not passive victims in a cruel world. We are cocreators. It is a responsibility we cannot take lightly.

According to the Gregorian calendar, people were so fearful of the year 1000 that they literally climbed onto tree limbs and rooftops to watch the end of the world. Imagine the disappointment when nothing happened. The message: Don't get caught up in the fear of doom; continue to live from your heart. Today, the question begs to be asked again: Are we setting ourselves up for the same event one thousand years later? From the looks of it, some people have already started climbing trees for a ringside seat, eagerly awaiting the main event in 2012: *The End Times*, now appearing at a city near you.

The French have an expression to describe this phenomenon. They call it *le cirque fin*—the end of the cycle.[4] In this case it is the prophetic end of time (as we know it)—the anticipation of the end—that is setting the frantic change in motion. Is the sky really falling? Not at all. While the perception of a falling sky may seem quite real at times, the sky, like our level of consciousness, is merely expanding.

Could the winds of change and the winds of grace be one and the same? I believe so. Either way, we must remember to raise our sails if we are to move forward on the human journey. By refusing to do so, we merely drift endlessly, feeling abandoned and lost at a time when we need to remain focused and connected. The expression, "May you live in interesting times," is quite appropriate in this day and age. Although it is most often cited as a Chinese curse, from a different perspective it could easily be regarded as a blessing. Ironically, cracks in the cosmic egg are not something to repair. They are the initial stage of a birthing process. Whereas at first we may be fearful of the cracks, by staying centered our apprehension will soon give way to the realization that the result is not impending disaster. Instead, each crack is really the beginning of a spiritual renaissance.

Evolution with an R = Revolution

There is an ancient proverb that states "Revolutions begin with a whisper." Among the whispers today, the conclusions are less than favorable. There is a growing consensus that suggests we must change—both our perceptions and behavior—if we are to continue to exist peacefully on this planet.

In some circles the word *revolution* may denote a conspiracy, but this is not always the case. Marilyn Ferguson, in her highly praised book *The Aquarian Conspiracy*, notes that the word *conspire* means to breathe together. In its truest sense, conspire speaks of the spirit of necessary change.[5] As a futurist and longtime follower of change, Ferguson has heard and listened to the whispers of the revolution of consciousness. Since the publication of her book in 1980, the level of these whispers has steadily increased from a murmur to a dull roar.

The split between science and religion might be better understood through their respective philosophies of life. Based on the law of entropy, science typically sees a steady disintegration of matter. Because we are made of matter, it would appear that we would naturally follow suit. However, we are not solely made of matter. The laws of spirit suggest that the evolution of creation continues to unfold. According to author Terence McKenna, it is not the nature of the universe to disintegrate. Instead, the universe continually unfolds in creation. What may look like chaos is only a lower form of order giving birth to a higher level of creation. There is, in fact, a strong association between the words *chaos* and *creation*.[6]

Ralph Abraham, an advocate of the chaos theory, notes that when the word *chaos* was first introduced into the English language, it didn't mean trouble or destruction. According to Abraham, the concept of chaos depicted a void between heaven and Earth, out of which form emerged. "Creation came out of chaos, but chaos did not mean disorder or anything negative."[7]

Ferguson has this to say: "Armed with a more sophisticated understanding of how change occurs, we know that the very forces that have brought us to planetary brinkmanship carry in them the seeds of renewal."[8] In her 2005 sequel to *The Aquarian Conspiracy* titled *Aquarius Now*, Ferguson feels the same way. From her research, Ferguson singled out a group of people who predicted that humanity would break through a period of chaos to a spiritually evolved species. Today we may think of these individuals as being before their time, but in reality, they were the ones who planted the seeds of revolution.

Ferguson believes that when enough people reach this level of consciousness, a critical mass forms. This opens the path for all people to rise to that level. Today, global links, through various forms of telecommunications, have enabled vast numbers of people to access information. This cosmic curiosity may be the catalyst for conscious evolution. Expressed in the jargon of stress and spirituality, the evolutionary process is moving from a motivation of fear toward a motivation of unconditional love. Those who embrace the aspect of love will find the transition a peaceful one. Those who are slow to release the illusion of fear may find the transition toward higher consciousness an extremely bumpy ride.

Uncomfortable Truths

Having Luke as a middle name, much less a nickname, has lead to a great many *Star Wars* jokes. If I had a dime for everyone who walked up behind me and claimed to be my father, I would be a rich man. Darth Vader not withstanding, I think it's fair to say, my friends, that there truly is "a disturbance in the force" these days. Perhaps many disturbances. While there are some problems we feel compelled to ignore or at least prioritize, global warming is very real, and nothing we can hide from. It is the quintessential wake-up call. As someone whose passion focuses on nature, the environment, and sustainable living, this topic is paramount to my life and livelihood. Amusingly, I recall a book signing I did for *Stand Like Mountain* in 1997 where a man walked up to me, picked up a book, read the cover, and asked, "Is this a book about the environment?" I should have said yes. If ever presented with the opportunity again, I will. Because of the interconnectedness to life, all issues, all topics relate to the environment. The health of the human spirit is certainly included.

The theater was packed, and yet people continued to stream down the aisles looking for a seat. The movie in this theater was *An Inconvenient Truth*, a documentary featuring former vice president Al Gore. The movie and subsequent book of the same title[9] presented the very sobering, if not disturbing, reality of global warming. Several times applause broke out in the theater during the presentation. I overheard many conversations as people exited the theater. Comments were a mix of accolades for the film, and expressions of frustration with politicians, lobbyists, and, perhaps most of all, greedy, corrupt, corporate executives in the oil and automotive industries.

While there were many facts to absorb regarding the how, what, and who of global warming, I was reminded of the Chinese expression that within every problem lies opportunity. Here, Gore presented a colossal problem, and opportunity was right there, staring us in the face. To be honest, it's staring Americans in the face the most because we not only pollute the most of any country, but use the greatest percentage of the world's resources per capita. Sustainability is a foreign concept to most Americans.

Just as fear can immobilize people to a point of paralysis, used correctly, fear can also serve as a motivation to respond. Global warming is more than just a political issue, although fear-mongering politicians (on both sides of the political aisle) tend to dramatically overshadow this with other issues. Issues of stem cell research, gay marriage, flag burning, terrorism, and school prayer have become distractions from a much greater issue: our own survival as a species.

When this book was first published in 1997, all eyes were focused on the turn of the coming millennium. Having survived that rite of passage, people now have their calendars marked similarly for the year 2012, a point in time regarded by many as the year of end times as predicted by the Mayans, the ancient Egyptians, the Hopi Indians, and perhaps several more indigenous peoples. I have since learned there is even a name for this fascination, *eschatology*: the study of the end times, a rather bleak if not morbidly disturbing career path to pursue.

Time and time again, the question is asked: Are we at a critical turning point? The answer is an unequivocal *yes!* But the real question is, are we willing to step up and answer this call, or will we collectively roll back over and doze off once again? The only viable answer is to wake up, get up, and show up. Despite the fact that many people have, it is not in our best interest to adopt a "cosmic codependency" attitude in which we support the belief that someone (aliens?) or something (God) will come save us at the last minute from ourselves. This we must do ourselves. Remember, we can send intentions to God, the Universe, or All That Is, but we are part of God, the Universe, and All That Is. We must take responsibility, and this is the meaning of Gandhi's words: "Be the change you wish to see in the world." John F. Kennedy said it differently: "God's work must truly be our own."

Part of the spiritual hunger aspect also needs to be addressed here. What benefit do we get? Perhaps more important, are we blinded by our belief systems? Is it the ego? If a new truth were to emerge to dislodge your belief system, would you adapt or crumble?

As the countdown to the new millennium neared its end, I secretly and selfishly hoped that the computer debacle known as Y2K would kick in, so I could finally get caught up on all my reading, including several stacks of enticing books that were begging for attention. Over the past twenty years I have read and listened to the many whispers of changes forecasted for the fate of humanity. The Hopis, the Mayans, the Egyptians, and scores of mystics and wisdom keepers have foretold of a time of great change, the dawn of a new chapter in the history of humanity. Many people feel that we are in the time of great change. Change, it should be remembered, is often met with fear, yet fear will not assist us in this process. Humanity, like each individual she comprises, is also on a hero's journey. As one people we are now beginning to realize that we have collectively entered what Joseph Campbell calls the initiation stage. Sooner or later we must realize that we have to put aside our differences and come together as one people. A wisdom keeper himself, Campbell was once asked to share his insights on humanity's progress on the hero's journey. He confided that mythology suggests the road of trials will have many potholes. We must navigate them very carefully, he warned. But with a smile, added, all will turn out well in the end, because, he said, "I know how the story will end."

Waking Up and Getting Up

The collective soul of humanity has been dormant for centuries—unaware of the dynamic reality of our divine nature and the connection of all of life. At this time in the history, each one of us—regardless of where we are in our spiritual evolution—is being called to awaken from this dream state. Consider the waking habits of your own household. Rarely does everyone rise from bed at the exact moment. So it is with the collective soul, for it does not awaken at once. The soul of humanity regains awareness slowly, one by one, until conscious thought echoes around the globe. Each wake-up call beckons us to recognize our highest human potential and realize that we are all one.

To roll over, hoping to gain five more minutes of sleep, is no longer an option. The cosmic clock doesn't have a snooze alarm.

In earlier days, the survival instinct of competition was strong. Today, this consciousness is neither appropriate nor healthy. As Vaclav Havel suggested, cooperation, not competition, is the only way to evolve as a species. Systems and institutions built on the fear-based premise of competition are showing signs of crumbling and will continue to do so until a shift is made. Collaboration and cooperation must be coupled with compassion in action. Those who keep their finger on the human pulse note that the transition is already in progress.

Charles Tart, in his book *Waking Up*, provides an analogy to the awakening process. Imagine, he explains, that each person has a personal computer, yet one that runs slowly and with an extremely limited memory.

What we have forgotten, in our attachment to and dependence on our little computer, is that it will act as a terminal to connect with a giant supercomputer. This supercomputer runs far faster than our personal computer, has an enormous memory full of vital facts ordinarily unknown to us, and uses two very sophisticated and powerful languages for computing that solve all sorts of important problems that can't be adequately dealt with in Intellectual Basic, Emotional Basic, or Bodily/Instinctual Basic. These languages are Higher Emotional and Higher Intellectual.[10]

Waking up from a long night's sleep, we open our eyes to the awareness of a new day. Waking up spiritually is no different. How do you know when you have fully awakened? Here are some clues:

- You begin to see, honor, and fully appreciate the connection of all life.
- You use judgment solely for the purpose of guiding the soul, not to support the fear-based whims of the ego.

- You practice meditation to lift the veils of illusion, which then allows you to freely cross back and forth from your conscious and unconscious minds.
- You minimize fear-based perceptions in favor of love-based thoughts regarding the evolution of your self and your interactions with all others.
- You live a sustainable lifestyle to honor the planet and all living creatures.
- You see the ordinary as extraordinary and the supernatural as quite natural.

Waking up means taking responsibility for your own evolution. The call to awaken has been spoken by the shamans, sages, wisdom keepers, and healers all over the world. Can you hear them? In his book *Sacred Earth: The Spiritual Landscape of Native America*, Arthur Versluis wrote:

> *The hour for spiritual awakening is still possible. . . . The key to regenerating our world lies in realizing the spiritual reality of which our world is a reflection. Only when we open ourselves to the transcendent reality with which humanity has always lived, can we begin to change the approach to the world around us.* [11]

HARNESSING THE POWER OF LOVE

Imagine that you are sitting under a waterfall of warm golden light as energizing particles cascade over your head and face, covering your shoulders, arms, chest, and entire body. Each particle of light becomes absorbed through the skin and is invited into each cell of every body tissue. This image of golden light is an ageless metaphor illustrating the dynamic energy of love. It can be seen depicted in various

Christian paintings and frescoes of the European Renaissance, as well as in the pagodas dedicated to the Buddha. Various impressions of this image can be found in the ancient wisdom of all cultures.

We may picture love as a ray of golden light, but love is not solely an external force. Love is also an internal energy that resides deep within our hearts. Like the embers of a smoldering campfire, which burst into flames when breathed upon with our spirit, the golden embers of love are deep within us. The energy of love is never extinguished; it merely lies dormant, waiting to awaken.

The ancient Mayans believed they were the sons and daughters of the sun. Like the Mayans, all of us carry the golden glow of love. It has been described as:

- the light found within
- the fire in the belly
- the fire in the soul
- human bio-circuitry.

In Eastern religions it is known as the Kundalini—a source of mystical energy that resides in all people. Symbolically it is represented as:

- a golden staff of light that runs from the base of the spine to the crown of the head
- tongues of fire over the heads of saints
- a sign of divine enlightenment.

Contemporary sages and healers indicate that only a tiny fraction of today's population has ever accessed this power. In the vast majority it still lies dormant, shadowed by the illusion of fear. The hour for spiritual awakening, however, is still possible!

There is a version of the Greek story, Pandora's Box, that resonates deep within my soul. In this unique rendition, Pandora closes the box before love can radiate its brilliance—thus balancing all that went before it. By closing the lid before the beams of light could emerge, Pandora did more harm than good. Before we can harness the power of love, we must open our hearts and allow the light of love to emerge.

I have spoken with many individuals who have shared their gift of healing with me. What I have learned is that the power they use to heal—bio-energy, therapeutic touch, reiki, and so on—is the channeling of love. Each healer said that the source of energy is divine love. What's more, they say that everyone has the ability to harness this energy. It is not a gift for a chosen few; it is a birthright for everyone, a right we must exercise daily.

The evolution from homo sapiens to homo spiritus is an evolution of the soul, where the mystical fire burns brightly to harness the power of love. Will stress be left behind? If we are to survive in the coming years, we must move from a motivation of fear to a motivation of love in our thoughts and actions. By doing so we learn to grow through the stress, through the illusion of fear, toward a new and better reality. Societies built on a foundation of fear cause wars, violence, and apathy. This is the antithesis of conscious evolution. Our human potential is capable of so much more.

Love is the glue that holds the universe together. Love is the most formidable power, for with love all things are possible. To harness the power of love, you must first invite love into your heart and make its presence known. Once awakened, the power of love is limitless.

An ancient Chinese voice of wisdom said it best this way: [12]

> *If there is light in the soul*
> *There will be beauty in the person*
> *If there is beauty in the person*
> *There will be harmony in the house*

If there is harmony in the house
There will be order in the nation
If there is order in the nation
There will be peace in the world.

ALPENGLOW

*As far as we can discern, the sole
purpose of human existence is to kindle a light
in the darkness of mere being.*

—Carl Gustav Jung

When the first beams of sunlight hit the snow-covered mountains of Colorado each morning, the reflection of the sun's rays turns the white snow pink. This hue is called *alpenglow*, and it is a beautiful sight to behold. Between the tilt of Earth's axis, rotational ellipse, and various cloud formations, the morning view of the mountains never seems to look the same way twice. Indeed, the mountain is the metaphor. Like the sun's rays which shine on Earth's topography giving illumination, there is a lot of information in this book that necessitates processing and reflection. And like the shades of pink, salmon, magenta, peach, and rose that briefly appear on the mountaintops, most likely you will absorb and reflect only those rays of illumination that are most significant to you at this point on your journey.

Years ago, I received the book *The Road Less Traveled* as a gift from a very dear friend. I recall being quite moved upon reading it. A few years later, the same book was assigned as a text in one of my graduate courses in health psychology. At first I thought I would simply flip through the pages to refresh my memory, but I ended up reading the entire book cover to cover again, often wondering why I had left significant passages unscathed by my pen and highlighter on the first read. It didn't take long to realize how much I had grown in the three years since I had first finished Peck's work. It is my wish that this book merits a second and possibly a third round, because like me, you will find the experiences on the human journey change your level of consciousness. Perhaps most important, glancing once again through these pages will serve as a reminder to stay focused as you journey forward.

In 2005 I was invited to speak at a conference sponsored by the Institute of Noetic Sciences (IONS) held in our nation's capital. An organization formed more than thirty years ago by astronaut Edgar Mitchell to expand the knowledge of nature and potentials of the mind and spirit, IONS has become a think tank for higher consciousness regarding mind-body-spirit healing, exceptional abilities, altruism, and the emergence of new paradigms in science, spirituality, and society. Today a group with more than 50,000 members, it attracts people from all over the world who wish to dialogue about change and efforts for a peaceful transformation. At this particular conference, the series of presentations was remarkable, but more astonishing were the conversations that took place in the halls, parking lots, and bathrooms. It was not uncommon to hear the expression "transition and transformation" in nearly every conversation. At one point I heard someone eloquently say, "We are members of the transition team." If you are reading this book, no doubt you too are a member of this group as well. It is my intention that the thoughts, ideas, and reflections presented here stimulate conversation and dialogue, for this is how the seeds of conscious evolution take root. Revolutions begin with a whisper!

Lastly, this thought. In my first book, *Managing Stress*, Larry Dossey, M.D., began the foreword with the proverb, "After ecstasy, the laundry." These words of wisdom hold significant meaning as we approach the summit of the metaphorical mountain. At some point we have to descend the mountain (or as the case may be, return from the conference workshop) and carry on with life, in essence, do the laundry! Figuratively speaking, this proverb underscores the nature of responsibility, for, once we know the way, we are obligated to help others who yearn for a similar experience. Welcome to the team!

Since *Stand Like Mountain* first came out, I have been invited to give presentations across the country and around the world on the topic of stress and human spirituality. I close each presentation with this passage, a poem I wrote up in Jackson Hole, Wyoming, at the foot of the Grand Tetons. It has since become my signature ending to these talks. It seemed only fitting to close this book, once again, with these words that auspiciously found their way to my pad of paper that cloudy, rainy day:

Stand Like Mountain, Flow Like Water

To walk the human path is hard,
To stay put is not an option.
At times my head is filled with doubt,
I pause, uncertain and insecure,
Then I hear these words aloud,
Stand like mountain, flow like water.

I walk each step in search of truth,
My quest brings both joy and sorrow.
Light and dark dance unified,
Yes! Balance is the key to life,
Again I hear the words aloud,
Stand like mountain, flow like water.

We come to Earth to learn to love,
A lesson we all must master.
To know and serve the will of God,
Is not a task for a chosen few,
We must each answer the call to love,
Stand like mountain, flow like water.

—Brian Luke Seaward
©1996 Inspiration Unlimited

HEALING WATER
MEDITATION

INTRODUCTION

New scientific discoveries reveal that water has the ability to hold intention and memory. As such, it can be a powerful means to deliver healing intentions. This meditation is based on the premise of mindfulness of water's tremendous healing potential.

1. Begin this meditation by filling a cup or glass with fresh water. Place it by your side or in front of you, as you sit with your back straight. Sit quietly and clear your mind of any and all random thoughts and nagging chitchat, coming to a still place of peace.

2. Then, focus on your breathing to still both your mind and body. Take several (five) slow, deep breaths. Feel a deep sense of relaxation with each exhalation.

3. Now, slowly reach for the glass of water and hold the glass in both hands, so that your hands surround the water. Taking another slow, deep breath, pause for a moment to reflect on the source of water in your glass. Let your mind flow backward toward the original source from where this water came. Allow your mind to travel to the source, a mountain stream, a deep well, an underground aquifer, raindrops.

4. Slowly, shift your focus from the source of the water to the many purposes of water, the gift of life. Water is used to cleanse and purify. It is used to hydrate and bring balance to that which craves balance. Water is a nutrient and is used as a source of sustenance, allowing life to flourish. Water is a symbol of the divine, and it is used to anoint and bless the vibration of divine spirit into dense matter. Think of all these and any other uses for this precious gift.

5. Holding the glass in both hands, bring the glass to your face and look at the water, first the surface, and then deep into the water. At room temperature, water is liquid, yet water can take many forms in the continuum of matter. Just as the glass holds water, so too does the water become a container to hold things. Water also amplifies our thoughts, feelings, and intentions.

6. In this meditation, allow the water in your hands to hold a special intention from your heart. Bring to your heart and mind a thought, prayer, or intention that surfaces regularly to your consciousness. Then allow this healing intention (personal or global) to float on the surface of the water and then slowly dissolve into the water, like a drop of blue coloring, so that soon the entire glass of water holds this intention in every molecule.

7. Still holding the glass in both hands, bring the glass to your lips and slowly sip from the edge, taking some of this water into your body. As you do this, feel the water move over your tongue, through your mouth, and gently pass down your throat. Although you cannot see it, use your mind's eye to follow these drops of water into the heart of every cell in your body, replenishing the fluid that bathes your DNA.

8. When you are through with the mindfulness of this experience, slowly get up and walk outside and pour half of the remaining

glass of water on the earthen soil, and as you do this, once again repeat the intention of your heart. Finally, place the glass of water in the sun to evaporate so that your healing intention may be carried by the four winds to be made manifest for the highest good of all concerned.

APPENDIX 2

ADDITIONAL READING

I am often asked by readers and workshop participants to recommend books that I have enjoyed. Since *Stand Like Mountain* was first published in 1997, a new wave of books has arrived on the scene that further explore many aspects on the topic of stress and spirituality. The following books are new favorites that I wholeheartedly recommend.

Adam, *The Path of the Dream Healer*. Viking Books, Toronto, Canada, 2006.

Arntz, W., et al., *What the Bleep Do We Know!?*. Health Communications Inc., Deerfield Beach, FL, 2005.

Dyer, W., *The Power of Intention*. Hay House, Carlsbad, CA, 2004.

Lipton, B., *The Biology of Belief*. Mountain of Love/Elite Books, Santa Rosa, CA, 2005.

Luskin, F., *Forgive for Good*. HarperCollins Publishers, NY, 2000.

Luskin, F., and Pelletier, K., *Stress Free for Good*. HarperCollins Publishers, NY, 2005.

McTaggart, L., *The Field*. HarperSanFrancisco, 2002.

Narby, J., *The Cosmic Serpent*. Tarcher Books, NY, 1999.

Radin, D., *Entangled Minds*. Paraview Pocket Books, NY, 2006.

Roman, S., *Soul Love*. H.J. Krammer, Tiburon, CA, 1997.

Schmidt, L. E., *Restless Souls*. HarperSanFrancisco, 2005.

Schwartz, G., *The G.O.D. Experiments*. Atria Books, NY, 2006.

Seaward, B. L., *Quiet Mind, Fearless Heart: The Taoist Path of Stress and Spirituality*. Wiley & Sons, NJ, 2005.

Seaward, B. L., *Achieving the Mind-Body-Spirit Connection*. Jones and Bartlett, Sudbury, MA 2005.

APPENDIX 3

STUDY-GUIDE QUESTIONS

Dear Readers,

Soon after *Stand Like Mountain* was first released in 1997, I learned that many church groups (of nearly all denominations), support groups, and community book clubs had chosen this book as one of their prime selections. A few colleges even selected *Stand Like Mountain* as a personal health text. Recently, I learned that many life coaches now recommend this book to their clients. In essence, the book developed a life of its own. Over the years, I have been approached through e-mails, letters, and directly by workshop participants to come up with a list of open-ended questions that might further the discussion of various topics highlighted in various chapters. I have found that adult learners tend to best augment their knowledge base by processing information verbally. For this reason, I encourage these types of study groups. Secondly, I think when groups come together, a synergy forms to balance the negative fear-based thinking so prevalent in the world today. With this in mind, as I went through this edition, I drafted several questions that I thought might be of interest for group discussion to further personal growth (and possibly world peace). Please feel free to use or adapt these questions in any way that may further your understanding of the relationship between stress and spirituality and the unique alchemy of humanity and divinity.

CHAPTER ONE:
STRESS WITH A HUMAN FACE

1. What is your definition of stress and what do you consider to be the primary cause (external sources) of stress in people's lives today?

2. In general do you feel there is more stress today than ten years ago? If so, what accounts for this? What are some practical means to "change the culture" even if it's a culture of one, as in *Tuesdays with Morrie*?

3. Of the four styles of mismanaged anger, which do you think is the most common in the United States? Why? (Which of these do you see as your most predominant mismanaged anger style?)

4. The association between stress and disease is huge! What is your understanding of this connection? Explain your interpretation of the concept of the human energy field and the stress and disease connection.

5. Describe the term "consensual hallucination" in your words. Why do you suppose people "give their power away" to physicians, movie stars, politicians, sports heroes, and so on?

6. List five ways you can build an immunity to stress. What steps can you take to incorporate these into your life?

CHAPTER TWO:
SPIRITS ON A HUMAN PATH

1. How would you best define the concept of human spirituality? In your opinion, what commonalities do religion and human spirituality share? How do they differ?

2. Pull out a piece of paper and write down your top ten stressors. Then next to each one place a check mark if they fall in the category of relationships, values or value conflicts, or a meaningful purpose in life. Some people say that stress and human spirituality are diametrically

opposed, but do you see a connection between stress and human spirituality here?

3. Take a moment to share with people in your group a time when the cosmic curtain was pulled back to reveal the divine mystery in your life (e.g., synchronistic moment, epiphany, angels).

4. Select a classic or contemporary story (fiction or nonfiction) and highlight the stages of Joseph Campbell's hero's journey. Where are you on your hero's journey?

5. According to M. Scott Peck (author of *The Road Less Traveled*) there are four stages of the spiritual path. Which stage do you think most Americans are in and why? What stage would you describe yourself being in at this time?

6. If you were to overlap the stages of the hero's journey with Peck's stages of spiritual growth (and the seasons of the soul in Chapter 4), you might notice some similarities. What comes to mind when you look at these more closely?

7. Let's assume that unresolved anger and fear are the two biggest road-blocks on the spiritual path. Do you recognize these behaviors in your life? How do you best work to resolve them so you can move on with your life? Distractions first begin as attractions. Our world is filled with distractions. Please share your thoughts on this aspect of the spiritual journey as well.

8. Have you encountered a divine paradox while traveling the spiritual path? Which of these four can you best relate to? Is there an additional divine paradox you wish to share?

CHAPTER THREE:
THE DANCE OF EGO AND SOUL

1. The ego is often described as the bad guy, but we need the ego as protection. Can you list four reasons why this is so?

2. The term, "domesticate the ego" is said to have come from the Eastern culture. What are some ways or suggestions to start this process?

3. Speculate on the connection between ego and our DNA.

4. Before reading this book, how would you have described the relationship between stress and human spirituality, more specifically the ego and the soul? Have the insights and stories in this book changed your perspective? If so, how?

5. The concept of soul work is one of the most profound aspects of human spirituality, and very unique to each individual. How can the ego help us accomplish our soul work? How can we nurture the soul work of others, including our children?

6. To respond rather than react is no small order. What are some ways to shift to this mind-set to make this become a healthy habit?

CHAPTER FOUR:
SEASONS OF THE SOUL

1. Describe the four seasons of the soul in your own words.

2. What season are you in the midst of right now?

3. The emptying process is thought to be the most difficult season of the soul. Why is this? How does getting stuck in this season manifest in signs and symptoms of everyday life? What are some ways to move through this process so you don't get stuck in it?

4. What season of the soul would you guess that America, as a whole, is in at this time? What season of the soul would you guess that the world/humanity is in at this time?

5. Share one of your favorite synchronistic moments or a time when you wanted to yell, Eureka!

CHAPTER FIVE:
THE SEEDS OF CHANGE

1. The phrase "muscles of the soul" is used to describe those inherent inner resources that are employed to overcome the issues, concerns, problems, stressors, and crises we encounter on a regular basis. What do you feel are your strongest muscles?

2. Of the four stories featured—Taylor (faith), Judith (compassion), Barbara (humor), and Slavomir (willpower)—which of these seeds was planted in the fertile soil of your mind and heart? Which of these stories could you most relate to and why?

3. In your opinion, what factors are associated with a decrease in spiritual fitness of these muscles?

CHAPTER SIX:
WORDS OF MERCY, WORDS OF GRACE

1. What does prayer mean to you?

2. Do you pray now in the same way or fashion that you prayed as a child? Why or why not?

3. What roles does your unconscious mind play in the detachment of your prayers?

4. Share your thoughts on this popular phrase: "When we pray, we talk to God. When we meditate, God talks to us."

5. Discuss the implications of the concept that all thoughts are prayer.

6. If indeed all thought is prayer, what are the implications of group thought on the various aspects of life, from politics to terrorism to global warming?

7. If indeed all thought is prayer, what effect does mass media (primarily television) have on group thought? Because fear sells (as illustrated in

the movie *Bowling for Columbine*), does the fear that is perpetuated by the media skew the efforts of higher consciousness? How?

CHAPTER SEVEN:
HEALTH OF THE HUMAN SPIRIT

1. There are many ways to promote the health of the human spirit. Of those described in the book, which do you most resonate with? Are there any additional means that you use to enhance the health of your human spirit?

2. Rituals are important, but over time they can become shallow. What are some ways you keep your rituals vibrant? Do we as a nation have any sacred rituals that haven't evolved with the times and perhaps have lost their shine?

3. Can you list five ways in which you can harness the power of love and compassion?

CHAPTER EIGHT:
A SPIRITUAL RENAISSANCE

1. If you have read this book, it's a fair guess that you have entered the spiritual quadrant of your life (regardless of your age). How would you describe your experience in this quadrant of the wellness paradigm? Which of the four quadrants do you see the majority of Americans (the entire global village) in at this time?

2. There is certainly a Chicken-Little phenomenon going on in the world today, from a great many directions, yet fear is not the answer. At what point does this become a self-fulfilling prophecy?

3. What have been your most significant spiritual wake-up calls?

4. There are many quotes to be found in this book from an eclectic collection of sages and wisdom keepers. Do you have a favorite, and if so, how does it speak to your heart?

5. Neither spiritual growth nor enlightenment is a contest, but can you begin to describe your waking-up process?

6. Waking up is one thing, getting out of bed is another. The expression "Wake up, get up, and show up" is a common theme in this book. Please speak to the nature of these three aspects individually and collectively (as your group and a part of humanity).

7. How attached or invested are you to your belief system? Why? If a new truth were to emerge to dislodge your belief system, would you adapt or crumble? Share your impressions of the expression: Don't believe everything you think! What is your reaction to this quote from renowned philosopher Buckminster Fuller: "God is not a noun, but a verb"?

8. BONUS QUESTION: What is THE most significant concept you received from this book?*
   (As the author, I would love to know the answer to this question. If you wish, please e-mail your answer to brianlukes@cs.com. Thanks!)

---

*If you liked this book and found it to be helpful, you may also like the sequel to this book, *Quiet Mind, Fearless Heart*, by the same author.

APPENDIX 4

ABOUT THE
STAND LIKE MOUNTAIN,
FLOW LIKE WATER CD AND
EVERSOUND MUSIC

F ew books have a soundtrack, but I am happy to announce that the tenth-anniversary edition of *Stand Like Mountain* indeed, has a phenomenal musical score that will raise you up above the clouds and keep a smile on your face the entire time, if not longer. As a follow-up to the success of Eversound's *One Quiet Night,* a CD that I was invited to compile in 2004, this *Stand Like Mountain* CD of instrumental selections surpasses the musical excellence of *One Quiet Night* and will become a perennial favorite in your CD collection. Selections of piano, guitar, cello, and a host of sublime orchestration are featured in eighteen compositions by John Adorney, Manuel Iman, Lino, John Mills, and many others. Additionally, this CD contains one of my favorite songs from the talented composer Jim Wilson from his bestselling CD, *Northern Seascape.* The *Stand Like Mountain* compilation also includes an original adaptation of *Amazing Grace,* performed by my good friend and colleague, Zach Bergen, and an acoustic version of Greg Tamblyn's hit song, *Stand Like Mountain, Move Like Water,* sung by Eversound artist Danny Ellis. In a day and age where good music is hard to find, look no further. It has been said that when you listen to great music, you eavesdrop on the thoughts of God. I think it is no exaggeration to say that when you listen to this CD, you will be eavesdropping on the divine. Selections of all songs from the *Stand Like Mountain* CD are available for your listening pleasure online at *www.eversound.com* and may be purchased there or at your favorite music store.

Notes

CHAPTER ONE:
STRESS WITH A HUMAN FACE

1. C. G. Jung, *Modern Man in Search of a Soul* (New York: Harcourt Brace Jovanovich, 1933).

2. H. Selye, *The Stress of Life* (New York: McGraw Hill, 1976).

3. R. Lazarus and S. Folkman, *Stress, Appraisal, and Coping* (New York: Springer, 1984).

4. M. Angelou, *Wouldn't Take Nothing for My Journey Now* (New York: Bantam Books, 1993) 33–34.

5. B. L. Seaward, *Managing Stress: Principles and Strategies for Health and Wellbeing 5E*, (Boston: Jones and Bartlett Publishers, 2006). In 1994, I published a textbook on the topic of stress management where the topic of anger and fear is described in great depth.

6. H. Lerner, *The Dance of Anger* (New York: Harper & Row, 1985). This critically acclaimed book is a wonderful reference about the issues women deal with regarding anger.

7. S. Greer and T. Morrit, "Psychological Attributes of Women Who Develop Breast Cancer: A Controlled Study," *Journal of Psychosomatic Research* 19 (1990): 147–153.

8. M. Freidman and D. Ulmer, *Type A Behavior and Your Heart* (New York: Knopf, 1984). There have been many studies and subsequent publications on Type A behavior. This is one of the classic resources on this topic.

9. N. Warner, *Make Anger Your Ally* (Colorado Springs, CO: Focus on the Family, 1990).

10. K. Casey and M. Vanceburg, *The Promise of a New Day* (New York: HarperCollins Publishers, Hazelden Meditations, 1983). Kenny's quote is the opening quote for the entry on February 8.

11. Ibid. Indira Gandhi's quote is the opening quote for the entry on August 5.

12. This quote came from Roger von Oech, *A Whack on the Side of the Head* (New York: Warner Books, 1983). This and his second book, *A Kick in the Seat of the Pants*, are excellent resources for creativity.

13. G. Jampolsky, *Love Is Letting Go of Fear* (Berkeley, CA: Celestial Arts Press, 1979).

14. I was on a Mind-Body Healing panel with Candace Pert at the 1996 National Wellness Conference in Stevens Point, Wisconsin, July 16, 1996, where she addressed the issue of emotions as the interface between the mind and body. This quote can also be found in the journal *Alternative Therapies* 1.3 (1995): 70–76.

15. R. Ader, *Psychoneuroimmunology*, 2nd ed. (San Diego, CA: Academic Press, 1990). The story of how the field of psychoneuroimmunology began is well-documented in the book *The Heart of Healing*, a Turner Book, compiled by the Institute of Noetic Sciences, 1993.

16. R. Gerber, *Vibrational Medicine* (Santa Fe, NM: Bear & Company, 1988). After reading his book, I was able to converse by phone with Dr. Gerber and learn a bit more about his insights on the human energy field, as well as his view of why all this is coming into the consciousness at this time.

17. B. O'Regan, "Healings, Remission, and Miracle Cures," *Noetic Science Collection* (Sausalito, CA: Institute of Noetic Sciences, 1991).

18. Adam, "The Path of the Dream Healer." The Prophet's Conference. Boulder, CO, May 21, 2006.

19. Lipton, B., *The Biology of Belief* (Santa Rosa, CA: Mountain of Love/Elite Books, 2005).

CHAPTER TWO:
SPIRITS ON A HUMAN PATH

1. A. Huxley, *The Perennial Philosophy* (New York: Perennial Library, 1944).

2. I heard Thomas Moore interviewed on New Dimensions Radio and it was here where he explained his views about psychology and spirituality.

3. World Health Organization, Geneva, Switzerland, 1992.

4. B. L. Seaward, *Managing Stress: Principles and Strategies for Health and Wellbeing 5E* (Boston, MA: Jones and Bartlett Publishers, 2006). What makes this book unique in its approach to stress management is its holistic approach and the inclusion of the spiritual dimension of health, where Chapter 7— "Stress and Human Spirituality"—is devoted to this whole topic and actually inspired the writing of this book.

5. M. Angelou, *Wouldn't Take Nothing for My Journey Now* (New York: Bantam Books, 1993) 33–34.

6. M. Fox, "What Is Medicine for the Soul?" (paper presented at the Body & Soul Conference sponsored by the *New Age Journal,* Boston, September 30-October 2, 1994). Actually, I have heard Matt speak on several occasions when he has made constant reference to a post-denominational age, partially influenced by his own encounters with the Catholic Church.

7. In the Eastern philosophy, it is suggested that we return to Earth to

learn the lessons of humanity. Each incarnation is a chance to know our divinity in human form through a host of experiences. There are many sources that describe this philosophy, including: J. Fisher, *The Case for Reincarnation* (New York: Carol Publishing Group, 1984).

8. K. Gibran, *The Prophet* (New York: Alfred A. Knopf, 1923, reprinted in 1981).

9. C. Castenada, *The Teachings of Don Juan: A Yaqui Way of Knowledge* (New York: Pocket Books, 1968).

10. K. Casey and M. Vanceburg, *The Promise of a New Day* (New York: HarperCollins Publishers, Hazelden Meditations, 1983), 188–200.

11. M. S. Peck, *The Different Drum* (New York: Simon & Schuster, 1987).

12. "CIRCLE" ©1972 THE CHAPIN FOUNDATION. Used by permission.

13. There has been much speculation that the phenomenon known as Attention Deficit Disorder is highly correlated to excessive television watching. Over the years, advertisements have gone from 60-second spots to as short as 15 seconds. This, coupled with the proliferation of channels and remote control viewing, has only added to the shortened attention span. More information can be found in this topic in T. Armstrong, *The Myth of ADD* (New York: Dutton Books, 1995).

14. This quote, which is often attributed to Nelson Mandela from his inauguration speech, is actually by Marianne Williamson.

Chapter Three: The Dance of Ego and Soul

1. C. Hall, *A Primer of Freudian Psychology* (New York: New American Library, 1954). The synthesis of information about Freud in this section comes not only from Hall's work but that of Duane Schultz (*Theories of Personality*, Pacific Grove, CA: Brooks/Cole, 1990) and Ken Wilber (*Sex, Ecology, Spirituality*, Boston, MA: Shambhala, 1995).

2. C. Jung, *Man and His Symbols* (New York: Anchor Press, 1964). There are

many sources of Jung's material to read from. Much of his own work is often difficult to understand. Jung once said, "I am glad I am Jung and not a Jungian." In a near-death experience Jung writes about in his autobiography, *Memories, Dreams, Reflections*, he was told that he needed to make his information more understandable to the lay public. *Man and His Symbols* is his successful attempt to do so.

3. Ibid.

4. C. S. Lewis, *The Screwtape Letters*, rev. ed. (New York: Collier Books, 1961) 20.

5. I came across this marvelous quote in Carlson and Shield, ed., *Handbook for the Soul* (New York: Little, Brown and Company, 1995) 85.

6. I first heard Brian Weiss use this quote at a presentation made at the Body and Soul Conference (Boston, September 30–October 2, 1994). He has since used it in his book *Only Love Is Real* (New York: Warner Books, 1996).

7. C. Hall, The synthesis of information about Freud in this section comes not only from Hall's work but also from Duane Schultz.

8. K. Wilber, *Sex, Ecology, Spirituality*. (Boston, MA: Shambhala Books, 1995) 226–230.

9. V. Froelicher, *Exercise and the Heart: Clinical Concepts* (Chicago, Year Book Publishers, Inc., 1983). The information cited here can also be found in any standard exercise physiology textbook regarding cardiovascular effects of anaerobic and aerobic work.

10. Dean Ornish, M.D., made a keynote presentation titled "Opening Your Heart, Anatomically and Spiritually" at the 1993 Institute of Noetic Sciences Conference, Alexandria, VA. (June 22–27) 1993. It was here he explained learning about meditation in India and the aspects of subtle anatomy and the chakras.

11. M. Fox., "What Is Medicine for the Soul?" Body and Soul Conference

sponsored by the *New Age Journal* (Boston, September 30–October 2, 1994). I have also heard Matt share this philosophy in a presentation he made in Boulder at the Fairview High School in November of 1993, and again at the Voices of the Earth Conference held in Boulder, July 1994.

12. G. Zukav, *The Seat of the Soul* (New York: Fireside Books, 1992). Zukav's work is an excellent summation of the nature of the soul and his vision of how soul work is necessary to evolve the human species.

13. As quoted in an essay written by Levine in Carlson and Shield, ed., *Handbook for the Soul* (New York: Little Brown and Company, 1996) 50.

14. I first heard Jean Houston use the term *entelechy* at a workshop she conducted several years ago. Reference to this term can also be found in her book *The Search for the Beloved* (Los Angeles: Tarcher, 1987) 31–32.

15. As quoted in an essay written by Carlson and Shield, ed., *Handbook for the Soul* (New York: Little, Brown and Company, 1996) 64.

16. J. Fisher, *The Case for Reincarnation* (New York: Carol Publishing Group, 1984) 8.

17. K. Wilber, 227–228.

CHAPTER FOUR:
SEASONS OF THE SOUL

1. "Turn! Turn! Turn! (To Everything There Is a Season)." Words from the Book of Ecclesiastes. Adaptation and Music by Pete Seeger. TRO ©1962 (Renewed) Melody Trails, Inc., New York, NY. Used by permission.

2. This interpretation comes from Diane Dreher's book *The Tao of Inner Peace* (New York: Harper Perennial, 1991) TAO 16. Diane has masterfully synthesized the Taoist philosophy into everyday use.

3. Paramahansa Yogananda has written extensively on a great many spiritual topics. This quote comes from the 1995 engagement calendar published by the Self-Realization Fellowship, an organization founded by Yogananda to teach Kriya Yoga and self-realization.

4. J. Krishnamurti, *On God* (San Francisco: HarperSanFrancisco, 1992) 31.

5. Herbert Benson has done a lot of research on the topic of meditation and relaxation. He Americanized TM and called it *The Relaxation Response*, which contains the significant findings and application of his research. His most recent book, *Timeless Healing*, expands on the concept of *The Relaxation Response* (New York: Scribner Books, 1996).

6. J. Krishnamurti, 85.

7. I have heard this story countless times from numerous people, including Ram Dass, Roger von Oech, and Jim Gordon. Von Oech described this story in his book *A Whack on the Side of the Head*.

8. K. Casey and M. Vanceburg, *The Promise of a New Day* (New York: HarperCollins Publishers, Hazelden Meditations, 1983). Jung's quote appears on the date of September 29 as the opening quote for this day's meditation.

9. K. Gibran, *The Prophet* (New York: Alfred A. Knopf, 1923, reprinted in 1981), 32–33.

10. Peck made this comment at a seminar he gave titled "Journeys Along the Road Less Traveled" (Life Cycle Learning Workshop, Alexandria, VA, December 2, 1989).

11. I have heard this story several times from various sources. It is most accurately described in *The Parabola Book of Healing* (New York: Spiritus Contra Spiritum Continuum, 1994) 128–133.

12. C. Grof, *Thirst for Wholeness* (San Francisco: HarperSanFrancisco, 1993).

13. Gibran, 62–63.

14. Studies on journal writing can be found in James Pennebaker's book *Opening Up: The Healing Power of Confiding in Others* (New York: William Morrow and Company, 1990).

15. This Native American prayer, "All Winter Long," (public domain) is reprinted from E. Roberts and E. Amidon, eds., *Earth Prayers* (New York: HarperCollins, 1991) 327.

16. I first heard Lily Tomlin use this line in a live performance at the University of Maine, Orono, in 1977, during one of her monologues. It has since been cited as her creation in several sources, primarily books on humor and prayer.

17. This story has been passed down through the ages through many a chemistry class (which is where I first heard it). Jung describes it as well in *Man and His Symbols* (New Orleans: Anchor Press, 1964), 38.

18. Roger Sperry first wrote about his research in "The Great Cerebral Commissure," *Scientific American* (1964) 44–52. He also published *The Reach of the Mind* (San Francisco: Saybrook Publishing Company, 1989). Several other colleagues have written extensively about the cognitive functions of the brain, including Naranjo and Ornstein, *On the Psychology of Meditation* (New York: Penguin Books, 1991) and Ornstein's book, *The Psychology of Consciousness* (New York: Penguin Books, 1972).

19. As a consultant to Ancilla Health Systems, I have had the good fortune to meet and work with Dr. Deepak Chopra. In both his seminars and casual conversations he uses the expression "infinite possibilities" quite extensively to describe the nature of the void and its relationship to divine consciousness.

20. J. Cameron, *The Artist's Way* (Los Angeles: Tarcher Books, 1992) 2.

21. J. S. Bolen, *The Tao of Psychology* (New York: Harper & Row, 1979) 14–15.

22. Ibid, 7.

23. S. Burnham states this throughout her book *A Book of Angels*. Living in Washington, D.C., I was fortunate to be invited to a dinner party where Sophy was also a guest, and she also shared these thoughts with those present.

24. There are many versions of Chief Seattle's reply to then-President Franklin Pierce. I have taken this text from a version read by Joseph Campbell on his taped series *The World of Joseph Campbell*, vol. 1, "The Power of Myth" (St. Paul, MN: High Bridge Productions), 1990.

25. This interpretation also comes from Diane Dreher's book *The Tao of Inner Peace* (New York: Harper Perennial, 1991), TAO 22.

26. Michael Talbot's book *The Holographic Universe* (New York: HarperCollins, 1992) is the source of this information. It is one of the most well synthesized and comprehensive books I have ever read on this topic. In a conversation I had with Marilyn Ferguson, she mentioned that there were additional aspects that Michael wanted to include in the book, but the publisher thought they were too far out.

27. I learned that Einstein and Jung conversed over lunch through a book in the Time-Life series titled *Mysteries of the Unknown*.

28. D. Chopra, *The Seven Spiritual Laws of Success* (San Rafael, CA: Amber-Allen Publishing), 1994.

29. A quote taken from M. Ferguson *The Aquarian Conspiracy* (Los Angeles: Tarcher Books, 1980).

30. V. Frankl, *Man's Search for Meaning* (New York: Pocket Books, 1963) 122.

CHAPTER SIX:
WORDS OF MERCY, WORDS OF GRACE

1. R. Byrd, "Positive Therapeutic Effects of Intercessory Prayer in a Coronary Care Unit Population," *Southern Medical Journal*, 81.7 (1988): 826–829.

2. L. Dossey, *Healing Words* (San Francisco: HarperSanFrancisco, 1993).

3. I came to this conclusion after exposure to several research findings presented at the Third Annual Conference of the Institute of Noetic Sciences, Chicago, IL, July 1994, where guest lecturers Charles Tart, Stan Groff, and others recounted their research explorations of human consciousness over the past thirty years. Tart, Groff, and Ram Dass, as well as others, have written several books that highlight their research efforts.

4. Charles Tart made this remark in his keynote address at both the annual conference for ISSSEEM in Boulder, June 1994, and at the IONS conference in Chicago, July 1994.

5. S. Groff, *Beyond the Brain* (Albany, NY: State University of New York Press, 1981).

6. K. Casey and M. Vanceburg, *The Promise of a New Day* (New York: HarperCollins Publishers, Hazelden Meditations, 1983). Bateson's quote is the opening entry on June 27.

7. Elmer and Alyce Green started ISSSEEM as a bridge between the mechanistic paradigm of science and the holistic art of energy healing. They host an annual conference each summer in Boulder, CO. ISSSEEM is located at 356 Goldco Circle, Golden, CO 80403, (303) 278-2228.

8. N. Shealy and C. Myss, *The Creation of Health* (Walpole, NH: Stillpoint Press, 1990).

9. R. Gerber, *Vibrational Medicine* (Santa Fe, NM: Bear and Company, 1988), 313–316.

10. In Mietek and Margaret's advanced class and subsequent workshops, they teach their students this technique; it was here they shared this story.

11. I learned of this through Larry Dossey; he also writes about it in his book *Healing Words* (San Francisco: HarperSanFrancisco, 1993), 120–121.

12. M. von Trapp, *The Trapp Family Singers* (New York: Doubleday, 1949). Maria von Trapp was a remarkable woman. The musical *The Sound of Music* is based on the first few chapters of this book. Life was no bed of roses for Maria and her family after they escaped the Nazis. A woman of great faith, Maria recounts many times throughout her autobiography how prayer was used as a means to cope with stress.

13. I learned of this story from my good friend Skylar Sherman, who befriended Burk Vaughn in Australia through his work with the Moral Re-Armament Program. Through my encounters with several people who have come to understand the culture of the Australian aborigines, I have come to learn that Vaughn's story is not unique. Author Marlo Morgan also recounts similar stories in her book *Mutant Message Down Under*.

14. L. Dossey, *Healing Words* (San Francisco: HarperSanFrancisco, 1993).

15. J. Borysenko, *Guilt Is the Teacher, Love Is the Lesson* (New York: Warner Books, 1990).

16. W. Dyer, *The Power of Intention*. (Carlsbad, CA: Hay House. 2004.)

17. B. Eadie, *Embraced by the Light* (Placerville, CA: Goldleaf Press, 1992), 103.

18. S. Burnham, *A Book of Angels* (New York: Ballantine Books, 1990), 223–226.

19. Joan Borysenko shares this story frequently in her seminars. I first heard it in Washington D.C., October 25–26, 1991.

20. E. Roberts and E. Amidon, eds., *Earth Prayers* (New York: HarperCollins, 1991), 211.

21. This Native American prayer (public domain) is reprinted in Earth Prayers.

CHAPTER SEVEN:
HEALTH OF THE HUMAN SPIRIT

1. C. Myss, *Anatomy of Spirit* (New York: Harmony Books, 1996) was first in a series of taped lectures that Caroline created for Sounds True Recording Company. I had the opportunity to sit in on two of these lectures and converse with her about her views on the art of self-renewal.

2. L. Buscaglia, *Love* (New York: Fawcett Books, 1972).

3. Stephan Rechtschaffen made a keynote address at the 1996 Noetic Science conference in Boca Raton, Florida, where he talked about the concept of time shifting. His book, *Timeshifting*, is published by Doubleday, New York, 1996.

4. B. L. Seaward, *Managing Stress: Principles and Strategies for Health and Wellbeing 5E* (Boston: Jones and Bartlett Publishers, 2006). The topic of self-esteem, which I synthesized from a great many works, including that of Nathaniel Branden and Harris Clemes, is described in great depth in Chapter 6.

5. I first heard this quote by Joseph Campbell cited by Larry Dossey in a keynote address of the second annual conference of the Institute of Noetic Sciences, Washington, D.C., June 1993.

6. A great source of information on the topic of forgiveness is the book *Forgiveness* by Sidney Simon and his wife, Suzanne (New York: Warner Books, 1990).

7. I found this quote in the article "The Sacred Path of Intimate Relationships," *Lotus Journal*, (Spring, 1996): 37.

8. D. Milman, *The Laws of Spirit* (Tiburon, CA: H.J. Kramer, 1996), 42.

9. Deepak Chopra shared these thoughts with me during a visit to South Bend, IN, where we were both doing some consulting work to open the Healing Arts Center of Ancilla Systems.

10. R. Ornstein and D. Sobel, *Healthy Pleasures* (Reading, MA: Addison-Wesley, 1989).

11. M. Seligman, *Learned Optimism* (New York: Pocket Books, 1990), 2.

12. J. Cameron, *The Artist's Way* (Los Angeles: Tarcher Books, 1992).

13. P. Long, "Laugh and Be Well," *Psychology Today 21* (1987): 28–29.

14. H. Selye, *Stress Without Distress* (New York: Lippincott, 1974).

15. D. Milman, *The Way of the Peaceful Warrior* (Tiburon, CA: H.J. Kramer, Inc., 1984).

16. R. Fitgergald. *The Hundred-Year Lie.* (New York: Dutton, 2006).

17. This story is recounted by Joseph Telushkin in his book *Words That Hurt, Words That Heal* (New York: William Morrow & Co., 1996), 155.

18. R. Dass and M. Bush, *Compassion in Action* (New York: Bell Tower, 1992), 5.

19. H. H. Dalai Lama, *Beyond Dogma* (Berkeley, CA: North Atlantic Books, 1989), 59–60.

CHAPTER EIGHT:
A SPIRITUAL RENAISSANCE

1. M. Ferguson, *The Aquarian Conspiracy* (Los Angeles: Tarcher Books, 1980), 48.

2. This comment was in response to a letter written to Einstein by a rabbi who himself was seeking words to comfort his daughter on the death of her sister. I came across this passage in Jon Kabat-Zinn's book *Full Catastrophe Living* and again in Larry Dossey's book *Recovering the Soul*.

3. The *New Age Journal* reprinted Havel's speech. It can be found in the October 1994 issue, pp. 45–48, 161–162.

4. I first heard of the expression "le cirque fin" from South African rock singer Johnny Clegg, on tour in the United States during a performance

in Vermont. The expression, I am told, dates back to the end of the first millennium. Clegg shared this wisdom as a polite warning that we are responsible for our destiny and must take appropriate action now.

5. M. Ferguson, 19.

6. Terence McKenna made these comments about his concept of the novelty theory during a lecture presentation in Boulder, CO on May 3, 1996.

7. R. Abraham, *Trialogues at the Edge of the West* (Santa Fe, NM: Bear and Company, 1991).

8. M. Ferguson, 29.

9. Gore, A. *An Inconvenient Truth*. Emmaus, PA: Rodale Press. 2006.

10. C. Tart, *Waking Up* (Boston: Shambhala Publications, 1986), 217–218.

11. A. Versluis, *Sacred Earth: The Spiritual Landscape of Native America*, (Rochester, VT: Inner Traditions & Bear Company, 1992).

12. J. Canfield and M.V. Hansen, *Chicken Soup for the Soul* (Deerfield Beach, FL: Health Communications, Inc. 1993).

Organizations of Interest

Institute of Noetic Sciences (IONS): Founded by astronaut Edgar Mitchell, IONS has become a think tank for higher consciousness uniting the realms of science and spirituality. IONS sponsors an annual conference with themes that range from mind-body healing and death and dying, to altruistic service and the ecology. Based in Petaluma, California, this organization hosts many regional conferences and community study groups on a host of topics. Call 707.779.8238. *www.noetic.org.* They also now have an interactive website: *www.shiftinaction.com.*

International Society for the Study of Subtle Energy and Energy Medicine (ISSSEEM): Founded by Elmer and Alyce Green in 1989, ISSSEEM is a group of healthcare professionals, scientists, physicists, physicians, and healers dedicated to understanding the dynamics of energy medicine ranging from Qi Gong and polarity therapy, to acupuncture and bio-energy healing. They hold an annual conference each summer in Boulder, Colorado. Call 303.425.4625. Or see their website: *www.issseem.org.*

National Wellness Institute: This organization was founded thirty years ago with the mission to expand the meaning of health beyond the standing definition of "the absence of disease." Dedicated to sharing information about all aspects of mind-body-spirit and emotions, its members include health educators, psychologists, physicians, nurses, teachers, college students, and healers. They hold a weeklong conference on the campus of the University of Wisconsin at Stevens Point every week in July. Call 800.243.8694. They can also be reached via their website: *www.nationalwellness.org.*

Index

About the Author

Brian Luke Seaward, Ph.D., is considered a pioneer in the field of health psychology, and he is internationally recognized for his contributions in the area of holistic stress management, human spirituality, and mind-body-spirit healing. The wisdom of Dr. Seaward can be found quoted in PBS specials, national magazines, medical seminars, boardroom meetings, church sermons, and college graduation speeches all over the world. It's been said several times that Brian Luke Seaward looks like James Taylor, dresses like Indiana Jones, and writes like Mark Twain. He is the author of several popular books, including *Stressed Is Desserts Spelled Backward, The Art of Calm, Health of the Human Spirit, Hot Stones & Funny Bones,* and *Quiet Mind, Fearless Heart.* His relaxation CDs include, *A Change of Heart, Sweet Surrender,* and *A Wing & a Prayer.* Highly respected throughout the international community as an accomplished teacher, consultant, lecturer, author, and mentor, when not instructing, writing, or consulting, he relaxes back home in the Colorado Rocky Mountains. He can be reached at *www.brianlukeseaward.net.*